Spanish Grammar

JOHN BUTT

OXFORD
UNIVERSITY PRESS

OXFORD
UNIVERSITY PRESS

Great Clarendon Street, Oxford OX2 6DP

Oxford University Press is a department of the University of Oxford.
It furthers the University's objective of excellence in research, scholarship,
and education by publishing worldwide in

Oxford New York

Athens Auckland Bangkok Bogotá Buenos Aires Calcutta
Cape Town Chennai Dar es Salaam Delhi Florence Hong Kong Istanbul
Karachi Kuala Lumpur Madrid Melbourne Mexico City Mumbai
Nairobi Paris São Paulo Singapore Taipei Tokyo Toronto Warsaw

with associated companies in Berlin Ibadan

Oxford is a registered trade mark of Oxford University Press
in the UK and in certain other countries

Published in the United States
by Oxford University Press Inc., New York

© Oxford University Press 1996, 2000

First published 1996
Reissued in new cover 2000

British Library Cataloguing in Publication Data

Data available

Library of Congress Cataloging in Publication Data

Data available

ISBN 0-19-860343-6

10 9 8 7 6 5 4 3 2 1

Printed in Great Britain by
Mackays of Chatham plc
Chatham, Kent

Introduction

Spanish is the main language of twenty-one countries and it will soon have 400 million speakers, so anyone who knows both it and English can communicate with a significant proportion of the Earth's inhabitants. Since each Spanish-speaking country has its own accents, colloquialisms and peculiarities of grammar and vocabulary, and since no one agrees about which country speaks the best Spanish, it is occasionally a problem to know which words foreign students should learn. For example, a ball-point pen is **un bolígrafo** in Spain, **una birome** in Argentina, **un lapicero** in Peru and Central America, **un esfero** in Colombia and **una pluma** or **una pluma atómica** in Mexico, although in this, as in many similar cases, the word used in Spain is understood by many people everywhere.

This problem should not be exaggerated. The problem of variety mainly affects familiar or popular vocabulary and slang. Variations in Spanish pronunciation are no great problem: they never amount to more than fairly minor regional differences of accent, so one does not run into the kind of problem that can face Americans or Englishmen in the countryside of Scotland or Ireland. The basic grammar of Spanish is moreover amazingly uniform considering the tremendous size of the Spanish-speaking world. And, above all, virtually every-body—except perhaps in remote villages—knows generally-used words. For example, Mexicans often say **cuate** for *friend*, but they all know and also use the word **amigo**, just as Americans who say *buddy* and Britons and Australians who say *chum*, *pal* or *mate* all share the common word *friend*—which is obviously the word any foreign learner of English would learn first.

As far as possible the examples given in this book avoid regional forms and reflect the sort of Spanish used in the media and by educated people when talking to people from other Spanish-speaking countries. Nevertheless, where differences are unavoidable the language used is that of Spain and important Latin-American variants are noted where they arise. As a result this basic grammar should be equally useful to students of the Spanish of Europe and of Latin America.

Grammatical terms written with capital letters (e.g. Subjunctive, Indicative, Mood) are explained in the Glossary on p.320. The description of pronunciation given on pp. 214–221 is rather more detailed than is usual in this kind of book, since many of the pocket grammars, dictionaries and phrase-books on sale in the English-speaking world contain badly misleading accounts of the sounds of Spanish.

Incorrect forms —i.e. forms that learners must avoid — appear in bold italics and are marked with an asterisk, e.g. *****‘quizá viene mañana’** for the correct **quizá venga mañana** *perhaps he's coming tomorrow.*

The American-English spelling 'preterit' (British 'preterite') is used throughout the book. In other cases where American and British English spelling differs, both forms are shown, e.g. *flavor/*(British *flavour*).

Acknowledgements

The author wishes to thank Ms Antonia Moreira Rodríguez, the staff and students of King's College London, and also the editorial staff of Oxford University Press for their help and advice on a number of points.

Contents

VERBS *1*

Forms of verbs *2*

Types of Verbs *3*

Uses of the Indicative Tenses *4*

    The present tense 4   The preterit tense 6

    The imperfect tense 7   The perfect tense 9

    The pluperfect tense 11   The future tense 11

    The conditional tense 12

Continuous forms of the tenses *13*

Less common tense forms *16*

Moods *18*

    The indicative 18   The subjunctive 20

    The imperative 36

Conditions *40*

Non-finite verb forms *42*

    The infinitive 42   The gerund 51

    The past participle 55

Modal verbs *60*

    (poder, deber, tener que, haber que, haber de,

    querer, saber, soler)

The Passive *64*

'Reflexive' (pronominal) verbs *66*

Ser, estar and 'there is'/'there are' *77*

ARTICLES *82*
The definite article *82*
The indefinite article *87*

NOUNS *91*
Gender of nouns *91*
Forms of nouns referring to females *97*
Plural of nouns *100*
Collective nouns *102*

PERSONAL PRONOUNS *104*
Forms of pronouns *104*
Use of subject pronouns *107*
Formal and informal modes of address *108*
Object pronouns *109*
Order and position of object pronouns *113*
Redundant pronouns *117*
Emphasis of pronouns *118*
'It's me', 'it's us', etc. *118*

INDEFINITE PRONOUNS *119*
el que, quien, el de, alguien, algo, alguno, cualquiera, uno,

RELATIVE PRONOUNS *124*

ADJECTIVES *127*
Forms *127*

Agreement *131*
Comparison *132*
-ísimo *134*
Position of adjectives *135*

DEMONSTRATIVE PRONOUNS AND ADJECTIVES *138*

POSSESSIVES *141*

NEUTER PRONOUNS AND ARTICLES *145*

ADVERBS *148*
Adverbs formed from adjectives *148*
Other adverbs *149*
recién *150*
Comparative and superlative of adverbs *151*
Adverbs of place *152*
Position of adverbs *153*

NEGATION *154*

PERSONAL *A* *157*

PREPOSITIONS *159*
Alphabetical list of prepositions *160*
Preposition finder (English-Spanish) *183*

CONJUNCTIONS *187*

NUMBERS, TIME AND QUANTITIES *191*
Cardinal numbers *191*
Ordinal numbers *194*
Approximate numbers *196*
Fractions *196*
Time *197*
Days, months, seasons *199*
The date *200*
Age *201*
Measurements *201*

QUESTIONS *202*

'FOR N DAYS/WEEKS', 'AGO', 'SINCE' AND SIMILAR EXPRESSIONS *205*

AFFECTIVE SUFFIXES (diminutive, augmentative & pejorative suffixes) *208*

WORD ORDER *211*

PRONUNCIATION *214*

SPELLING AND PUNCTUATION *222*
The alphabet *222*
Writing accents *222*
Diphthongs and triphthongs: Spelling and accent rules *225*

Miscellaneous spelling rules *226*
Punctuation *227*

TRANSLATION TRAPS *230*
'afternoon'/'evening' *230*
'American'/'Latin-American', 'Spanish-American' *230*
'any' *231*
aun and *aún* *232*
'to become' *232*
de que and *de* *233*
'-ing' forms of English verbs *234*
'to like' *235*
'only'/'alone' *236*
'some' *236*
'Spanish'/'Castilian' *237*
'would' *237*
ya *238*

VERB FORMS *239*
Forms of regular verbs *239*
Conjugation of *hablar*, *beber* and *vivir* *240*
Spelling rules affecting all verbs *249*
Spanish Verbs: hints and tips for learners *250*
Tables of model irregular and radical-changing verbs *253*
List of irregular and radical-changing verbs *302*

GLOSSARY OF GRAMMATICAL TERMS *320*

INDEX *336*

Verbs

Forms of verbs: Tense, Mood, Person and
Number *2*
Types of verb *3*
Uses of the indicative tenses   The Present
tense *4* The Preterit tense *6*   The Imperfect
tense *7*   The Perfect tense *9*   The Pluperfect
tense *11*   The Future tense *11*   The
Conditional tense *12*   Continuous forms of the
tenses   *13*   Less common tense forms *16*
Mood   The Indicative *18*   The Subjunctive
20   The Imperative *36*
Conditions *40*
Non-finite forms of verbs   The infinitive *42*
The Gerund *51*   The Past participle *55*
Adjectival Participles *59*
Modal verbs *60*
The passive *64*
Pronominal ('reflexive') verbs *66*
Ser and estar *76*

Spanish verbs have different forms that show *Tense*[1]
(Present, Future, various kinds of Past Tense,

---

[1] Grammatical terms beginning with a capital letter are defined
in the Glossary on p. 320.

Conditional, etc.), *Mood* (Indicative, Imperative or Subjunctive), *Person* (first, second or third) and *Number* (singular or plural). There are also three Non-Finite Forms of verbs: the *Gerund*, the *Past Participle* and the *Infinitive*. The latter, which always ends in **-r**, is the Dictionary Form of the verb.

FORMS OF VERBS

The various forms of Spanish Regular and Irregular verbs are shown on pp. 239–302.

■ Tense

Spanish tenses are of two basic kinds: Simple Tenses, consisting of a single word, and Compound Tenses, consisting of an appropriate form of the verb **haber** plus a Past Participle:

Simple Tenses	**bebo, beberé, bebí** *I drink, I'll drink, I drank*
Compound Tenses	**he bebido, había bebido** *I have drunk, I had drunk*

All the various tenses of verbs can also appear in the Continuous Form, made from the verb **estar** *to be* plus the Gerund, which always ends in **-ndo**:

> **estoy bebiendo** *I'm (in the middle of) drinking*
> **estaba bebiendo** *I was drinking*
> **he estado bebiendo** *I have been drinking*

The Continuous form is discussed further on pp.13–16.

■ Mood

Verbs appear either in the Indicative Mood, used for making statements as explained on p.18, the Subjunctive Mood, explained on pp.20–35, or the Imperative Mood, which is used for making orders or requests and is explained on pp. 36–40.

■ Person and Number

Spanish verbs are unlike English verbs in that their endings show the Person and Number of their Subject:

hablo *I speak*	**hablamos** *we speak*
hablas *you speak*	**habláis** (Spain only) *you (plural) speak*
habla *he/she speaks, you* (singular) *speak*	**hablan** *they/you* (plural) *speak*

As a result, a verb on its own can form a Spanish sentence: **voy** means *I'm going*, **duermen** means *they're sleeping*. The Spanish words for *I*, *you*, *he/she/it*, *we*, *they* have special uses that are discussed later (p.107).

TYPES OF VERB

As far as the task of learning their various forms is concerned, there are three broad types of Spanish verb:

■ Regular Verbs

The vast majority of Spanish verbs are regular. If one knows the endings of the various tense forms and the spelling rules shown on p.249, one can predict every form of every regular verb.

   Regular verbs are divided into three Conjugations according to whether their Infinitive ends in **-ar**, **-er** or **-ir**. Three commonly encountered regular verbs are **hablar** *to speak* (first conjugation), **beber** *to drink* (second conjugation), **vivir** *to live* (third conjugation). The various forms of these three verbs in all their tenses are shown on pp.239–249, and these forms should be learned first.

■ Radical Changing Verbs

The endings of Radical Changing Verbs are the same as for regular verbs, but their stem vowels change in certain forms, cf. **dormir** *to sleep*, **duermo** *I sleep*, **durmió** *he slept*, etc. These irregularities appear only in the Present Tenses (Indicative and Subjunctive), in the **tú** Imperative and, in the case of some -**ir** verbs, in the Preterit, the Imperfect Subjunctive and the Gerund. Radical changing verbs are quite numerous and many are in everyday use. The most important are listed on pp.253–302.

■ Irregular verbs

Some Spanish verbs are truly irregular: some of their forms are unpredictable and must be learned separately. These verbs are not very numerous, but they include the most common verbs in the language like 'to go', 'to come', 'to be', 'to have', 'to put', and they must therefore be memorized thoroughly. The irregularities are usually most obvious in the Present Indicative and the Preterit: with some exceptions one can usually predict most of the other forms from these two sets of forms.

Irregular verbs are listed on pp.253–302.

USES OF THE INDICATIVE TENSES

Present Indicative Tense

Present Indicative forms like **hablo, bebes, vivimos** mean *I speak, you drink, we live* and also *I'm speaking, you're drinking, we're living*. They are also often used for future actions and occasionally for past ones as well. This imprecision can sometimes be removed by using the Present Continuous forms of the verb to stress the idea that an action is actually in progress in the present: see p.13.

The main uses of the simple Present Indicative tense are:

■ To show that an action happens habitually or is timeless (i.e. is an eternal truth):

> **Me peino todos los días** *I do my hair every day* (habit)
>
> **Los españoles comen mucho ajo** *The Spanish eat a lot of garlic* (habit)
>
> **Trabajas demasiado** *You work too much* (habit)
>
> **El carbón de piedra produce calor** *Coal produces heat* (timeless)

■ To show that something is happening in the present:

> **Hoy hace mucho calor** *It's very hot today*
>
> **¿Qué haces hoy?** *What are you doing today?*
>
> **¡Cómo llueve!** *Look at the rain!* (literally *how it's raining*)
>
> **Nos hospedamos en el Hotel Palace** *We're staying at the Palace Hotel*

It is more appropriate to use the Present Continuous if we need to stress the fact that the action is in progress *at this very moment*:

> **Roberto está pintando la puerta** *Roberto is (in the middle of) painting the door*

■ To show that an event is imminent, i.e. is just about to happen:

> **¡Socorro! ¡Que me caigo!** *Help! I'm falling!*
>
> **¿Le pago ahora?** *Do I pay you now?/Shall I pay you now?*
>
> **¡Que se va el tren!** *The train's leaving!*
>
> **¿Vienes conmigo?** *Are you coming with me?*

■ To show that an event in the future is scheduled or pre-arranged. In this case it is often like the English present form ending in *-ing* in *next year **we're going** to Miami*:

> **La fiesta es mañana a las ocho** *The party's tomorrow at eight o'clock*

> **Te llamo esta noche a las nueve** *I'll call you
> tonight at nine*
> **En diciembre voy a París** *In December I'm going
> to Paris*
> **El avión sale mañana a las ocho** *The plane
> leaves tomorrow at eight*

■ As a past tense (the 'Historic Present'). The present is often used as an alternative to the Preterit tense to make narrative in the past sound exciting. This is found both in formal literary styles and in informal speech:

> **Unos días después empieza la Guerra Civil**
> *A few days later the Civil War began* (literally
> *begins*)
> **Entra y me dice . . .** *She/He comes in and says to
> me . . .* (familiar style)

■ The present tense is also used in sentences of the type *'I've spoken/been speaking French since I was a girl'*, *'it's the first time we've seen her in years'*. See p.205.

The Preterit Tense

■ To look back on an event as completed in the past. It is therefore used to report the fact that event A happened and *finished*, *then* event B happened, *then* event C, and so on.

> **Se sentó, sacó un cigarrillo y lo encendió** *He
> sat down, took out a cigarette and lit it*
> **Anoche vi dos veces a tu madre** *I saw your
> mother twice last night*
> **Fue intérprete y después profesor** *He was an
> interpreter and then a teacher*
> **El viernes estuve en casa de la abuela** *on Friday
> I visited grandmother's house*

■ For events that lasted for a specific period of time and then ended:

Fue presidente durante ocho años *He was President for eight years*

Su enfermedad duró varios meses *Her/his illness lasted several months*

Estuve esperando varias horas or **Esperé varias horas** *I waited several hours* (the Continuous stresses the action as long drawn-out)

English speakers often have difficulty in distinguishing between the Preterit and the Imperfect (see next section), especially in sentences of the following kind:

Tuve que decírselo *I had to tell it to him* (and I did)

Tenía que decírselo *I had to tell it to him* (I may or may not have done)

Fue un día magnífico *It was a magnificent day* (all day)

Era un día magnífico *It was a lovely day* (at the time, but perhaps it rained later during the day)

The last example shows how the Preterit of **ser**—**fue**—indicates a different point of view compared with the Imperfect **era**. The Preterit looks back on the event after it finished, whereas the Imperfect describes an event while it was still going on. This is clear in English with most verbs other than *to be*. Compare *what **did you do** in the garden yesterday?* (looks back on the event as finished, therefore Preterit: **¿qué hiciste ayer en el jardín?**) and *what **were you doing** in the garden yesterday?* (the action is described as not yet finished at the time, therefore Imperfect: **¿qué hacías ayer en el jardín?**).

The Imperfect Tense

■ To show that an event was not yet completed. The Imperfect is therefore used for events that *were continuing* when something else happened:

Ignacio estaba en la habitación cuando se hundió el techo *Ignacio was in the room when the roof caved in*

Llovía muy fuerte, así que cerré la ventana *It was raining very hard, so I shut the window*

Esta puerta era azul *This door was blue* (i.e. at the time)

Ana tenía diecinueve años cuando se casó *Ana was nineteen when she got married*

Cuando yo era pequeño yo adoraba a mi madre *When I was little I adored my mother*

As these examples show, the Imperfect gives us no clear information about whether the event continued or when it ended: Ignacio probably left the room after the roof collapsed, but the point is that he was still there when it happened. As a general rule, if an English verb can be rewritten using *was* and the *-ing* form, Spanish will use the Imperfect: **Ana llevaba una falda azul cuando la vi** *Ana was wearing a blue skirt when I saw her*. But, as the examples above show, this rule does not usually apply to the verb *to be*.

■ To express habitual or timeless events in the past, i.e. events that had no clearly defined end even though they may no longer be happening now:

De niño yo tenía ojos azules *I had/used to have blue eyes as a child*

Mi madre era vegetariana *My mother was/used to be a vegetarian*

Yo iba todos los días a casa de mi amigo *I went/used to go to my friend's house every day*

Londres era más grande que Nueva York *London was/used to be bigger than New York*

As a general rule, if the meaning of the English verb can be expressed by the formula *used to . . .* Spanish will use the Imperfect Tense.

■ To denote something that was just going to happen (usually the same as **iba a . . .** *was going to*):

> **Yo me marchaba cuando sonó el teléfono** *I was leaving when the phone rang*

The Perfect Tense

Spanish distinguishes between the Perfect Tense and the Preterit, much the same as English does between the Perfect *I have seen* and the Simple Past *I saw*. The Perfect Tense is common in written styles everywhere and it is constantly heard in speech in Spain, but in some Latin-American varieties of spoken Spanish the Preterit may more or less completely replace the Perfect, although practice varies from country to country. The Perfect Tense is used:

■ For past events that have happened in a period of time that has not yet ended. Compare **fui dos veces el año pasado** *I went twice last year* and **he ido dos veces este año** *I have been twice this year* (this year hasn't ended yet):

> **La bolsa ha subido mucho hoy** *The stock market has gone up a lot today*
> **Ha llovido menos durante este siglo** *It has rained less this century*
> **No han contestado todavía** *They haven't replied yet*
> **Hemos estado trabajando toda la mañana** *We've been working all morning*

Latin Americans often use the Preterit in this context:

la bolsa subió mucho hoy, no contestaron todavía, estuvimos trabajando . . . , etc.

■ To show that the effects of a past event linger in or are relevant to the present. Compare **estuvo enfermo** *he was unwell* (in the past, but now he's recovered) and **ha estado enfermo** *he's been unwell* (that's why he's pale, late for work, irritable, etc.):

> **Alguien ha fumado/ha estado fumando en esta habitación. Huele a humo** *Someone has smoked/been smoking in this room. It smells of smoke*
>
> **Está contento porque lo/le² han ascendido** *He's pleased because they've promoted him*

Latin Americans may also prefer the Preterit tense in these cases.

■ In Spain, optionally, to show that an event happened today (i.e. since midnight). This is the 'Perfect of Recency':

> **Me he levantado temprano** *I got up early (today)*
>
> **Quién ha llamado?** *Who phoned (just now)?*
>
> **Perdona, no he podido hacerlo** *Sorry, I couldn't do it (today)*
>
> **Hemos ido al parque esta mañana** *We went to the park this morning*

If the event is very recent, the Perfect is usual in Spain, but for events earlier in the day the Preterit or the Perfect may be used. Latin Americans use the Preterit: **me levanté temprano, ¿Quién llamó?**, etc.

---

² **Lo/le** shows that either pronoun can be used here for *him*, **lo** being more common in Latin America, and **le** preferred in Spain (although **lo** is also widely used).

The Pluperfect Tense

In general, the same as the English Pluperfect form (*had* + Past Participle), i.e. to show that an event in the past had finished before the next one started:

> **Ya habían dejado dos mensajes en el contestador cuando yo llegué** *They had already left two messages on the answering machine when I arrived*
> **La policía encontró el revólver que el asesino había comprado dos días antes** *The police found the revolver that the murderer had bought two days before*

The Future Tense

As was mentioned earlier, future time can be expressed by the simple Present Tense when the event is felt to be pre-scheduled or pre-arranged: **la película empieza a las ocho** *The film starts at eight.* Furthermore, the Future Tense forms shown here are often replaced by **ir a** + the Infinitive in informal styles, especially in Latin-American speech, e.g. **si me habla de esa manera, me enojaré** *if he talks like that to me I'll get angry* becomes **si me habla de esa manera, me voy a enojar/voy a enojarme**[3].

The Future Tense is used:

■ For future events that are not pre-scheduled or fixtures:

> **Algún día se casará con ella** *He'll marry her one day*
> **Ya te cansarás** *You'll get tired eventually/in the end*

---

[3] In Spain **enfadarse** is the normal word for *to get angry*.

Para entonces yo ya no estaré aquí *By then I won't be here any more*

■ For approximations, guesses and suppositions:

Miguel tendrá unos cincuenta años *(I guess) Miguel's about fifty*
Estará durmiendo a estas horas *(I guess) he'll be sleeping at this time*

Latin Americans tend to prefer the construction **deber** or **deber de** + Infinitive (which is also used in Spain): **debe (de) tener unos cincuenta años, debe (de) estar durmiendo . . .** The **de** is often dropped, but learners should retain it so as to distinguish between suppositions and obligations. Compare **debes hacerlo** *you've got to do it* (obligation).

■ In questions, to express wonder or amazement:

¿Qué habrá sido de él? *What (on earth) can have happened to him?*
¿Quién será éste? *I wonder who this is?*

The Conditional Tense

■ As an equivalent of the English *would* form in conditions:

En ese caso te dejarían en paz *In that case they would leave you in peace*
El pastel estaría mejor con menos azúcar *The cake would be better with less sugar*
Eso sí costaría más! *That **would** cost more!*

■ With **poder, querer,** to make polite requests or express polite wishes:

¿Podría usted abrir la ventana un poquito? *Could you open the window a bit?*

Querría terminarlo antes de las ocho *I'd like to finish it before eight*

■ To express the future in the past (i.e. the same as **iba a** + Infinitive):

Aquel día empezó la que sería su última película *That day he began what would be his last film*

Yo sabía que no me devolvería el dinero *I knew he wouldn't/wasn't going to give the money back to me*

■ To express guesses or suppositions about the past:

Aquella semana la habríamos visto más de cinco veces *That week we must have seen her more than five times*

Pesaría unos cien kilos *It must have weighed about 100 kilos*

Deber or (preferably) **deber de** + Infinitive is more usual in this construction: **debía de pesar más de cien kilos**.

Note: the **-ra** form of the Imperfect Subjunctive is constantly found as an alternative for the Conditional of **haber** and **querer**:

Te hubiera/habría ayudado antes *I would have helped you sooner*

Quisiera/querría verte mañana *I'd like to see you tomorrow*

Continuous Forms of the Tenses

Spanish Continuous forms of the tenses (all formed with **estar** + the Gerund) either (a) stress that an event is, was or will be actually in progress at the time spoken of, or (b) in the case of the Preterit and Perfect Tenses, show that it continued for a certain amount of time in the past before ending.

As far as the Present, Imperfect and Future Continuous Tenses are concerned, English-speakers must remember to use the Continuous only for events actually *in progress*. The following is definitely *not* good Spanish: *'**mañana estoy viajando a Los Ángeles**' tomorrow I'm (in the middle of) traveling* (British *travelling*) *to Los Angeles*, correctly **mañana viajo a Los Ángeles.**

The Continuous is used:

■ In all tenses except the Preterit, Perfect and Pluperfect, to stress that an event is, was or will be actually in progress. Usually the non-Continuous tenses can also be used, but the Continuous is preferred nowadays when the event is actually in progress at the time:

> **Esto se está convirtiendo en una pesadilla** *This is turning into a nightmare*
>
> **Yo estaba durmiendo cuando sonó el despertador** *I was sleeping when the alarm clock went off*
>
> **Miguel está leyendo** *Miguel's reading*
>
> **Lo que pasó fue que ella estaba deseando irse** *What happened was that she wanted/was wanting to leave*
>
> **No puedes ir a las cinco porque estarás haciendo tus deberes** *You can't go at five o'clock because you'll be doing you're homework*

■ To show that an event is surprising or temporary:

> **¡¿Pero qué tonterías le has estado contando?!** *But what nonsense have you been telling him?!*
>
> **Es una zapatería, pero últimamente están vendiendo periódicos** *It's a shoe-shop, but lately they're selling newspapers*

> **María estaba trabajando de intérprete** *Maria was working as an interpreter* (at the time, temporarily)

■ To emphasize the idea of repetitive actions that are or were still continuing:

> **Está bebiendo mucho últimamente** *He's drinking a lot lately*
> **Siempre estaba pensando en ella** *He was always thinking of her*

■ In the Preterit, Perfect or Pluperfect Tenses, to show that an event (a) lasted a certain length of time and (b) that it finished:

> **Anoche estuvimos viendo la televisión** *We watched TV last night*
> **Te he estado esperando toda la mañana** *I've been waiting for you all morning*
> **Había estado leyendo durante horas** *He had been reading for hours*

Here the non-Continuous forms **vimos, he esperado, había leído** would not emphasize the long drawn-out nature of the events.

The Spanish Continuous *cannot* be used (at least in standard forms of the language):

■ For events that are not actually in progress:

> **Yo creo que este libro defiende una postura revolucionaria** *I think that this book is defending/defends a revolutionary position* (not **está defendiendo**, which means *is in the middle of defending*)
> **Yo iba a verme con ella al día siguiente** *I was seeing her the following day* (it hadn't happened yet)
> **Vamos mañana** *We're going tomorrow* (it hasn't happened yet)

> **Su padre[4] está enfermo de muerte** *His father is dying* (i.e. he is fatally ill. **Está muriendo** would mean that he is actually dying at this moment)
>
> **Está sentado** *He's sitting down* (**está sentándose** has the unlikely meaning *he's in the middle of sitting down*)

■ Normally, for events that are not really actions but conditions or states:

> **Llevaba una pajarita de seda** *He was wearing a silk bow-tie*
>
> **Parecías más joven aquella noche** *You were looking younger that night*
>
> **Un aroma delicado flotaba en el aire** *A delicate smell was floating in the air*

■ Never with the verb **estar**. One cannot say *‘estar estando’*, although **estar siendo** occasionally occurs:

> **Está siendo debatido en este momento** *It's being debated at this moment*

■ In standard varieties of Spanish, the Continuous is not used with the verbs **ir** *to go* and **venir** *to come*:

> **¿Adónde van ustedes?** *Where are you going?*
>
> **Ya vienen** *They're coming*

Less Common Tense Forms

The following forms are occasionally found, all of them (except for **tengo hecho**, etc.) being more common in writing than in speech:

■ **Tener** ‘to have’ is sometimes used to form compound tenses instead of **haber**. This is only possible if the verb

---

[4] Latin Americans tend to use **papá** for *father* and **mamá** for *mother*, but these words mean *daddy* and *mummy* in Spain.

has a direct object, and the difference between **lo he terminado** and **lo tengo terminado** is about the same as between *I've finished it* and *I've got it finished*: the latter emphasizes successful completion or acquisition of something—

> **Ya tengo pintadas tres de las paredes** *I've got three of the walls painted*
>
> **Ya tenemos compradas las flores** *We've got the flowers bought/We've bought the flowers*

As the examples show, the past participle agrees in number and gender with the direct object of the verb.

■ The **-ra** form, used for the Imperfect Subjunctive in normal styles, is often found in flowery writing, but not in spoken Spanish, as an alternative for the Pluperfect in Relative Clauses. This is especially common in Latin America but is gaining ground in Spain:

> **Se casó con la que *fuera* la esposa de su padre** *He married the woman who had been his father's wife* (everyday style . . . **había sido la esposa . . .**)

■ **-ra** forms (and sometimes also **-se** forms) of verbs frequently appear after **después de que** *after* and **desde que** *since* instead of the Preterit tense:

> **Este es el primer discurso que pronuncia desde que lo/le nombraran presidente** *This is the first speech he has delivered since he was appointed President*

This use of the **-ra** forms rather than the Preterit after **desde que** and **después de que** is the preferred construction in Spain, but the Preterit is possible, as this example from the Colombian novelist Gabriel García Márquez shows:

> **. . . su simple evocación le causaba un estremecimiento de pavor hasta mucho después**

de que se casó, y tuvo hijos . . . *the mere mention of him caused her a shudder of fear until long after she had married and had children*

However, the Subjunctive is obligatory after **después de que** and **desde que** when they point to events that are or were still in the future. See pp.29–30.

■ The Preterit of **haber** + the Past Participle is occasionally used to form the Anterior Preterit tense (**Pretérito anterior**). This is found only in literary styles before words meaning *as soon as* or *when*, to emphasize that an event *had just* finished before the next started. It can be replaced by the Pluperfect or, much more commonly, by the Preterit:

Apenas hubo terminado la cena, todos los invitados se fueron *Scarcely had supper finished when all the guests departed* (more usually **apenas terminó** . . .)

MOOD

The Indicative Mood

The uses of the various tenses of the Indicative Mood have already been discussed. The Indicative Mood is overwhelmingly the most commonly used verbal mood: in most types of Spanish well over 85% of the verbs are in the Indicative mood.

The Indicative is used:

■ In all Main Clauses (see Glossary) other than those that give orders (which require the Imperative mood):

En invierno no hacía mucho frío *It wasn't very cold in Winter*

> **No me gusta el sabor de la cerveza** *I don't like the taste of beer*
>
> **Me voy a comprar unos zapatos** *I'm going to buy some shoes*

■ In Subordinate Clauses after statements meaning *it is true/correct/a fact/certain* **that** . . .

> **Es verdad/cierto/correcto/un hecho que los limones son agrios** *It's true/certain/correct/a fact that lemons are sour*

But the Subjunctive is normally used when such statements are negated or denied: **no es cierto que los limones *sean* dulces** *It isn't true that lemons are sweet.*

■ After statements that express beliefs or opinions:

> **Creo que llegan el martes** *I think that they're coming on Tuesday*
>
> **Parece que no pudo solucionarlo** *It seems he didn't manage to solve it*

Again, the Subjunctive is normally used when such statements are denied: **no creo que *lleguen* el martes** *I don't think they're coming on Tuesday*

■ When the clause is introduced by a Subordinator (see Glossary) that refers to a time when the action has or had happened: compare **yo estaba viendo la televisión cuando llegaron**[5] *I was watching TV when they arrived.* This is discussed below on pp.29 ff.

■ In Relative Clauses, when the antecedent (the thing referred to by the Relative Pronoun) is known to exist (see p.34):

> **Conozco una cafetería donde sirven té inglés** *I know a café where they serve English tea*

[5] In Spain one usually says **ver la televisión** *to 'see' TV,* although **mirar** *'to watch'* is heard in Latin America

■ After **si** *if* in 'open' conditions: **si llueve me quedo en casa** *if it rains I'm staying at home.* Conditional Sentences are explained on p.40.

The Subjunctive Mood

The basic function of the Subjunctive is not to make statements of fact, but either (a) to show that the speaker is reacting emotionally in some way to the event referred to or (b) that the event mentioned in a Subordinate Clause is still not a reality (e.g. because it hasn't happened yet). Most learners of Spanish postpone the Subjunctive until the last moment, but there are good reasons for tackling it early, since it is common in all styles of language.

The Subjunctive can be explained under five headings:

(a) Cases in which it appears in Subordinate Clauses (see Glossary) introduced by **que**, following some statement indicating want, necessity, possibility, emotional reaction, fear, doubt, etc.

(b) Cases in which it appears after a number of words which are mostly Subordinators (see Glossary), for example **cuando** *when*, **apenas** *scarcely*, **quizá** *perhaps*, **posiblemente** *possibly*, **antes de que** *before*, **después de que** *after*, **con tal de que** *provided that*, etc . . .

(c) Cases in which it appears in Relative Clauses, e.g. **quiero comprar una casa que *tenga* muchas ventanas** *I want to buy a house that has a lot of windows.*

(d) Cases in which the Subjunctive can appear in the Main Clause of a sentence, i.e. cases in which the Subjunctive could stand as the first word in a sentence (rare—the Imperative excepted).

(e) Cases in which it appears in the if-clause of Conditional Sentences, e.g. **si *tuviera* más tiempo lo**

haría mejor *if I had more time I'd do it better.* This is discussed on p.40.

Forms of the subjunctive

The Subjunctive has three simple tense forms (the fourth tense form, the Future Subjunctive, is virtually obsolete. See below).

Present:

> **(que) yo hable** *that I should speak . . .*
> **(que) él diga** *that he should say . . .*

-ra Past:

> **(que) yo fuera** *that I should have been . . .*
> **(que) usted pensara** *that you should have thought . . .*

-se Past:

> **(que) yo fuese** *that I should have been . . .*
> **(que) usted pensase** *that you should have thought . . .*

The Subjunctive can also appear in compound tenses:

Perfect:

> **(que) yo haya hablado** *that I should have spoken . . .*
> **(que) él haya dicho** *that he should have said . . .*

Pluperfect:

> **(que) yo hubiera/hubiese hablado** *that I should have spoken* (before then)
> **(que) él hubiera/hubiese dicho** *that he should have said* (before then)

Continuous forms are also possible, e.g. **(que) yo esté hablando** *that I should be (in the middle of) speaking,* etc.

These are formed from the appropriate tense of the Subjunctive of **estar** + the Gerund.

The English translations shown above are very approximate and misleading. The Spanish Subjunctive cannot usually be translated clearly into English since the latter language has lost most of its Subjunctive forms.

■ The Future Subjunctive

This is virtually obsolete. It is formed by replacing the last **a** in the -**ra** Imperfect Subjunctive by **e**: **hablare hablares hablare habláremos hablareis hablaren**, **comiere, comieres, comiere, comiéremos, comiereis, comieren**, etc.

It is nowadays rarely seen outside legal documents and similar very formal texts. In all other cases it is replaced by the Present or Imperfect Subjunctive, so foreign learners will not need to use it.

■ Equivalence of the -**ra** and -**se** Subjunctives

When they are used as Subjunctives, the -**ra** forms and the -**se** forms are interchangeable, the -**ra** forms being nowadays much more frequent than the -**se** forms:

> **Yo quería que me _llamaras_ = Yo quería que me _llamases_** *I wanted you to call me*

In this book, unless otherwise stated, whenever the -**ra** form appears the -**se** form could have been used, and vice-versa.

Tense Agreement with the Subjunctive

The basic rules, which apply to ninety per cent of Spanish sentences, are:

Tense of verb in Main Clause	*Tense of Subjunctive in Subordinate Clause*
Present	Present
Future	" "
Perfect	Present (sometimes Imperfect)
Conditional	Imperfect (-**ra** or -**se**)
Imperfect	" "
Preterit	" "
Pluperfect	" "

> **Es/será/ha sido necesario que vengas** *It is/will be/has been necessary for you to come*
> **Sería/era/fue/había sido necesario que vinieras/vinieses** *It would be/was/had been necessary for you to come*

Replacement of a finite verb by an infinitive

When the subject of the Main Clause in a sentence and the subject of the Subordinate Clause refer to the same person or thing, the Infinitive is often used and not the Finite verb form: **quiero hacerlo** *I want to do it* (**yo** is the subject of both **querer** and **hacer**), but **quiero que *él* lo haga** *I want **him** to do it*.

In this respect English differs sharply from Spanish in allowing the Infinitive to refer to a new subject: *I prefer **him** to go*. The fact that Spanish does not allow this (with the few exceptions mentioned below) is the chief reason why it constantly uses the Subjunctive: **yo prefiero que él *vaya***.

The use of the Infinitive is also found after certain Subordinators (note the appearance of **que** when the Infinitive is not used):

¿Te voy a ver antes de irme? *Will I see you before I go?*

¿Te voy a ver antes de que te vayas? *Will I see you before **you** go?*

Lo hizo sin darse cuenta *He did it without realizing*

Lo hizo sin que yo me diera cuenta *He did it without **my** realizing*

Other Subordinators that allow this are:

con tal de (que) *provided that*
después de (que) *after*
en caso de (que) *in the event of*
hasta (que) *until*
para (que)/a (que) *in order to*
a pesar de (que) *in spite of*

But most Subordinators require a Finite verb form (Subjunctive or Indicative) whether the subjects are the same or not:

Lo haré cuando termine esto *I'll do it when I finish (or he/she/you finish(es)) this* (never **lo haré cuando terminar esto*')

Nos vamos en cuanto/apenas terminemos esto *We're going as soon as we finish this*

No digo nada, aunque sé la verdad *I'm saying nothing although I know the truth*

Lo hace bien porque sabe mucho *He does it well because he knows a lot*

The rules that determine whether the Finite verb is in the Indicative or Subjunctive are discussed below.

Subjunctive in clauses introduced by *que*

The Subjunctive is required in Subordinate Clauses after the word **que** when this word is introduced by a statement meaning:

■ Wanting, wishing, requesting

> **Quiero que me contestes** *I want you to answer*
> **Estaba deseando que se fueran** *He was wanting them to go*
> **Mi sueño de que mi hijo fuera médico** *My dream that my son would be a doctor*
> **Pidió que lo/le dejaran en paz** *He asked them to leave him in peace*
> **Prefiero que ustedes me lo entreguen a domicilio** *I prefer you to deliver it to me at home*

■ Ordering, obliging, causing, recommending, insisting

> **Le dijeron que se quedara** *They told him to stay*
> **Les ordenó que cargasen sus fusiles** *He ordered them to load their rifles*
> **El médico le recomendó que dejara de fumar** *The doctor recommended him to stop smoking*
> **Hizo que se quedaran en casa** *He made them stay at home*
> **Insistió en que se hiciera así** *He insisted that it should be done like this*

The verbs **ordenar, mandar, hacer, recomendar, aconsejar** *to advise*, **obligar** *to oblige* can optionally take the Infinitive: **les ordenó/mandó apagar las luces** or **ordenó/mandó que apagaran las luces** *he ordered them to put out the lights*; **los hizo quedarse en casa** *he made them stay at home*; **te recomiendo no hacerlo** *I recommend you not to do it*.

Decir que with the indicative mood means *to tell* (i.e. *inform*) *someone that*: **le dijeron que se quedaba** *they told him he that he was staying*.

■ Allowing and forbidding

> **No permito que mi hija viaje sola** *I don't allow my daughter to travel alone*

> **Les prohíbe que fumen en casa** *He forbids them to smoke at home*

And similarly **dejar** *to let*, **tolerar/aguantar** *to tolerate*, **oponerse a que** *to oppose*. However, **permitir, prohibir** and **dejar** also allow the infinitive construction: **no le permito/dejo a mi hija viajar sola, les prohíbe fumar en casa**

■ Needing

> **Es necesario/preciso que nos pongamos en contacto con ellos** *It's necessary that we contact them*
>
> **Hace falta que trabajen más** *They need to work more*

■ Possibility and impossibility

> **Es posible/probable/previsible que no lo terminen a tiempo** *It's possible/probable/likely that they won't finish it on time*
>
> **No puede ser que tenga tanto dinero** *It can't be (possible) that he's got so much money*

Use of the subjunctive with words meaning *perhaps* is discussed later in this section.

■ Emotional reactions, e.g. surprise, pleasure, displeasure, puzzlement

> **Me irrita que tengas esa actitud** *It irritates me that you have that attitude*
>
> **Fue increíble que no se diesen cuenta** *It was incredible that they didn't realize*
>
> **Estoy hasta la coronilla de que siempre tengamos tanto trabajo** *I'm sick to death of the fact that we have so much work*
>
> **Siento mucho que no puedan venir** *I'm sorry you/they can't come*

Nos extrañaba que no hubiese escrito *It puzzled us that he hadn't written*

■ The verb **quejarse de que** *to complain that* usually takes the Indicative: **siempre se queja de que tiene frío** *he's always complaining that he feels cold.*

■ Value judgments, i.e. any phrase meaning *it's good/bad that . . .* , *it's natural/logical/preferable/undesirable/satisfying that . . .* , etc.:

Conviene que llueva de vez en cuando *It's good that it rains from time to time*

Era absurdo que lo dejasen sin pintar *It was absurd for them to leave it unpainted*

Es natural que usted se sienta cansado *It's natural that you should feel tired*

Es importante que sepamos la verdad *It's important for us to know the truth*

The expression **menos mal que . . .** *it's a good thing that . . .* takes the Indicative: **menos mal que lo hiciste ayer** *it's a good thing you did it yesterday.*

■ Denial of truth, opinion, appearance or knowledge

No es verdad que la haya llamado *It isn't true that he called her*

No parece que esté dispuesta a hacerlo *It doesn't seem that she's prepared to do it*

No creo que sea posible *I don't think it's possible*

No sabía que fueras tan inteligente *I didn't know you were so intelligent*

No es que sea incorrecto, sino que es increíble *It isn't that it's incorrect but that it's incredible*

But these verbs take the indicative when they are positive: **es verdad que la ha llamado** *It's true that he called her,* etc. The indicative is also possible with **no saber que** when the thing referred to is not an opinion but a fact: **no**

sabía que ya había pagado *I didn't know that he'd already paid.*

■ Doubt

> **Dudo que sepas hacerlo** *I doubt you know how to do it*

■ Fear

> **Temo que la paz no sea posible** *I fear peace isn't possible*
>
> **Tengo miedo de que me muerda ese perro** *I'm scared that dog's going to bite me*

The indicative is usual after **temerse** when it expresses a regret: **me temo que he cometido un error** *I fear I've made a mistake.*

■ Hoping, depending on, sympathizing with, avoiding, explaining the cause of something:

> **Espero que ustedes estén bien** *I hope you're well*
>
> **Dependo de que me dé dinero periódicamente** *I depend on him giving me money regularly*
>
> **Esto sólo hacía que él se riera más** *This only made him laugh more*
>
> **Comprendo que no quieras hablar de ello** *I understand you not wanting to talk about it*
>
> **Intentaba evitar que su suegra se enterase** *He was trying to avoid his mother-in-law finding out*
>
> **Esto explicaba el que prefiriera quedarse en casa** *This explained the fact that he preferred to stay at home*

■ *The fact that . . .*

Use of the Subjunctive is common after **el hecho de que** . . . *the fact that*, and also after **el que** . . . or **que** . . . when they mean the same as **el hecho de que**. The question of when the Subjunctive is used after these words is complex, but the general rule is that the Subjunctive is usual except when **el hecho de que** is preceded by a preposition:

> **El hecho de que los gramáticos no siempre estén de acuerdo deja perplejos a muchos estudiantes** *The fact that the grammarians aren't always in agreement leaves many students perplexed*
>
> **El que lo hayamos visto tres veces no puede ser una coincidencia** *The fact that we've seen him/it three times can't be a coincidence*
>
> **Que fuera él quien lo hizo no debería sorprender a nadie** *The fact that he was the one who did it should surprise no one*

but

> **No quiso contestar por el hecho de que no se fiaba de la policía** *He refused to answer due to the fact that he didn't trust the police*

Use of the subjunctive after subordinators

The Subjunctive is required in certain cases after clauses introduced by Subordinators, e.g. words that introduce clauses and mean *when, as soon as, in order to, after, without, as long as*, etc. Most, but not all, of these are phrases that include the word **que**.

The Subjunctive is used after these words whenever the action that follows them has not or had not yet happened at the time referred to in the Main Clause. Compare **me acosté cuando llegó mamá** *I went to bed when* (i.e. *after*) *mother arrived* and **me acostaré cuando llegue mamá** *I'll go to bed when mother arrives* (she hasn't arrived yet).

With some subordinators the Subjunctive is always necessary: these include **antes de que** *before*, **sin que** *without*, **para que** and **a que** *in order to*, **con tal de que** and **a**

condición de que *provided that*. In a few cases the Indicative is always used, but with most subordinators either the Indicative or the Subjunctive is used, according to whether the event has or has not happened at the time:

> **Te llamaré en cuanto/apenas llegue** *I'll call you as soon as I arrive/he arrives*
>
> **Te llamé en cuanto/apenas llegó** *I called you as soon as he arrived*
>
> **Bebíamos champán siempre que nos traía una botella** *We drank champagne whenever he brought us a bottle*
>
> **Beberemos champán siempre que nos traigas una botella** *We'll drink champagne whenever/provided you bring us a bottle*
>
> **Lo compré después de que lo repararon**[6] *I bought it after they fixed it*
>
> **Lo compraré después de que lo reparen/hayan reparado** *I'll buy it after they've fixed it*

The following list includes the most common subordinators. Those marked 'variable' obey the rule just explained, while the others either always or never take the Subjunctive:

> **cuando** *when* (variable)
> **antes de que** *before* (always)
> **después de que** *after* (variable, but see p.17)
> **desde que** *since, from the moment that* (variable, but see p.17)
> **a partir del momento en que** *from the time that* (variable)

---

[6] However, as explained on page 17, the **-ra** form is common in Spain after **después de que** and **desde que** *since*, to refer to any event in the past: **después de que lo repararan, desde que la viera** *since he had seen her*.

según *as* (as in *he answered the letters as they arrived* **contestaba a las cartas según iban llegando**) (variable)

a medida que *as* (as **según,** but implies *without delay*; variable)

tan pronto como, nada más, en cuanto, nomás (the latter in Lat. Am. only), **apenas** all meaning *as soon as, scarcely* (variable)

a que, para que, a fin de que, con el objeto de que *in order to* (always)

no sea que, no fuera que *lest, in order that . . . not* (always)

de ahí que *hence the fact that* (always)

sin que *without* (always)

de manera que, de modo que, de forma que *in such a way that, so* (indicating manner or result) (variable)

en caso de que *in the event of . . .* (always)

por si *in case* (usually indicative)

suponiendo que *supposing that* (always)

hasta que *until* (variable)

siempre que *whenever, every time that* (variable)

mientras (que) when it means *provided that, as long as,* always takes the Subjunctive. When it means *while* and refers to some future event it optionally takes the Subjunctive **tú puedes descansar mientras que yo trabajo/trabaje** *you can rest while I work;* otherwise it takes the Indicative

con tal de que, siempre que, a condición de que *provided that* (always)

salvo que, excepto que, a menos que *unless* (nearly always take Subjunctive)

aunque *although* takes the Subjunctive when it refers to an uncertainty: **dile que venga aunque esté enfermo** *tell him to come even if he is sick*. It takes the indicative when it refers to past events: **fuimos al parque, aunque llovía a cántaros** *we went to the park although it was pouring with rain*

a pesar de que, **pese a que** *despite the fact that* (variable)

puesto que, **ya que**, **en vista de que**, **debido a que** *seeing that, in view of the fact that, due to the fact that* (never)

pues *because* (literary styles only; see p.189), *well . . . , in that case* (never)

como (see p. 187)

como si *as if* (always)

porque *because*. Only takes Subjunctive after the phrase **no porque . . .** *not because . . .* and also when it means an emphatic *simply because* or *just because*: **no voy a quedarme en casa sólo porque tú me lo digas** *I'm not staying at home simply because you tell me to* (you may not have said it yet, but even if you do . . .). **Porque** plus the subjunctive occasionally means *in order that* after a few verbs, especially those meaning *to make an effort*: **se esforzaba para que/porque todo el mundo lo aceptara** *he was making an effort to get everyone to accept it/him*

Subjunctive after words meaning 'perhaps'

■ After **a lo mejor,** which is colloquial (like *maybe* in British English), the appropriate tense of an Indicative verb form is used:

A lo mejor pensaba que no estabas en casa
Maybe he thought you weren't at home
A lo mejor es ella *Maybe it's her*

■ After **quizá**[7], **tal vez** (Lat. Am. **talvez**), **acaso** (literary style) and **posiblemente** *possibly*, the Subjunctive is always correct. However, modern Spanish increasingly prefers the Indicative in certain circumstances, and the following remarks reflect current tendencies:

The Present Subjunctive must be used if the event refers to the future:

> **Quizá/tal vez/acaso llegue mañana** *Perhaps it'll arrive tomorrow* (not **'**quizá llega mañana**')
> **Quizá/tal vez/posiblemente sea mejor** . . .
> *Perhaps/possibly it would be better* . . .

Either the Present Subjunctive or Present Indicative can be used if the verb refers to the present, the Subjunctive being more formal or rather more hesitant or hypothetical:

> **Quizá/tal vez sea/es verdad que** . . . *Perhaps it's true that*

An Indicative past tense or the Imperfect Subjunctive may be used if the event is in the past, the Subjunctive being slightly more hesitant:

> **Quizá pensaba/pensara/haya pensado que nadie se enteraría** *Perhaps he thought no one would find out*

The Imperfect Subjunctive or the Imperfect of **ir a** . . . is used for a future in the past:

> **Quizá/posiblemente me lo diera/iba a dar cuando llegase al día siguiente** *Perhaps/*

---

[7] The form **quizás** is generally avoided in writing.

possibly he would give it to me when he arrived
*the next day (not *'**Quizá me lo daba**')*

■ The word **igual** is nowadays constantly heard in Spain with the meaning *maybe* or *probably*, but it is not used in writing or formal speech. It always takes the Indicative mood.

The subjunctive in relative clauses

The Subjunctive must be used in relative clauses when the thing referred to by the relative pronoun does not exist or is not yet known to exist. Compare **quiero vivir en un país donde nunca *haga* frío** *I want to live in a country where it's never cold* (we don't know yet which country) and **los guatemaltecos viven en un país donde nunca *hace* frío** *the Guatemalans live in a country where it's never cold*. Further examples:

> **Nunca hubo guerra que no fuera un desastre**
> *There was never a war that wasn't a disaster*
> **Tienes que hablar con alguien que te com-**
> **prenda** *You have to talk to someone who under-*
> *stands you*
> **Dame algo que no tenga alcohol** *Give me some-*
> *thing/anything that doesn't have alcohol in it*

This construction requires practice since English does not make the distinction clear. Compare **va a casarse con una mujer que *tiene* mucho dinero** *he's going to marry a woman who has a lot of money* (Indicative, because he has found her) and **quiere casarse con una mujer que *tenga* mucho dinero** *he wants to marry a woman who has a lot of money* (Subjunctive: he's still looking for her).

There are a number of words and phrases that correspond to English words ending in *-ever*, e.g. *whatever, whenever, however, whoever, wherever*. These take the Subjunctive and can be conveniently included under discussion of the Subjunctive in relative clauses:

> **sea lo que seá** *whatever it is*
> **Tome lo que usted quiera** *Take whatever you like*
> **Pueden comer cuando quieran** *You can eat whenever you like*
> **Hazlo como quieras** *Do it however you like*
> **sea quien sea/quienquiera que sea** *whoever it is*
> **sea cual sea** *whichever it is*
> **esté donde esté/dondequiera que esté** *wherever he is*

The Subjunctive is also found in relative clauses—at least in formal styles—after a superlative when the idea of *ever* is stressed:

> **la temperatura más alta que se haya registrado en treinta años** *the highest temperature that has **ever** been recorded in thirty years*

but

> **Éstos son los mejores zapatos que tengo** *These are the best shoes I've got*

The subjunctive in main clauses

The Subjunctive can also appear in Main Clauses, i.e. it is possible for a Subjunctive verb to be the only verb in the sentence. This occurs:

■ In all forms of the **usted/ustedes** imperative: **dígame** *tell me*, **dénmelo** *give it to me*, **no me diga** *don't tell me*.

■ In the *negative* form of the **tú** and **vosotros** imperatives: **no me digas (tú)**, **no me digáis (vosotros)** *don't tell me*.

■ In third and first-person imperatives: **que pasen** *let them come in*, **pensemos** *let's think*.

■ After **ojalá** *let's hope that* . . . and after **quién** when it means *if only*: **¡Ojalá no llueva!** *Let's hope it doesn't rain!*, **¡Quién tuviera tanto dinero como tú!** *If only I had as much money as you!*

The imperative

The Imperative mood is used for orders and requests.

There are four second-person forms of the Imperative corresponding to the four pronouns meaning *you*: **tú, usted, vosotros/vosotras** and **ustedes**. There are also first-person plural imperatives (*let's go, let's wait*) and third-person imperatives (*let him go, let it be*). These are discussed below.

Vosotros/vosotras is not used in Latin America, where the only form used for *you* in the plural, whether one is speaking to intimate friends, little children, strangers or even animals, is **ustedes**.

■ The **tú** imperative is formed by removing the **-s** of the second-person singular of the present indicative: **habla** s*peak*, **cuenta** *count/tell* (from **contar**), **escribe** *write*. There are eight common exceptions:

decir *to say*	**di**
hacer *to make*	**haz**
ir *to go*	**ve**
poner *to put*	**pon**
salir *to go out*	**sal**
ser *to be*	**sé**[8]
tener *to have*	**ten**
venir *to come*	**ven**

The imperative of **estar** *to be* is usually formed (but not in every Latin-American region) from the Pronominal Form of the verb (see Glossary): **¡Estate quieto!**[9] *Sit still!*

These forms of the **tú** imperative are used only for *positive* orders. All *negative* orders in Spanish are based on the Present Subjunctive: **no hables** *don't speak!*, **no escribas**

---

[8] The accent distinguishes it from the pronoun **se**.
[9] **Quieto** = 'still', **callado** = 'quiet'.

don't write!; **sal** *leave!/get out!*, **no salgas** *don't leave/don't go out.*

In Argentina and in most of Central America (but not in Mexico) the pronoun **vos** replaces **tú** in ordinary speech. The imperative forms used vary from country to country, but in Argentina and in most other places they are created by dropping the -d from the standard Spanish **vosotros** imperative (see below): **decí, vení, contestame** (standard forms **di, ven, contéstame**). In the negative the standard Subjunctive forms should be used: **no digas, no vengas, no me contestes**.

■ The **vosotros/vosotras** Imperative is considered archaic in Latin America (and in the Canary Islands) and it is replaced by the **ustedes** form; but it is constantly heard in Spain. It is used for two or more close friends, children, family members or animals. It is formed by replacing the -r of the Infinitive by -d: **hablad** *speak!*, **venid** *come!*, **id** *go!* This form ending in -d is often nowadays replaced in familiar styles by the Infinitive: **hablar, venir, ir**, etc. However, careful speakers may consider this slovenly, so foreigners should use the -d forms.

All *negative* imperatives are based on the present Subjunctive, so one says **no habléis** *don't speak!*, **no vengáis** *don't come!*, **no vayáis** *don't go!*

■ The **usted** imperative is used when addressing a stranger (other than a child or another young person if you are also young), and the **ustedes** form is used for addressing more than one stranger (in Spain) or for more than one person, friend or stranger, in Latin America. All the **usted** and **ustedes** imperative forms, positive and negative, are identical to the third-person Present Subjunctive: **venga (usted)** *come!*, **contesten (ustedes)** *answer!*, **¡No se queden atrás!** *Don't fall behind!*

Object pronouns with the imperative

In the case of positive imperatives, Object Forms of Personal Pronouns are attached to the imperative as suffixes, in the order shown on page 113.

> **Dime la verdad** *Tell me the truth* (**tú**)
> **Llámala ahora** *Call her now* (**tú**)
> **Siéntate** *Sit down* (**tú**)
> **Decídnoslo** *Tell it to us* (**vosotros**)
> **Deme** *Give me*[10] (**usted**)
> **Déselo** *Give it to him/her/them* (**usted**)
> **Envíenmelos** *Send them to me* (**ustedes**)

Note that an accent is often necessary to show that the stress is not shifted when the pronouns are added: **da** *give* (**tú** form), **dame** *give me*, **dámelo** *give me it/give it to me*.

When the pronoun **os** is added to a **vosotros** imperative, the **d** is dropped: **lavad** + **os** = **lavaos** *get washed*; also **callaos** *be quiet*, **decidíos** *make up your minds* (from **decidid** + **os**; note accent). There is one exception: **idos** *go away* (instead of ★'**íos**'). Familiar speech nowadays usually avoids these forms by using the Infinitive—**lavaros, callaros, decidiros, iros**—although non-fluent foreigners should not do this. The **vosotros** form is replaced by the **ustedes** form in Latin America: **lávense, cállense, decídanse, váyanse**, etc.

Personal pronouns are put *before* negative imperatives in the same order as above:

> **No me digas la verdad** *Don't tell me the truth* (**tú**)
> **No la llames ahora** *Don't call her now* (**tú**)
> **No te sientes** *Don't sit down* (**tú**)
> **No nos lo digáis** *Don't tell it to us* (**vosotros**)

[10] Or **déme**. There is some disagreement about whether the accent of **dé**, the third-person present subjunctive of **dar**, should be retained when one pronoun is attached to it. The accent is required on the word **dé** when it stands alone to avoid confusion with **de** *of*.

No se lo dé *Don't give it to him/her/them* (**usted**)

No nos los envíen *Don't send them to us* (**ustedes**)

Third-person imperatives

These translate English forms like *let him . . .* , *tell him/her to . . .* , etc. They consist of **que** plus the third-person present Subjunctive:

> **Que diga quién es** *Tell him to say who he is*
>
> **Que vuelvan más tarde** *Tell them to come back later*

The Passive **se** construction (see p.73) used with the Subjunctive forms an imperative often used in recipes, instructions and official forms to give impersonal orders:

> **Pónganse en una cacerola las patatas** (Lat.-Am. **papas**) **y los tomates** *Put the potatoes and tomatoes in a saucepan*

Ponga en una cacerola las patatas, etc. would have meant the same thing.

First-person imperatives

The first-person plural of the Present Subjunctive translates the English *let's . . .* , *let us . . .* :

> **Pensemos un poco antes de hacerlo** *Let's think a bit before doing it*

When the pronoun **nos** is added to this imperative form, the final -**s** of the verb is dropped:

> **Sentémonos** *Let's sit down.*

The verb **ir** is unusual in that the Present Indicative is used for *let's go*: **vamos, vámonos**

Other forms of the imperative

■ There is a tendency to use the Infinitive for second-person Imperatives, singular and plural, especially in

written instructions but also sometimes in speech: **re-
llenar el cupón y enviarlo a . . .** *fill in the coupon and
send it to . . .,* **no fumar** *no smoking,* **tirar** *pull!*
Grammarians and schoolteachers disapprove of this, but it
is becoming increasingly frequent.

■ The ordinary Present Indicative is often used for the
Imperative, but it can sound angry: **¡Te duermes en
seguida o me voy a enfadar!** (Lat-Am. **me voy a eno-
jar**) *you're going to sleep right now or I'm going to get mad!*

■ The Imperative may be softened or replaced in polite
speech by one of the following constructions, which are
more friendly in tone:

> **¿Podría usted guardar mi maleta?** *Could you
> look after my suitcase?*
> **¿Le importaría llamar a mi mujer?** *Would you
> mind phoning my wife?*
> **¿Quisiera hacerme el favor de llamarme
> cuando sepa algo?** *Would you call me when
> you know something?*
> **Hagan el favor de permanecer sentados** *Please
> remain seated*
> **¿Me da una cerveza?** *Would you give me a beer,
> please?* (Question form used for polite request)

CONDITIONS

There are three basic kinds of Conditional Sentence in
Spanish:

■ Conditions that do not require the Subjunctive in the *if*-
clause[11]. These are conditions in which the condition is

---

[11] The Spanish for *if* is **si**. However, foreign learners are often
confused by the widespread tendency to use **si** simply as a way of
turning a remark into a protest: **¡Si te lo dije anoche!** *But I told you
last night!*

equally likely or unlikely to be fulfilled. The verbs are in the Indicative Mood, and their tense is the same as in their English equivalents:

> **Si me das dinero, te compraré un helado** *If you give me some money I'll buy you an ice-cream*
> **Si te pones esa corbata, no voy contigo** *If you put that tie on, I'm not going with you*

The Imperfect Indicative is used if these conditions are reported by someone, but the Imperfect Indicative is not used in any other kinds of Conditional Sentence[12]:

> **Me dijo que no iría conmigo si me ponía esa corbata** *She said she wouldn't go with me if I put that tie on*

Como + Subjunctive is sometimes used instead of **si** in this kind of condition. This is particularly common in threats and apparently more frequent in Spain than Latin America:

> **Como vuelvas a hacerlo, llamo a la policía** *If you do it again, I'm calling the police*

■ Conditions that require the Imperfect Subjunctive in the *if*-clause and the Conditional in the other clause. The condition is less likely to be met or impossible to meet:

> **Si yo tuviera veinte años menos, sería feliz** *If I were twenty years younger, I'd be happy* (impossible)
> **Si trabajaras más te darían mejores notas** *If you worked harder they'd give you better grades/marks* (some doubt about whether it's possible)

The best styles of Spanish prefer the **-ra** form of the Imperfect Subjunctive in the *if*-clause of these sentences, although the **-se** form is common in speech.

[12] Except in familiar speech as an occasional alternative for the Conditional Tense, although beginners should avoid this.

■ Conditions that require the Pluperfect Subjunctive in the *if*-clause and the Pluperfect Conditional in the other clause. In this case the condition was not fulfilled:

> **Si se hubiera casado con ella, habría sido rico**
> *If he had married her he would have been rich*
> (but he didn't)
>
> **Si te hubiera visto, te habría saludado** *If I had seen you I would have said hello to you* (but I didn't)

Either the Conditional or the **-ra** form of **haber** can be used in the second clause (e.g. **hubiera saludado** or **habría saludado**).

The **si** and the Subjunctive in this kind of clause are occasionally replaced by **de** + Infinitive, but only if the verbs in each clause are in the same person:

> **De haberte visto, te habría saludado** *Had I seen you, I'd have said hello*

NON-FINITE VERB FORMS (SEE GLOSSARY)

The infinitive

This non-finite form always ends in **-ar**, **-er**, **-ir** or **-ír**: **andar** *to walk*, **convencer** *to convince*, **insistir** *to insist*, **reír** *to laugh*.

It is used:

■ After Modal Verbs (see p.60), e.g. **poder** *to be able*, **deber** *must*, **tener que** *to have to*, **hay que** *it's necessary to*, **saber** *to know how to*:

> **No puedo salir hoy** *I can't go out today*

> **Debiste llamarla** *You should have called her*
> **Tenemos que esperar** *We've got to wait*
> **Habrá que hacerlo** *It'll be necessary to do it*
> **No sé nadar** *I don't know how to swim*

■ After prepositions and prepositional phrases

> **Ha ido a América a estudiar** *He's gone to study in America*
> **Tosía por haber fumado demasiado** *He was coughing from having smoked too much*
> **Corrió hasta no poder más** *He ran until he could (run) no more*
> **Roncaba sin darse cuenta** *He was snoring without realizing*
> **lejos de pensar que . . .** *far from thinking that . . .*
> **En lugar de ir a España . . .** *Instead of going to Spain*

If the subject of the Infinitive and the subject of the Main Clause do not refer to the same thing or person, the Infinitive cannot be used (at least in careful Spanish): **tosía porque ella había fumado demasiado** *he was coughing because* **she** *had smoked too much* (not ***'*por ella haber fumado demasiado*').

After some prepositions, the Spanish Infinitive may have a passive meaning: **una carta sin terminar** *an unfinished letter*, **cosas por hacer** *things to be done*.

■ After many other verbs

With some verbs no preposition is required before the Infinitive, and with other verbs a preposition is necessary. This list shows the construction with some of the most common verbs. Where no preposition is shown none is required, e.g. **quiero hacerlo** *I want to do it*:

abstenerse de *to abstain from*
acabar de: acabo de verla *I've just seen her*
acabar por *to end by*
acercarse a *to approach*
aconsejar *to advise*
acordarse de *to remember*
acostumbrar a *to be accustomed to*
acusar de *to accuse of*
admitir *to admit*
afirmar *to claim/state*
alegrarse de *to be happy at/to*
amenazar or **amenazar con** *to threaten*
anhelar *to long to*
animar a *to encourage to*
aparentar *to seem to, to have the look of . . .*
aprender a *to learn to*
arrepentirse de *to regret/repent*
asegurar *to assure/insure*
asombrarse de *to be surprised at*
asustarse de *to be frightened by*
atreverse a *to dare to*
autorizar a *to authorize to*
avergonzarse de *to be ashamed of*
ayudar a *to help to*
buscar *to seek to*
cansarse de *to tire of*
cesar de *to cease from*
comenzar a *to begin to*
comprometerse a *to undertake to*
condenar a *to condemn to*
conducir a *to lead to*
confesar *to confess*
conseguir *to succeed in*
consentir en *to consent to*
consistir en *to consist of*
contar con *count on*

contribuir a *to contribute to*
convenir en *to agree to*
convidar a *to invite to*
cuidar de *to take care to*
deber *must*
decidir *to decide to*
decidirse a *to make up one's mind to*
declarar *to declare*
dejar *to let/allow*: **me dejó hacerlo** *he let me do it*
dejar de *to stop/leave off, e.g.* **dejó de fumar** *he stopped smoking*
demostrar *to demonstrate*
depender de *depend on*
desafiar a *to challenge to*
desear *to desire/wish to*
desesperarse de *to despair of*
dignarse *to deign to*
disponerse a *to get ready to*
disuadir de *to dissuade from*
divertirse en *to amuse oneself by*
dudar *to doubt*
dudar en *to hesitate over*
echar(se) a *to begin to*
empeñarse en *to insist on*
empezar a *to begin to*
empezar por *to begin by*
enfadarse de *to get angry at*
enojarse de *to get angry at*
enseñar a *to show how to/teach how to*
escoger *to choose to*
esforzarse por *to strive to*
esperar *to hope/expect/wait*
evitar *to avoid*
fingir *to pretend to*
forzar a *to force to*

guardarse de *to take care not to*
habituarse a *to get used to*
hartarse de *to get tired of*
imaginar(se) *to imagine*
impedir *to prevent from*
incitar a *to incite to*
inclinar a *to incline to*
insistir en *to insist on*
intentar *to try to*
interesarse en (or **por**) *to be interested in*
invitar a *to invite to*[13]
jactarse de *to boast of*
jurar *to swear to*
juzgar *to judge*
limitarse a *to limit oneself to*
luchar por *to struggle to*
llevar a *to lead to*
lograr *to succeed in*
mandar *to order to*
mandar a *to send to*
maravillarse de *to marvel at*
merecer *to deserve to*
meterse a *to start to*
mover a *to move to*
necesitar *to need to*
negar *to deny*
negarse a *to refuse to*
obligar a *to oblige to*
ofrecerse a *to offer to*
olvidar, olvidarse de, olvidársele a uno[14] *to forget*
oponerse a *to oppose/resist*

[13] Note one special use of this verb in bars, restaurants etc.: **te invito** *I'm paying for you,* **¿Quién invita?** *Who's paying for us?*

[14] Note construction: **me olvidé de decirte** or **se me olvidó decirte** *I forgot to tell you.*

optar por *to opt to/for*
ordenar *to order to*
parar de[15] *to stop*
parecer *to seem to*
pasar a *to go on to*
pasar de *to pass from, to be uninterested in*
pedir *to ask to*
pensar: pienso hacerlo *I plan to do it*
pensar en *to think about*
permitir *to allow to*
poder *to be able to*
preferir *to prefer to*
prepararse a *to get ready to*
pretender *to claim to*
procurar *to try hard to*
prohibir *to prohibit from*
prometer *to promise to*
quedar en *to agree to*
querer *to want to*
recordar *to remember*[16]
renunciar a *to renounce*
resignarse a *to resign oneself to*
resistirse a *to resist*
resolver *to resolve to*
sentir *to regret/be sorry for*
soler: solía ir *he used to go*
solicitar *to apply to*
soñar con *to dream of*
sorprenderse de *to be surprised that*
tardar en *to be late in/be a long time*
temer *to fear to*
tender a *to tend to*

[15] **Pararse** means *to come to a halt* in Spain, *to stand up* in Latin America.
[16] Note alternatives: **recordar algo** or **acordarse de algo** *to remember something*.

tener que *to have to*
terminar de *to finish*
terminar por *to finish by*
tratar de *to try to*
vacilar en *to hesitate over*
venir de *to come from . . .*
volver a (hacer) *to (do) again*

The Infinitive is normally only possible with the above verbs when the subject of both verbs is the same. Compare

Soñaba con ser bombero *He dreamt of being a fireman*

and

Soñaba con que su hijo *fuese* bombero *He dreamt of his son being a fireman.*

Verbs of permitting and forbidding allow either construction:

Te permito hacerlo/Te permito que lo hagas / *allow you to do it*

Te prohibía ir/Te prohibía que fueses *He forbade you to go.*

■ With verbs of stating, believing, claiming

In this case the Infinitive construction is *optionally* allowed when both verbs share the same subject:

Dice ser de Madrid/Dice que es de Madrid *He says he's from Madrid* (he is talking about himself)

Afirmaba haberlos visto/que los había visto *He claimed to have seen them*

Parecía conocerla/Parecía que la conocía *He seemed to recognize her/It seemed that he recognized her*

Similarly with **pretender** *to claim*, **imaginar** *to imagine*, **creer** *to believe*, **recordar/acordarse de** *to remember*, **reconocer** *to recognize*, **admitir** *to admit*, **confesar** *to confess*.

■ After **ver** *to see* and **oír** *to hear*

> **Le oí decir que tenía mucho dinero** *I heard him say that he had a lot of money*
>
> **Te vi entrar en su casa** *I saw you enter his/her house*

For the possible use of the Gerund as an alternative to the Infinitive in this construction, see p.53.

■ In the common construction **al** + Infinitive, which translates *on doing something . . . , when . . .* **al llegar a Madrid** . . . *on arriving at Madrid . . .*

> **al levantarse** . . . *on getting up . . .*

■ After Subordinators (other than **cuando** *when*, **en cuanto**, *as soon as*, **apenas** *as soon as/scarcely* and a few others mentioned on p.24) when the subject of the first verb is identical to the subject of the second verb: Compare **comí antes de salir de casa** *I ate before leaving home* and **comí antes de que tú salieras de casa** *I ate before you left home*:

> **Entró sin hacer ruido** *He entered without making any noise*
>
> **Redecoraremos la casa en lugar de venderla** *We'll redecorate the house instead of selling it*

■ In combination with an adjective, and with noun phrases

> **Es difícil hacerlo** *It's difficult to do it*
>
> **Parecía imposible equivocarse** *It seemed impossible to make a mistake*
>
> **Cuesta trabajo pensar eso** *It's hard to think that*

If the Infinitive has no object and is not followed by **que**, **de** is required:

> **Es que ella es difícil *de* olvidar** *The fact is she's difficult to forget*
> **Sería imposible *de* probar** *It would be impossible to prove*

But this construction is usually avoided and **es que es difícil olvidarla, sería difícil probarlo**, etc. are used instead.

■ **As a noun.** In this case it often corresponds to the English form ending in *-ing*. When used as a noun, the Spanish Infinitive is masculine and singular:

> **No me gusta esperar** *I don't like waiting*
> **Cansa mucho viajar en avión** *Traveling* (British *travelling*) *in planes makes one very tired*
> **Sería mejor dejarlos aquí** *It would be better to leave them here*

This kind of sentence must never be translated using the Spanish Gerund: **'hablando da sed'* is definitely not possible for **(el) hablar da sed** *talking makes you thirsty*.

Use of the Definite Article with the Infinitive in such sentences is more or less optional, although it is common in literary styles at the head of a sentence or clause:

> **(El) decir esto le iba a causar muchos problemas** *Saying this was to cause him many problems*
> **Los médicos afirman que (el) comer mucho ajo es bueno para el corazón** *Doctors claim that eating a lot of garlic is good for the heart*

■ To make a quick answer to a question

> **—¿Qué hacemos? —Pensar** '*What are we going to do?' 'Think.'*

■ In familiar speech, as an alternative for the Imperative

This construction is discussed under the Imperative, p.36 ff.

■ In combination with **que,** or with the prepositions **por** or **a,** as an alternative for a relative clause.

The construction with **a** is commonly seen, but foreigners should use it only in set phrases like the ones shown:

> **Tengo mucho que hacer** *I've got a lot to do*
> **Queda mucho que/por hacer** *There's a lot left to do*
> **total a pagar** *total to pay/payable*
> **asuntos a tratar** *matters to be discussed*

> **Para** is used after verbs of wanting, needing:

> **Quieren algo para comer** *They want something to eat*
> **Necesito dinero para vivir** *I need money to live*

The gerund

The Gerund always ends in -**ndo**. It is formed:

In the case of all -**ar** verbs, by replacing the -**ar** by -**ando: hablar**—**hablando** *talking,* **andar**—**andando** *walking.*

In the case of most -**er** and -**ir** verbs, by replacing the Infinitive ending by -**iendo: comer**—**comiendo, vivir** -**viviendo, ser** -**siendo,** etc.

-**iendo** is written -**yendo** when it follows another vowel: **destruir**—**destruyendo** *destroying,* **creer**—**creyendo** *believing,* **caer**—**cayendo** *falling,* **oír**—**oyendo** *hearing.* The Gerund of **ir** is regularly formed: **yendo** *going.*

-**iendo** becomes -**endo** after **ñ** or **ll: gruñir**—**gruñendo** *growling,* **reñir**—**riñendo** *scolding,* **engullir**—**engullendo** *gobbling up, swallowing whole.*

Poder, venir, morir and **dormir**, and all verbs conjugated like **pedir, sentir** and **reír** base their Gerund on the stem of the third-person Preterit:

Infinitive	3rd-person Preterit	Gerund
poder	**pudo**	**pudiendo** *being able*
venir	**vino**	**viniendo** *coming*
repetir	**repitió**	**repitiendo** *repeating,*
pedir	**pidió**	**pidiendo** *asking for*
sentir	**sintió**	**sintiendo** *feeling*
corregir	**corrigió**	**corrigiendo** *correcting*
freír	**frió**	**friendo** *frying*
dormir	**durmió**	**durmiendo** *sleeping*
morir	**murió**	**muriendo** *dying*

The gerund of **decir** is not based on the preterite form (**dijo**): **diciendo** *saying*.

The Gerund is used:

■ To show that an action is simultaneous with another:

> **Entró riendo** *He came in laughing*
> **Se lo diré, pero no estando aquí este señor** *I'll tell you, but not while this gentleman is here*

■ To show the method by which something is done

> **Se hizo rico vendiendo vídeos ilegales** *He got rich selling illegal videos*
> **Verás el jardín asomándote al balcón** *You'll see the garden by looking out of the window*
> **Me molestaba cada cinco minutos diciéndome que no tenía dinero** *He bothered me every five minutes saying that he didn't have any money*

■ With **estar** to make the Continuous Form of verbs: **está trabajando** *he's (in the middle of) working*. This is discussed on p.13 ff.

■ With verbs meaning *see, imagine, paint, draw, photograph, meet, find, catch, surprise, remember*:

> **Los cogieron robando manzanas** *They caught them stealing apples*
>
> **Le sacaron una foto cenando con el presidente** *They took a photo of him/her having dinner with the President*
>
> **La vi jugando en el parque** *I saw her playing in the park*

Other verbs found with this construction are **recordar** *to remember*, **describir** *to describe*, **dibujar** *to sketch*, **pintar** *to paint*, **mostrar** *to show*, **representar** *to represent*.

With the verb **ver** *to see* the Infinitive is used if the action is complete: **lo/le vi bajarse del autobús** *I saw him get out of the bus* but **la vi jugando en el jardín** *I saw her (while she was) playing in the garden*.

The Infinitive is used after **oír** *to hear*: **te oyeron entrar** *they heard you come in*. The Infinitive is also always used with the verbs **venir** *to come* and **ir** *to go*: **la veíamos venir** *we could see her coming*, **lo/le vi ir hacia la puerta** *I saw him go towards the door*.

With **ver** and **oír** the idea of ongoing action can be stressed in colloquial language by using **que** + Imperfect Indicative: **la vi que iba en bicicleta** *I saw her riding a bicycle*.

■ With **venir** and **ir** to show that an event is drawn out over a period of time:

> **Iba apuntando todo lo que decían** *He was noting down everything they were saying*
>
> **Los problemas vienen siendo cada vez más complicados** *The problems are getting more and more complicated*

■ With **llevar** *to carry* to translate the idea of *to do something for n days/months/years*, etc.

> **Lleva varios días pintando la casa** *He's been painting his house for several days*

See page 205 for more remarks on this construction.

■ Occasionally as alternative for **aunque** *although* or **a pesar de que** *despite*

> **Un día se confesó que, amando inmensamente a su hija, le tenía envidia** *One day she admitted to herself that, despite loving her daughter immensely, she envied her*

■ As an alternative to **porque** *because* or **ya que** *since*:

> **Calló, viendo que el otro no le hacía caso** *He fell silent, seeing that the other was not paying attention to him*

■ In combination with **como**, as an alternative to **como si** *as if*

> **Se agachó como preparándose para saltar** *He squatted down, as if preparing to jump*
>
> **Emitió una tosecilla, como llamándonos al orden** *He made a slight cough, as if calling us to order*

The gerund as a participle

English regularly uses the *-ing* form of verbs to form an adjective: *an exhausting task*, *a surprising attitude*, *a freezing wind*. The Spanish Gerund is not possible in these cases: an adjective or a participle in **-nte** must be used (if one exists: see below): **una tarea agotadora, una actitud sorprendente, un viento helado**. The only exceptions are the two invariable adjectives **hirviendo** and **ardiendo**—**agua hirviendo** *boiling water*, **un árbol ardiendo** *a burning tree*.

English also constantly uses the *-ing* form to replace a relative pronoun plus a finite verb: *passengers waiting for*

the train, a woman driving a car. In Spanish a Relative
Pronoun and a Finite Verb must be used: **los pasajeros
que esperan el tren, una mujer que conduce/con-
ducía un coche**. The only exception that need concern
beginners is captions to pictures: **una foto de una mujer
dando de comer a un niño** *a photo of a woman feeding a
child.*

In general, foreign students should respect the rule that
the Spanish Gerund is basically a kind of adverb and must
therefore modify a verb. If there is no verb, as in the
phrase *a plane carrying passengers* there can be no Gerund:
un avión que lleva/llevaba pasajeros, not **'un avión
llevando pasajeros'.*

The past participle

Forms

from **-ar** verbs	by replacing the **-ar** by **-ado**
from **-er** and **-ir** verbs	by replacing the ending by **-ido**

hablar	*to speak*	**hablado**	*spoken*
comer	*to eat*	**comido**	*eaten*
ser	*to be*	**sido**	*been*
vivir	*to live*	**vivido**	*lived*
ir	*to go*	**ido**	*gone*

When the Infinitive ends in **-ír**, **-aer** or **-eer** the Past
Participle ending is written with an accent: **reír—reído** *to
laugh,* **traer—traído** *to bring,* **creer—creído** *to believe.*
Verbs whose Infinitive ends in **-uir** do not have an accent:
construir—construido *to build.*

The following forms are irregular:

abrir	*to open*	**abierto**	*opened*
absolver	*to absolve*	**absuelto**	*absolved*

cubrir	*to cover*	**cubierto**	*covered*
decir	*to say*	**dicho**	*said*
descomponer	*to put out of order*	**descompuesto**	*disordered*
describir	*to describe*	**descrito**	*described*
descubrir	*to discover*	**descubierto**	*discovered*
devolver	*to give back*	**devuelto**	*given back*
encubrir	*to cover up/ conceal*	**encubierto**	*concealed*
envolver	*to wrap up*	**envuelto**	*wrapped up*
escribir	*to write*	**escrito**	*written*
freír	*to fry*	**frito**	*fried*
hacer	*to make/do*	**hecho**	*made/done*
imponer	*to impose*	**impuesto**	*imposed*
inscribirse	*to sign on*	**inscrito**	*signed on*
morir	*to die*	**muerto**	*dead/died*
poner	*to put*	**puesto**	*put*
posponer	*to postpone*	**pospuesto**	*postponed*
prever	*to predict*	**previsto**	*foreseen*
resolver	*to resolve*	**resuelto**	*resolved*
revolver	*to turn over/ around*	**revuelto**	*turned over/ scrambled*
romper	*to break*	**roto**	*broken*
suponer	*to suppose*	**supuesto**	*supposed*
ver	*to see*	**visto**	*seen*
volver	*to return*	**vuelto**	*returned*

Another kind of irregularity involves a distinction between the verbal past participle and the past participle used as an adjective. The forms in the second column are used to form the Compound Tenses (e.g. **ha absorbido** *it has absorbed*, **habían soltado** *they had set free*), while the words in the third column form adjectives: **estaba absorto en su trabajo** *he was engrossed/absorbed in his work*, **unos papeles sueltos** *some loose sheets of paper*.

Infinitive	Verbal	Adjectival	
absorber	absorbido	absorto	*absorbed*
bendecir	bendecido	bendito	*blessed*
confesar	confesado	confeso	*confessed*
confundir	confundido	confuso	*confused*
despertar	despertado	despierto	*woken up*
elegir	elegido	electo	*chosen/elect*
imprimir	imprimido	impreso	*printed*
maldecir	maldecido	maldito	*cursed*
prender	prendido	preso	*taken prisoner*
presumir	presumido	presunto	*presumed*
proveer	proveído	provisto	*equipped with*
soltar	soltado	suelto	*let out*
suspender	suspendido	suspenso	*failed (exams)*

Uses of the past participle

The uses of the Spanish Past Participle resemble that of the English past participle. The main uses are:

■ In combination with the appropriate form of **haber,** to form Compound Tenses (e.g. the Perfect, Pluperfect, etc.):

> **Los científicos han descubierto una nueva droga** *Scientists have discovered a new drug*

> **No se habían dado cuenta** *They hadn't realized*

In these tenses the participle is invariable in form: it does not agree with either the subject or the object of the verb. The use of the Compound Tenses is discussed on p. 9 ff.

■ In combination with the verb **ser**, and also sometimes with the verb **estar**, to form the Passive Voice of verbs (which is discussed further on pp. 64 ff):

> **El nuevo proyecto será presentado por el ministro de Obras Públicas** *The new project will be presented by the Minister for Public Works*

As in English, the passive participle frequently appears without the verb *to be*:

> **Han encontrado a las niñas perdidas** *They've found the lost girls (i.e. the girls that were lost)*
>
> **Preguntados sobre el aumento a los mínimos para este año, los portavoces contestaron que . . .** *Asked about the increase in minimum salaries for this year, the spokespersons replied that . . .*

As the examples show, the participle must agree in number and gender with the noun it refers to.

■ To form adverbial phrases which describe the manner or appearance of the subject of a verb. As the examples show, this construction is used with a much wider range of participles than in English:

> **Gritó alborozado** *He shouted in glee/gleefully*
>
> **Me miraba fascinada** *She looked at me in fascination*
>
> **Salió contrariado del cuarto** *He came/went out of the room in an upset state*
>
> **Llegados a este punto, podríamos preguntarnos si . . .** *Having got this far, we might ask ourselves whether . . .*
>
> **un autor nacido en España y muerto en Francia** *an author who was born in Spain and died in France*

■ To form absolute participle clauses, i.e. ones that do not depend on the finite verb in the sentence:

> **Cometido este acto de vandalismo, se guardó la navaja** *Having committed this act of vandalism, he put away his knife*

> **Pero, una vez compradas las flores y la tarjeta,
> me di cuenta de que me había olvidado de su
> dirección** But, having bought the flowers and the
> card, I realized that I'd forgotten her address

Adjectival participles

Many Spanish verbs have an adjectival participle formed
by adding **-ante** to **-ar** verbs, and **-iente** (or, in some
cases, **-ente**) to **-er** and **-ir** verbs:

preocupar *to worry*   **preocupante** *worrying*
cambiar *to change*   **cambiante** *changing/fickle*
excitar *to arouse*   **excitante** *arousing*
crecer *to grow*   **creciente** *growing*
sorprender *to surprise*   **sorprendente** *surprising*
conducir *to lead/drive*   **conducente a** *leading to*
consistir en *to consist of*   **consisente en** *consisting of*
existir *to exist*   **existente** *existing*

There are a few irregular forms, the most common
being

convencer *to convince*   **convincente** *convincing*
dormir *to sleep*   **durmiente** *sleeping*
herir *to wound*   **hiriente** *wounding*
provenir de *to come from*   **proveniente de** *coming from*
seguir *to follow*   **siguiente** *following*

The suffix **-nte** is very productive, although many of
the new formations are seen only in newspaper and technical language. But foreigners should not attempt to
invent new words by using it: many verbs, for no obvious
reason, do not form adjectives in **-nte**, e.g.

aburrir *to bore*   **aburrido** *boring*
asombrar *to amaze*   **asombroso** *amazing*
aterrar *to terrify*   **aterrador** *terrifying*
cansar *to tire*   **cansado** *tiring*

confiar *to trust*   **confiado** *trusting*
venir *to come*   **venidero** *coming*

MODAL VERBS (SEE GLOSSARY)

These are **poder** *to be able*, **deber** *must*, **querer** *to want*, **tener que** *to have to*, **haber que** *to be necessary*, **saber** *to know how to*, **soler** *to be accustomed to*. They are followed by an Infinitive, although **poder + que** + Subjunctive is used to mean *it is possible that* and **querer** requires the Subjunctive when its subject is not the same as that of the following verb. **Saber** is also followed by **que** and an indicative tense when it means *to know* rather than *to know how to*.

■ Poder

This differs little in meaning and use from the English *can, may*:

> **No puedo ir hoy** *I can't go today*
> **Podría llover** *It might rain*
> **Puede que la situación mejore** *It may be that the situation will improve* (Lat. Am. also **pueda que . . .**)

The Preterit often means *managed to* (i.e. *could and did*) whereas the Imperfect means *was able* (but *may not have*)

> **No pudo abrir la puerta** *He didn't manage to get the door open*
> **Como no podía hacerlo, pidió ayuda** *Since he couldn't do it, he asked for help*

The Preterit can also refer to something that could have happened but definitely did not:

> **Tuviste suerte. Te pudiste matar** *You were lucky. You could have got killed*

▪ Deber

This translates *must*. As in English, it may indicate obligation or likelihood: *you must do it/you've got to do it, he must
be fifty*. The strict rule is that when it refers to likelihood it
should be followed by **de**:

> **Debe de tener cincuenta años** *He must be fifty*
> (guess)
>
> **Debían de pensar que no era verdad** *They must
> have been thinking that it wasn't true* (guess)
>
> **Debes hacerlo ahora** *You've got to do it now*
> (obligation)
>
> **Deberías llamarlos ahora mismo** *You ought to
> call them right now* (obligation)

The form **deber de** is never used for obligations, but
the form without **de** is constantly used nowadays for both
meanings, which can be confusing for learners. When it is
used for suppositions, **deber (de)** does not appear in the
Future or Conditional tense: **deben (de) ser las cinco** *(I
guess) it must be five o'clock*, not **'deberán (de) ser . . . '*
or **'deberían (de) ser . . . '*

The Imperfect of **deber** either implies *was/were supposed
to . . .* or it may be a familiar alternative for the
Conditional: *ought to do it*: **debías hacerlo tú** *you were
supposed to do it/you ought to do it* (i.e. **deberías hacerlo
tú**). The Preterit of **deber** may mean *should have done it
but didn't*, or *must have done it*:

> **Debí haberme ido, pero me quedé** *I should have
> left, but I stayed*
>
> **Debió de pensar que estamos todos locos** *He
> must have thought we're all mad*

The idea of *had to* (i.e. *was obliged to and did*) is translated by the Preterit of **tener que**:

> **Tuve que ponerme un suéter porque tenía frío** *I
> had to put on a sweater because I was cold*

■ **Tener que**

Tener que implies a strong obligation:

> **Tienes que decirnos la verdad** *You've got to tell us the truth*
> **Tuve que dárselo** *I was obliged to give it to him (and did)*

■ **Haber que**

Haber que (Present Indicative **hay que**) is an impersonal verb followed by the Infinitive and meaning *it is necessary to*:

> **Hay que añadir un poco de agua** *It's necessary to/We'll have to add a bit of water*
> **Hubo que encerrar al perro** *it was necessary to shut the dog in*

■ **Haber de**

Haber de is much used in Mexico for suppositions, where standard Spanish uses **deber de**, e.g. **ha de tener más de cincuenta años** for **debe de tener más de cincuenta años** or **tendrá más de cincuenta años** *he must be more than fifty*. In Spain **haber de** is a rather old-fashioned form that usually expresses a mild obligation: **si viene has de decirle lo que ha pasado** *if he comes you must tell him what has happened*; . . . **debes/tienes que decirle** . . . are more usual.

■ **Querer**

This verb translates *to want*. It also means *to love*, but in the latter sense it can refer only to human beings and animals: **quiero a mis padres, a mi perro** *I love my parents, my dog* but **adoro las novelas de amor** *I love novels about love*.

The conditional form, **querría** or, more commonly, **quisiera**, is used to make polite requests:

**Quisiera/querría expresar mi agradecimiento a
los organizadores . . .** *I'd like to express my
gratitude to the organizers*

The Imperfect means *wanted to*. The Preterit has two
mutually exclusive meanings that can only be clarified by
context. It usually implies *tried to . . .* (i.e. *wanted to but
couldn't*):

Quiso acercarse al Rey, pero no pudo *He tried
to get close to the King was, but he couldn't manage it*

However, it may imply *wanted to and did* when some idea
of getting one's own way is involved: **lo dije porque
quise, nada más** *I said it because I felt like it, and that's
that*. The negative of the Preterit means *refused* (i.e. *didn't
want to and didn't*): **no quiso decir su nombre** *he refused
to give his name.*

▪ Saber

The basic meaning of **saber** is *to know* (a fact); it must be
distinguished from **conocer** *to know* (a person or place).
Combined with an Infinitive it means *to know how to*, as in

Casi me ahogué por no saber nadar *I nearly
drowned because of not knowing how to swim*
**Me despidieron porque no sabía escribir a
máquina** *They fired me because I couldn't type*

▪ Soler

This basically means *to be accustomed to*, *usually*. It is not
used in the future or conditional tenses:

Solía limpiar mi coche (Lat. Am. **carro/auto**)
todos los días *I used to clean my car every day*
Suele hacer menos calor en septiembre *It's usually less hot in September*

THE PASSIVE

The Passive construction makes the Direct Object of an Active sentence into the Subject of a Passive one. Active: *I chose the red one*. Passive: *the red one was chosen by me*.

The Spanish Passive is formed in one of two ways:

(a) In a way similar to English, by using the verb meaning *to be* (**ser,** or occasionally **estar**) + the Past Participle, which must agree in number and gender:

> **Mis dos novelas fueron publicadas el año pasado** *My two novels were published last year*
> **El proyecto fue rechazado por el comité** *The project was rejected by the committee*

(b) By using the Passive **se** construction:

> **Mis dos novelas se publicaron el año pasado** *My two novels were published last year*

Construction (a) and construction (b) are usually interchangeable, but only if the preposition **por** does not appear. In other words, if **se** is used we cannot go on to say *by* whom or what the action was done. For this reason one should not say **'el proyecto se rechazó por el comité'*. The Passive with **se** is further discussed at pp. 73–4.

The following points about the Spanish Passive with **ser** should be noted:

■ It is only used in written Spanish (where it is common, especially in newspapers)

This is a bold generalization, but English-speaking learners of Spanish will do well to avoid the Passive with **ser** when speaking Spanish and to master first the use of the much more common Passive **se** (p.73). Usually a simple active construction produces the best and most idiomatic Spanish: passive sentences like **estoy muy con-**

tento porque *fui besádo por* una actriz muy famosa
I'm really happy because I was kissed by a famous actress
sound natural to English-speakers but they are very
clumsy in Spanish. The active construction is more normal: . . . **porque me besó una actriz muy famosa** . . .
because a very famous actress kissed me.

Examples of the passive from written Spanish:

> **El derrumbamiento del edificio fue causado por
> un terremoto** *The collapse of the building was
> caused by an earthquake*
>
> **Los hechos serán investigados por las autori-
> dades** *The facts will be investigated by the
> authorities*
>
> **Varias personas han sido expulsadas del par-
> tido** *Several people have been expelled from the
> party*

■ It must *never* be used when the subject of the verb **ser**
would be the Indirect Object

English allows two passive versions of sentences like
*they gave fifty dollars **to** me*: *fifty dollars were given to me* or *I
was given fifty dollars*. The second of these two construction is *never* possible in Spanish and the best translation in
both cases is **me dieron cincuenta dólares** *they gave me
fifty dollars.* **'Fui dado cincuenta dólares'* is definitely
not Spanish. Further examples

> **Nunca me contaban la verdad** *I was never told
> the truth/They never told me the truth.*
>
> **Me preguntaron varias cosas** *I was asked sev-
> eral things/They asked me several things*
>
> **Le enviaron una carta** *He/She was sent a
> letter/They sent him/her a letter*

Fue enviada una carta can only mean *a letter was sent.*

■ *Never* with verbs combined with a preposition. Compare
*this bed has been slept **in*** and **alguien ha dormido en esta**

cama (*someone has slept in this bed*), *never* **'esta cama ha sido dormido en'* which is emphatically not Spanish.

■ Usually only with the Preterit, Perfect and Future tenses of **ser**

Sentences like **fue interrogado por la policía** *he was interrogated by the police*, **ha sido interrogado . . .** and **será interrogado . . .** sound more natural than **es interrogado por la policía** *he is interrogated . . .* or **era interrogado por la policía** *he was being interrogated . . .* (although **estaba siendo interrogado . . .** is not unusual). Use of the Present or Imperfect of **ser** with the Passive is rather more common in Latin America than in Spain.

Use of *estar* to form the passive

■ A passive construction may be formed with **estar**

Use of **estar** draws attention to the state something is in, whereas use of **ser** describes the event that caused the state. Compare

> **La ciudad estaba inundada por las lluvias** *The city was covered in water as a result of the rains* (describes the state the city was in)
> **La ciudad fue inundada por las lluvias** *The city was flooded by the rain* (describes an event)

PRONOMINAL ('REFLEXIVE') VERBS

Pronominal verbs are verbs like **llamarse** *to be called*, **defenderse** *to defend oneself/to 'get by'*, **inhibirse** *to be inhibited*, **irse** *to go away*. These verbs are often called 'reflexive verbs', but the name is inaccurate. 'Reflexive' refers to only one of the various meanings of the Pronominal forms of verbs.

Pronominal verbs have an object pronoun that is of the same person and number as the subject of the verb:

> **(Yo) me lavo** *I wash (myself)*
> **(Tú) te vas** *You go away*
> **(Él/ella/usted) se cayó** *He/she/you fell over*
> **(Nosotros) nos queremos** *We love one another*
> **(Vosotros) os arrepentisteis** *You repented*
> **(Ellos/eilas/ustedes) se imaginan** *They/you imagine*

As the examples show, the third-person pronoun used for singular and plural is **se**. This pronoun may variously be translated *himself/herself/itself/yourself/themselves/yourselves*, but it also has several other uses.

Pronominal verbs have many uses in Spanish—far more than in French—and some of them are rather subtle. The picture is made more complicated by the fact that, as explained on p. 114, the pronoun **le** becomes **se** before **lo/la/los/las**, as in **se lo dije a mi madre** *I told it to my mother* (instead of the impossible * **'le lo dije a mi madre'**). This is an entirely different use of **se** not related to the issues discussed in this section.

The various uses of Pronominal verbs are best clarified by considering cases in which the subject of the verb is animate (human or some other animal) and cases in which the subject is inanimate.

Pronominal verbs with animate (human or animal) subjects

In this case the Pronominal form of verbs is used:

■ To show that the action is *not* done to someone or something else. Compare **asustas** *you frighten/you're frightening* (i.e. for someone else) and **te asustas** *you get frightened* (no one else involved). English often requires translation by *get . . .* + adjective or by *become*. Further examples:

Casó a su hija con un abogado *He married his daughter off to a lawyer*

Su hija se casó con un abogado *His daughter married/got married to a lawyer*

Convence cuando habla así *He's convincing (to others) when he talks like that*

Se convence cuando habla así *He gets convinced when he talks like that*

Se divorciaron al cabo de tres años *They got divorced after three years*

Me matriculé para el curso de inglés *I registered for the course of English*

Me canso fácilmente *I get tired easily*

Se irrita por nada *He gets irritable over nothing*

No te enojes/enfades *Don't get cross*

- Simply to give the verb a different meaning altogether:

admirar *to admire*	**admirarse** *to be surprised*
despedir *to fire*	**despedirse** *to say good-bye*
dormir *to sleep*	**dormirse** *to go to sleep*
fumar *to smoke*	**fumarse** *to skip a class, meeting* (colloquial)
guardar *to guard*	**guardarse de** *to refrain from*

Some verbs are only found in the pronominal form. The following are common:

abstenerse *to abstain*
acatarrarse *to get a cold*
arrepentirse *to repent*
atreverse a *to dare*
enfermarse *to get ill* (but **enfermar** is used in Spain with the same meaning)
quejarse de *to complain about*
suicidarse *to commit suicide*

There are also certain commonly occurring verbs in which the pronominal form merely has a special nuance that needs separate explanation for each verb. A list of these appears on pp.75 ff.

■ To show that an action is done *to* or *for* oneself: this is the 'reflexive' use of pronominal verbs.The action can be accidental or deliberate. The subject is human or animal for the obvious reason that cups, doors etc. don't usually do things to themselves:

> **Me rasqué** *I scratched myself*
> **Te peinaste** *You did your hair* (literally *you combed yourself*)
> **Mario se ensució** *Mario got himself dirty*
> **Ustedes se van a matar haciendo eso** *You're going to kill yourselves doing that*
> **Se quitó el sombrero** *He took off his hat*
> **Se sacó el dinero del bolsillo** *He took the money out of his (own) pocket*

■ When the verb is plural, to mean *to do something to or for one another*:

This is the 'reciprocal' use of the pronominal form, and again the subjects are usually humans or other animals since doors or bricks don't usually do things to one another:

> **Se escriben todas las semanas** *They write to one another every week*
> **Se daban golpes** *They were hitting one another*
> **Nos respetamos el uno al otro** *We respect one another*

The phrase **el uno al otro** or (when more than two subjects are involved) **los unos a los otros** *one another* may be added to clarify the meaning. **La una a la otra** and **las unas a las otras** are used only when only females are involved.

■ To give the sentence a passive meaning. This is rare with animate subjects because of the clash of meanings with the other uses of the Pronominal form listed above. However, it occurs when the noun does not refer to specific individuals, as in **se ven muchos turistas en agosto** *a lot of tourists are seen in August*. This construction is very common with inanimate subjects (see below).

When the noun refers to specific individuals, a special construction exists which makes Passive **se** unambiguous with human subjects:

> **Se detuvo *a* un narcotraficante** *A drug-pusher was arrested*
> **Se admiraba mucho *a* estos profesores** *These teachers were much admired*

In this case the verb is always singular and the preposition **a** is put before the noun. This construction avoids the problem raised by **estos profesores se admiraban mucho**, which would mean *these teachers admired themselves a lot* or . . . *admired one another a lot*.

Students must not confuse this construction with Passive **se** used with nouns referring to inanimate things, as described on page 73. It is possible to rewrite **se admiraba mucho a estos profesores** as **se les**[17] **admiraba mucho** *they were admired a lot*. But this is not possible when the original sentence refers to an inanimate thing, as in **se venden manzanas** *apples are sold*, which can only be rewritten **se venden** *they are sold*, not *★'se las vende'*. This is discussed in more detail in note (c) on page 74.

[17] There is a tendency everywhere to use **le/les** for *him/her/you* (i.e. ~~usted or ustedes~~)/*them* in this construction rather than **lo/la/los/las**, although the latter is not incorrect.

■ With singular intransitive verbs (like *to go*, *to arrive*, *to be*), as an equivalent of English impersonal sentences that have the subject *one*, *people* or *you* used impersonally:

> **En España se duerme por la tarde** *In Spain people sleep in the afternoon*
> **Por esta carretera se llega al castillo medieval** *Along this road one arrives at the medieval castle*
> **Se está mejor al sol** *One's better off in the sun*

This construction cannot be used with a verb that already has **se** attached for some other reason. In this case the pronoun **uno** *one* is required or, in less formal language, **tú**:

> **Si uno se levanta tarde, se pierde lo mejor del día** *If one gets up late one misses the best part of the day* (**levantarse** *to get up* is already a pronominal verb)
> **Uno se olvida de esas cosas/Te olvidas de esas cosas** *One forgets such things/you forget such things* (**olvidarse de** *to forget*)

■ With singular transitive verbs which in English would have the pronoun *people*, *one*, *you*.

This construction is sometimes difficult to distinguish from the Passive use of **se** described later. If the sentence contains no noun or pronoun that could be understood as the subject, the impersonal meaning is intended. Thus, if we are talking about olive oil, the sentence **en España se come mucho** means *a lot of it is eaten in Spain* (passive: implied subject *olive oil*). But if the conversation is on general eating habits, the same sentence means *people eat a lot in Spain* (impersonal: the verb has no subject):

> **Se habla de ello, pero no lo creo** *People talk about it, but I don't believe it*
> **En este país se escribe y se lee poco** *In this country people don't write or read much*

■ With a few verbs, to give the meaning *to get something done*

> **Me voy a hacer un traje** *I'm going to get a suit made* (or *I'm going to make myself a suit*)
> **El rey se construyó un palacio de mármol** *The king built (i.e. had himself built) a marble palace*
> **Me tuve que operar de apendicitis** *I had to have an operation for appendicitis*
> **Me peino en Vidal Sassoon** *I get my hair done at Vidal Sassoon's*

This construction is not used in some parts of Latin America, where **mandar** plus the Infinitive is used to express the idea of ordering something to be done: **mandó construir un palacio** *he had a palace built* (this construction is also possible in Spain).

■ With verbs meaning *eat*, *drink* or other types of consumption, *know*, *see*, *learn* and one or two others, to emphasize the quantity consumed, learned, seen, etc. This device is optional (but usual) and is only possible when a specific quantity is mentioned:

> **Me bebí tres vasos de ron** *I drank three glasses of rum*
> **Te has comido una pizza entera** *You've eaten a whole pizza*
> **Se leyó el libro entero** *He read the whole book*
> **Se lo creyó todo** *He believed every word of it*

Pronominal verbs with inanimate subjects (neither human nor animals)

In this case the verb can only be third-person (since stones, trees, etc. can't speak for themselves). The Pronominal form of the verb shows

■ That the verb has no outside subject (i.e. that the verb is Intransitive). Compare **abrió la puerta** *he/she opened the door* and **se abrió la puerta** *the door opened*.

> **Esta madera se está pudriendo** *This wood is going rotten*
> **El agua se ha enfriado** *The water's got cold*
> **Se le hinchó la mano** *His hand swelled up*

This construction does not apply to all verbs. Several non-pronominal verbs can also refer to more or less spontaneous actions (i.e. actions that have no external subject):

> **La situación ha mejorado** *The situation has improved*
> **El globo reventó** *The balloon burst*
> **La hierba ha crecido** *The grass has grown*
> **Las cantidades han aumentado** *The quantities have increased*

■ To make the passive. This is much more common with inanimate than with human and other animal subjects:

> **Se rehogan la cebolla y el ajo en aceite caliente** *The onion and garlic are sautéed/lightly fried in hot oil*
> **Se compran libros de ocasión** *Second-hand books bought*
> **Esas cosas no debieron decirse** *Those things shouldn't have been said*

Se acepta la propuesta de la oposición *The opposition's proposal is accepted*

Three important points about this construction are:

(a) The verb should agree in number with the subject. Foreign students should respect this rule whatever they may hear or see: sentences like **'se compra libros de ocasión'* are usually considered incorrect.

(b) This construction should not be followed by **por** + the agent of the action. If the person or thing that performed the action must be mentioned, only the Passive with **ser** (p.64) can be used: **el programa fue diseñado por J. González** *the program* (British *programme*) *was designed by J. González* is correct and **'el programa se diseñó por J. González'* is generally considered to be bad Spanish.

(c) The noun in this construction cannot be replaced by a pronoun. In other words one cannot change **se solucionó el problema** *the problem was solved* into **'se lo solucionó'* for *it was solved*, which is **se solucionó**. Use of an object pronoun is only possible if the original sentence referred to a human being and included the preposition **a** (the construction described on p.70). The following examples should make this clear:

Se admira mucho a Cervantes *Cervantes is admired a great deal*
Se *le* admira mucho *He is admired a lot*

Su novela se publicó el año pasado *His novel was published last year*
Se publicó el año pasado *It was published last year*

Se *le* puede ver *He/she can be seen*
Se puede ver (or) **puede verse** *It can be seen*

Unclassifiable pronominal verbs (subject either animate or inanimate)

A number of Spanish pronominal verbs are unclassifiable. The pronominal form merely has an extra nuance of meaning and these verbs must be learned as separate items. This type of verb raises problems that are not appropriate for a grammar of this size, so the following list includes only a brief description of some frequently encountered forms:

Infinitive	*non-Pronominal*	*Pronominal*
aparecer	*to appear*	*to materialize (ghosts, visions)*
bajar	*to go down stairs drop* (prices, etc.)	*to get out of to get down from (trees, etc.)*
caer	*to fall/drop*	*to fall down/over*
conocer	*to know (a person)*	*to know only too well*
dejar	*to leave something*	*to leave behind accidentally*
devolver	*to give back, to vomit*	*parts of Lat. Am. to come back*
encontrar	*to find*	*to find by chance*
estar	*to be* (somewhere)	*to stay put in a place*
ir	*to go*	*to go away, leave*
llegar	*to arrive*	*to approach*
llevar	*to carry, wear*	*to take away*
marchar	*to march*	*to go away*
morir	*to die*	*same, but used of loved ones or for lingering deaths*
parecer	*to seem*	*to resemble*
pasar	*to pass (by) to spend time*	*to go over the mark*

Infinitive	non-Pronominal	Pronominal
regresar	to come back	to return before time (only Lat. Am.)
salir	to leave, exit (normally)	to walk out, (fluid, gas) to leak
subir	go up stairs rise (prices, temperature)	get in (cars, etc.) climb (trees, etc.)
volver	to come back (normally)	to turn back, return before time

In some cases the difference is more or less simply stylistic, the non-pronominal form being rather more formal:

> **Olvidé decírtelo/Me olvidé de decírtelo/Se me olvidó decírtelo** *I forgot to tell you*
> **Espera/Espérate** *Wait!*
> **Calla/Cállate** *Be quiet!*
> **(Me) gasté todo el dinero que traía** *I spent all the money I had*
> **(Se) inventa cada cuento . . .** *He makes up all sorts of stories . . .*

Often the pronominal form suggests an unplanned or accidental action. Compare

> **La lluvia cae del cielo** *Rain falls from the sky* (natural)
> **(Se) cayó de la mesa** *It fell off the table*
> **Me caí en la calle** *I fell over in the street*

Ser, estar and 'there is'/'there are'

Spanish has two words that both translate as *to be*. They can only rarely be used interchangeably

ESTAR

The verb **estar** must be used:

■ To indicate *where* an object or person is (but not where something is *happening*, in which case use **ser**, as explained below):

> **Madrid está en España** *Madrid's in Spain*
> **Dile que no estoy** *Tell him I'm not at home*
> **¿Dónde está la piscina[18]?** *Where's the swimming-pool?*

■ With adjectives and participles to show the state or condition that something or someone is in, not an inherent characteristic. The condition or state is usually temporary—but not always, as the word **muerto** shows:

> **Estoy cansado/deprimido/contento** *I'm tired/depressed/pleased*
> **Está muerto/vivo** *He's dead/alive*
> **La ventana estaba rota** *The window was broken*
> **Las manzanas están verdes** *The apples are unripe* (**las manzanas son verdes** = *apples are green*)

[18] **Piscina = la alberca** in much of Latin America.

> **Estoy con gripe** *I've got the flu*
> **Estoy bien** *I'm feeling fine*

Compare **la nieve está negra** *the snow's black* (because of the soot, dirt) and **la nieve es blanca** *snow is white* (its natural state), or **eres muy guapa** *you're very attractive* and **estás muy guapa** *you're **looking** very attractive*.

■ To show that someone's or something's condition has altered (e.g. since you last saw it):

> **Manuel está calvo** *Manuel has gone bald*
> **Me han dicho que estás casado** *They tell me you're married*
> **¡Qué delgada está!** *Hasn't she got thin!*

Use of **ser** implies something more long-standing: **es casado** *he's a married man*, **es delgada** *she's thin/a thin person*.

■ To describe the taste or appearance of something:

> **Esta sopa está muy buena/rica** *This soup tastes very good/appetizing*
> **Está muy vieja** *She's looking very old*

SER

Ser must be used

■ To link two nouns or a pronoun and a noun:

> **La cebolla es una planta** *The onion is a plant*
> **Mario es profesor** *Mario is a teacher*
> **Yo soy psicólogo** *I'm a psychologist*
> **Esto es un problema** *This is a problem*

The pronoun may be implicit in the verb:

> **Era un hermoso día** *It was a lovely day*
> **Son estudiantes** *They're students*
> **Son las ocho** *It's eight o'clock*

The verb **estar** + a Noun or Pronoun means *to be at home*, *to be there*:

> **Está Mario** *Mario's there*
> **No está** *He's not at home*

Exceptions to this rule are so rare that beginners can ignore them, although the phrase **está un día hermoso** *it's a lovely day* is commonly heard in Spain.

■ To indicate *where* or *when* an event is happening

> **¿Dónde es la fiesta/clase/conferencia?** *Where's the party/class/lecture (being held)?*
> **La Guerra Civil fue en 1936** *The Civil War was in 1936*

But **estar** must be used for location of a thing: **¿Dónde está la habitación?** *Where's the room?*

■ With adjectives and participles, to show that a quality is an intrinsic part of something's nature rather than its condition or state:

> **Soy americano** *I'm American*
> **Eso es diferente** *That's different*
> **Son míos** *They're mine*
> **Son muy grandes** *They're very tall/big*
> **La Tierra es redonda** *The earth is round*

It is true that in such cases **ser** usually refers to a *permanent* quality, compare **soy rubio** *I'm blond* and **estoy irritado** *I'm irritated*. But **muerto** *dead* takes **estar** and the following possibly temporary states take **ser** in standard Spanish:

> **Soy feliz/desgraciado** *I'm happy/unhappy*
> **Soy rico/pobre** *I'm rich/poor* (or **estoy rico/pobre** for a temporary condition)
> **Soy consciente** *I'm aware* (**estoy consciente** in Lat. America)

Note however the phrase **estoy feliz y contento** *I'm happy and contented*. **Estar feliz/desgraciado** is commonly heard in Latin America, but it is usually avoided in writing.

■ In the phrase **ser de** *to be from, to be made from*

> **Soy de Madrid** *I'm from Madrid*
> **Es de oro** *It's made of gold*

CHANGES OF MEANING WITH *SER* AND *ESTAR*

Some adjectives change meaning according to which verb is used:

Adjective	Meaning with **ser**	Meaning with **estar**
aburrido	boring	bored
bueno	good	tasty
cansado	tiresome	tired
consciente	aware	conscious (not knocked out)
despierto	sharp-witted	awake
interesado	self-seeking	interested
listo	clever/smart	ready
malo	bad	ill
orgulloso	proud/haughty	proud (of something)
rico	rich	delicious
verde	green/smutty	unripe
vivo	alert	alive

THERE IS/THERE ARE

The Spanish for *there is/are* is **hay**. This is a special form of the verb **haber**, and the usual forms of this verb are used for the other tenses of **hay**. When used with this meaning, the verb is always third-person and always singular (although use of the plural for *there were/will be*, e.g. **habían/habrán muchos** for **había/habrá muchos** *there were/will be a lot* is extremely common in spoken Latin-American Spanish and also in Castilian as spoken by Catalans. It should be avoided in writing and it is not accepted in Spain). Examples

> **Hay cinco árboles** *There are five trees*
> **Había varias personas** *There were several people*
> **Hubo una tremenda explosión** *There was a tremendous explosion*

■ When **haber** refers back to some noun already mentioned in the sentence it normally requires an object pronoun:

> **Hay un error, o si no *lo* hay, entonces estas cifras son increíbles** *There's a mistake, or if there isn't then these figures are incredible*

■ The basic meaning of **haber** is *exist*. If the meaning is *is there* (i.e. rather than somewhere else) the verb **estar** is used:

> **Está Antonio** *Antonio is there/There's Antonio*
> **Para eso está el diccionario** *That's what the dictionary is there for*

Compare

> **¿Quién hay que sepa ruso?** *Who is there (i.e. who exists) who knows Russian?*

Articles

The Definite Article *82*
The Indefinite Article *87*

THE DEFINITE ARTICLE

The four forms of the Spanish Definite Article (the equivalent of *the*) are:

	singular	*plural*
masculine	**el**	**los**
feminine	**la**	**las**

There is also a 'neuter article', **lo**, discussed on pp.145 ff.

These words stand in front of a noun and agree in number and gender with it: **el hombre** *the man*, **los hombres** *the men*, **la ventana** *the window* (fem.), **las ventanas** *the windows*.

■ When a feminine noun begins with a stressed **a-** sound, the masculine article is used in the singular, but the noun remains feminine and the feminine articles, definite and indefinite, are used in the plural: **el/un águila** *the/an eagle*, but **las águilas** *the eagles*. The following are some common nouns beginning with stressed **a-** or **ha-**:

África	*Africa*
Asia	*Asia*
el agua	*water*
el/un alma	*soul*
el/un ama de casa	*housewife*
el asma	*asthma*
el hambre	*hunger*

el hampa	*criminal underworld*
el/un abra	*mountain pass* (Lat. Am., Spain **el puerto**)
el/un alza	*rise/increase*
el/un ancla	*anchor*
el/un área	*area*
el/un arma	*weapon*
el/un aula	*lecture room/seminar room*
el/un haba	*bean*
el/un habla	*language/speech form*
el/un hacha	*ax/*(British *axe*)
el/un hada	*fairy*
el/un haya	*beech tree*

If any word comes between these nouns and the article, the normal feminine form reappears: **el agua** *the* water, but *la* **misma agua** *the same water*. **La/una** is always used before *adjectives* beginning with stressed **a**: **la/una amplia área** *the/a wide area*.

Feminine words beginning with an *unstressed* **a-** sound take the normal feminine articles:

> **la/una amnistía** *the/an amnesty*
> **la/una hamaca** *the/a hammock*

La is used before letters of the alphabet beginning with stressed **a-**: **la a, la hache**.

■ **A** *to* and **el** compound to form **al**. **De** *of* and **el** compound to form **del**: **voy al mercado** *I'm going to market*, **vengo del banco** *I've just come from the bank*. This is not done if the article is part of a proper name: **los lectores de** *El País* *the readers of El País*, **vamos a El Paso** *we're going to El Paso*.

USES OF THE DEFINITE ARTICLE

Article usage is subtle, prone to exceptions and may vary slightly between regions, but the general rule is that the

Spanish Definite Article is used as in English except that:

■ It is required before countable nouns that are generalizations:

> **Las ardillas son animales** *Squirrels* (in general) *are animals*
> **Me gustan las fresas** *I like strawberries* (i.e. strawberries in general)

■ It is used before abstractions or substances in general when they are the subject or object of a verb or when they stand on their own:

> **la astronomía** *astronomy*
> **la democracia** *democracy*
> **el espacio** *space*
> **la gripe** *flu*
> **el oxígeno** *oxygen*
> **El odio destruye todo** *Hatred destroys everything*
> **Admiro la generosidad** *I admire generosity*

Such nouns often appear without the article after prepositions, especially when they are the second noun in the combination noun + **de** + noun and the English translation could be a compound noun (two nouns joined together): **una lección de filosofía** *a philosophy lesson*, **una carta de amor** *a love letter*, **una fábrica de pan** *a bread factory*.

The article is also not used with nouns describing abstractions and substances after **con** *with* and **sin** *without*: **con entusiasmo** *with enthusiasm*, **sin dinero** *without money*, **los españoles nunca comen nada sin pan** *the Spanish never eat anything without bread*.

■ Articles are omitted before quantities and abstractions that refer only to a part, not to the whole (partitive nouns):

> **Trae azúcar** *Bring some sugar*

> **No he puesto sal** *I haven't put any salt in*
> **Repartieron armas** *They distributed weapons*

See the section on Translation Traps for further remarks on the Spanish equivalents of *some* and *any*.

■ The Definite Article replaces Possessive Adjectives (**mi** *my*, **tu** *your*, **su** *his*, etc.) with parts of the body and with personal belongings, especially when these are the object of a verb or whenever an Indirect Object Pronoun identifies the owner:

> **Mario levantó la mano** *Mario raised his hand*
> **Le robaron la cartera** *They stole his/her note-book/wallet*
> **Yo me quité las botas** *I took off my boots*
> **Te torciste el tobillo** *You twisted your ankle*
> **Póngase el sombrero** *Put on your hat*

■ The article should be used before each noun when more than one occurs, whenever the nouns refer to different things or people:

> **el perro y el gato** *the dog and cat*
> **el padre y la madre de Antonio** *Antonio's father and mother*

but

> **el presidente y secretario del comité** *the chairman and secretary of the committee* (same person)

■ It is used before titles like **señor, señora, señorita**, but not when the person is directly addressed and not before foreign titles:

> **Buenos días, señor/señora Rodríguez** *Good morning Mr/Mrs Rodríguez*
> **Le dije buenos días al señor/a la señora Morán/a míster Brown** *I said Good Day to Sr/Sra Morán/to Mister Brown*

■ It is used before the names of a few countries. There is much disagreement on this matter, but students should note the following points:

(a) Always use the article when a country is modified by an adjective or some other word or phrase that does not form part of its official name: **la España contemporánea** *modern Spain*, **el México de los aztecas** *The Mexico of the Aztecs*, but **Gran Bretaña** *Great Britain*, **Corea del Norte** *North Korea*. The United States is either **Estados Unidos** (singular, the usual form) or **Los Estados Unidos** (plural):

> **Estados Unidos denuncia la actitud de Ruritania** or (less commonly) **Los Estados Unidos denuncian . . .** *USA denounces the attitude of Ruritania*

(b) Use the article with **la India** *India*, **el Reino Unido** *the United Kingdom* and **El Salvador**. The article is more often than not used with **el Líbano** *Lebanon* and, in Latin America, with **la Argentina**. It is also frequent in Latin America with **Perú, Ecuador, Paraguay, Uruguay, Brasil**.

■ It is used with names of languages, except after the verb **hablar** and, usually, after **aprender**: **el español es una lengua latina** *Spanish is a Latin language*, **domina el chino** *he's totally fluent in Chinese*, but **hablo/aprendo inglés** *I speak/am learning English*.

■ The article is used with days of the week and seasons (but not after **en**):

> **Viene los lunes** *He comes on Mondays*
> **Las hojas caen durante el otoño** *The leaves fall during Fall/Autumn*
> **El invierno es la peor estación** *Winter is the worst season*

but

> **En invierno nieva mucho** *It snows a lot in Winter*

■ It is used before the names of streets and squares:

> **Vivo en la Plaza de España** *I live in the Plaza de España*
> **un pequeño hotel de la calle de las Monjas** *a little hotel on Nuns' street*

■ It is used before percentages:

> **El cinco por ciento de los mexicanos** . . . *five percent of Mexicans*

■ It is omitted before the second of two nouns joined by **de** when these form a compound noun. Compare:

> **una voz de mujer** *a woman's voice*
> **la voz de la mujer** *the voice of the woman*
>
> **el agua de manantial** *spring water*
> **el agua del manantial** *the water from the spring*

THE INDEFINITE ARTICLE

The forms of the Spanish Definite Article (the equivalent of *a/an*) are:

	singular	plural
masculine	**un**	**unos**
feminine	**una**	**unas**

Un is used before feminine nouns beginning with stressed **a**, e.g. **un arma** *a weapon,* **un área** *an area.* See p.82.

The Indefinite Article is used in much the same way as its English counterpart, except that:

■ It is omitted after **ser**, and after verbs meaning *to become*, before the names of professions and, often, before words denoting sex:

> **Es profesora** *She's a teacher*
> **Quiere hacerse diplomático** *He wants to become a diplomat*
> **No digo eso sólo porque yo sea mujer** *I don't say that just because I'm a woman*

But it is retained if the noun is qualified or modified by some word or phrase:

> **Es un profesor magnífico** *He's a magnificent teacher*
> **Es una mujer inteligente** *She's an intelligent woman*

■ It is omitted after **tener** *to have*, **llevar** *to wear*, **sacar** *to take out* and a few other common verbs, when the direct object is something of which we usually only have one:

> **Tiene mujer/secretaria/paraguas** *He's got a wife/secretary/umbrella*
> **Mi casa tiene jardín y garaje** *My house has a garden and garage*
> **Busca novia** *He's looking for a girlfriend*
> **Lleva corbata** *He's wearing a tie*

but **tengo un dólar** *I've got a dollar*, **tengo una hermana** *I've got a sister* (because in both cases it would be normal to have more than one). But the article reappears if the noun is qualified: **lleva *una* corbata de seda** *he's wearing a silk tie*, **tiene *una* mujer muy atractiva**[19] *he has a very attractive wife*.

■ It is usually omitted after **sin** *without*, **con** *with* and **como** when it means *for/as*:

---

[19] **Guapo/guapa** is the usual word in Spain for *good-looking*, but it tends to mean *brave/tough* in Latin America, where **buen mozo/buena moza** is often used for *good-looking*. **Atractivo** is used internationally.

un sobre sin estampilla (Spain **sin sello**) *an envelope without a stamp*
un hombre con pasaporte *a man with a passport*
Me lo dio como regalo *He gave it to me as a present*
Ha venido como asesor *He's come as an adviser*

But it is used before **con** when it means *accompanied by*: **ha venido con un amigo** *he's come with a friend*.

■ It is not used before **otro** *another*, or after **qué** *what*, **medio** *half* and **tal** *such a*:

Hay otra película que quiero ver *There's another movie/film I want to see*
¡Qué pena! *What a pity!*
medio kilo *half a kilo*
tal día *such a day*

■ It is used with percentages:

Los precios subieron en un cinco por ciento *Prices rose five percent*

USES OF *UNOS/UNAS*

Spanish is unusual in that the Indefinite Article has a plural form. This is used:

■ To mean *approximately*

Trajeron unos mil kilos *They brought about 1000 kilos*

■ To mean *a/an* before nouns that do not appear in the singular, or to mean *a pair of* before nouns like *scissors*, *shoes*, *pants* that either come in pairs or are symmetrically shaped:

unos zapatos de cuero *a pair of leather shoes*
unas tijeras *a pair of scissors*

> **unos pantalones** *a pair of pants* (Brit. *trousers*)

In the case of nouns that always appear in the plural, e.g. **los celos** *jealousy*, **las vacaciones** *vacation/holidays*, **las ganas** *urge/desire*, and before nouns that would mean a profession if the Indefinite Article were omitted, **unos/unas** must be used whenever **un/una** would be used before a singular noun:

> **unas vacaciones magníficas** *a magnificent vacation/holiday*
> **Yo tenía unas ganas terribles** *I had a terrible urge*
> **Sentía unos celos incontrolables** *She/he felt an uncontrollable jealousy*
> **Sois/son unos payasos** *You're a bunch of clowns* (in the way you act)

Compare

> **Sois/son payasos** *You're clowns* (profession).

■ To mean *a few, a couple of*:

> **Me dejó unos libros** *He left/lent me a few books*
> **Dale unas pesetas** *Give him a couple of pesetas*
> **Unas veces sí, otras no** *Sometimes yes, others no*

Nouns

Gender of nouns *91*
Forms of Nouns referring to Females *97*
Plural of Nouns *100*

GENDER OF NOUNS

Spanish nouns are either masculine or feminine and this has major consequences for the shape of any adjectives, articles or pronouns that may be associated with a noun.

The gender of nouns is not related to questions of sex, except when the nouns refer to human beings or to a few well-known animals. There are few absolutely foolproof rules for predicting the gender of the other nouns in the language, so the best rule is to learn every noun with its definite article, which will soon become instinctive. It must be remembered that the grammatical gender of nouns referring to objects and abstractions is basically arbitrary and has nothing to with their meaning. The fact that **el árbol** *tree* is masculine in Spanish is arbitrary: 'tree' is feminine in the closely-related languages Portuguese and French.

The following generalizations can be made:

■ Nouns referring to men or boys are masculine, and nouns referring to women or girls are feminine:

el hombre *man*	**la mujer** *woman*
el modelo *male model*	**la modelo** *female model*
el juez *male judge*	**la juez** *female judge*

This generalization also applies to a few domestic and

well-known wild animals that have special forms to denote the female of the species:

el caballo *horse*	**la yegua** *mare*
el león *lion*	**la leona** *lioness*
el toro *bull*	**la vaca** *cow*

A longer list of these words appears below at p.97.

There are only a few words that are of invariable gender and apply to human beings of either sex, e.g.:

el bebé *baby*
el genio *genius*
el personaje *character* (in film, etc.),
la estrella *star* (in films, etc.)
la persona *person*
la víctima *victim*
la visita *visitor* (and *visit*)

■ Apart from those already mentioned and few others like **el lobo/la loba** *wolf/she-wolf*, **el gato/la gata** *tom-cat/she-cat*, **el perro/la perra** *dog/bitch*, the names of animals are of fixed arbitrary gender. The gender of these nouns must be learned separately from the dictionary:

la ardilla *squirrel*
el avestruz *ostrich*
la culebra *grass snake*
el lagarto *lizard*
la langosta *lobster*
el salmón *salmon*

The invariable words **macho** *male* and **hembra** *female* can be added if necessary:

el salmón hembra *the female salmon*
las ardillas macho *the male squirrels*

■ Nouns referring to inanimate things (and to plants) are of fixed gender. As was mentioned before, the gender of these words cannot be deduced from the meaning of the word: compare **el cuarto** (masculine) and **la habitación** (feminine) which both mean *room*.

However, the ending of a Spanish nouns that does not refer to a human being often gives a clue to the likely gender of a word:

■ Nouns ending in **-o** are masculine, e.g. **el libro** *book*, **el hombro** *shoulder*. Common exceptions are:

> **la foto** *photo*
> **la libido** *libido*
> **la mano** *hand*
> **la moto** *motor-cycle*
> **la radio** *radio* (in Spain and Argentina, but masculine in northern Latin America)

■ Nouns ending in **-r** are masculine, except **la flor** *flower*, **la coliflor** *cauliflower*, **la labor** *labor*/(Brit. *labour*):

> **el bar** *bar*
> **el calor** *heat*
> **el color** *color/colour*
> **el valor** *value*

■ Nouns ending in a stressed vowel are masculine:

> **(el) Canadá** *Canada*
> **el bisturí** *scalpel*
> **el tisú** *tissue*
> **el sofá** *sofa/couch*

■ Nouns ending in **-aje** are masculine:

> **el viaje** *journey*
> **el equipaje** *baggage*
> **el paisaje** *landscape*

■ Nouns ending in **-ie** are feminine:

> **la intemperie** *bad weather*
> **la serie** *series*

■ Other nouns ending in **-e** are unpredictable and must be learned separately:

> **el arte** (masculine) *art*
> **las artes** (feminine) *the arts*
> **la fuente** *fountain*
> **el puente** *bridge*
> **la parte** *part*
> **el parte** *bulletin*

■ Nouns ending in **-a** are feminine, with the important exceptions listed at (a) through (c) below:

> **la cama** *bed*
> **la casa** *house*
> **la mariposa** *butterfly*
> **la pera** *pear*

Exceptions:

(a)   **el alerta** *alert*
        el cometa *comet*
        el día *day*
        el insecticida *insecticide*
        el mañana *the morrow/tomorrow* (cf. **la mañana** *morning*)
        el mapa *map*
        el mediodía *noon*
        el planeta *planet*
        el tranvía *street-car/tram*
        el vodka *vodka*
        el yoga *yoga*

(b) Compound nouns consisting of a verb + a noun:

> **el montacargas** *freight elevator/service lift*
> **el guardarropa** *check room/cloakroom*

(c) Words ending in **-ma** that are of Greek origin. These are usually words that have a faintly technical or 'intellectual' character, e.g.

el aroma *aroma*
el clima *climate*
el coma *coma*
el crucigrama *crossword puzzle*
el diagrama *diagram*
el dilema *dilemma*
el diploma *diploma*
el dogma *dogma*
el enigma *enigma*
el esquema *scheme*
el fantasma *ghost*
el panorama *panorama*
el pijama *pajamas/pyjamas* (feminine in Latin
   America)
el plasma *plasma*
el poema *poem*
el problema *problem*
el programa *program/programme*
el síntoma *symptom*
el sistema *system*
el telegrama *telegram*
el tema *theme/topic/subject*

Words that end in **-ma** and are not of Greek origin are
feminine, e.g. **la cama** *bed*, **la forma** *shape*, **la lima** *lime*
(the fruit) or *file* (i.e. for wood or fingernails). Two words
that are of Greek origin but are nevertheless feminine are
la lágrima *tear* (i.e. the sort that one weeps) and **la
estratagema** *stratagem*.

■ Nouns ending in **-tad**, **-dad** and **-tud** are feminine:

   la ciudad *city*
   la libertad *liberty*
   la verdad *truth*
   la virtud *virtue*

■ Nouns ending in **-ción** are feminine:

> **la intuición** *intuition*
> **la nación** *nation*
> **la reproducción** *reproduction*

■ Nouns ending in **-is** are feminine:

> **la tesis** *thesis*
> **la crisis** *crisis*
> **la apendicitis** *appendicitis*

Exceptions: **el análisis** *analysis*, **el énfasis** *emphasis*, **el éxtasis** *ecstasy*, **el oasis** *oasis*, **los paréntesis** *brackets*.

■ Feminine words beginning with *stressed* **a-** or **ha-** take the masculine definite article in the singular despite always being feminine in gender: **el agua** *water*, **el alma** *soul*. See p. 82 for discussion.

■ Some words have different meanings according to gender:

el capital *capital (money)*	**la capital** *capital (city)*
el cólera *cholera*	**la cólera** *wrath/anger*
el coma *coma*	**la coma** *comma*
el cometa *comet*	**la cometa** *kite* (the sort you fly)
el corte *cut*	**la corte** *the Court*
el cura *priest*	**la cura** *cure*
el editorial *editorial*	**la editorial** *publishing house*
el frente *front (military)*	**la frente** *forehead*
el guardia *policeman*	**la guardia** *guard*
el mañana *tomorrow/morrow*	**la mañana** *morning*
el margen *margin*	**la margen** *riverbank*
el orden *order* (opposite of disorder)	**la orden** *order* (=command or *religious order*)
el Papa *Pope*	**la papa** (Lat. Am.) *potato*[20]
el parte *bulletin*	**la parte** *part*

[20] The word used in Spain is **la patata**.

el **pendiente** *earring*   la **pendiente** *slope*
el **pez** *fish*   la **pez** *pitch (i.e. tar)*
el **policía** *policeman*   la **policía** *police force*
el **radio** *radius/radium*   la **radio** *radio (masc. from
                                     Colombia northwards)*

FORMS OF NOUNS REFERRING TO FEMALES

The following remarks apply to nouns referring to female
human beings and to those few animals for which there is
a special word denoting the female.

■ There are special words for the female of some persons
and animals:

    el **actor**/la **actriz** *actor/actress*
    el **alcalde**/la **alcaldesa** *mayor/mayoress*
    el **caballo**/la **yegua** *stallion/mare*
    el **macho**/el **cabrío** *billy-goat* la **cabra** *she-goat*
    el **carnero**/la **oveja** *ram/ewe (sheep)*
    el **conde**/la **condesa** *count/countess*
    el **duque**/la **duquesa** *duke/duchess*
    el **emperador**/la **emperatriz** *emperor/empress*
    el **gallo**/la **gallina** *rooster/hen (chicken)*
    el **héroe**/la **heroína** *hero/heroine*
    el **león**/la **leona** *lion/lioness*
    el **marido**/la **mujer** *husband/wife*[21] or *woman*
    el **padre**/la **madre** *father/mother*
    el **príncipe**/la **princesa** *prince/princess*
    el **rey**/la **reina** *king/queen*
    el **toro**/la **vaca** *bull/cow*
    el **yerno**/la **nuera** *son-in-law/daughter-in-law*

[21] In Latin America **el esposo/la esposa** should be used for *hus-band/wife*, the word **mujer** being reserved for *woman*.

el varón/la hembra *male/female*[22]

With the exception of **la oveja** *sheep/ewe*, **la gallina** *chicken/hen*, **la cabra** *goat/she-goat* and **el toro** *bull*[23], the masculine form of words referring to humans and animals also refers to mixed groups or the species in general:

> **los reyes** *kings/the king and queen/kings and queens*
> **los hermanos** *brothers/brothers and sisters*
> **los padres** *fathers/parents*
> **los tíos** *uncles/uncles and aunts*
> **los zorros** *male foxes/foxes*

■ With the exceptions shown, words referring to females are formed from the words referring to males in various ways, according to the ending:

-és > -esa
> **el francés—la francesa** *Frenchman/woman*
> **el inglés—la inglesa** *Englishman/woman*

-o > -a
> **el abogado—la abogada** *lawyer*
> **el americano—la americana** *American*
> **el cerdo** *pig*—**la cerda** *sow*
> **el gitano** *gypsy*—**la gitana** *gypsy woman*
> **el perro** *dog*—**la perra** *bitch*
> **el psicólogo—la psicóloga** *psychologist*

Exceptions: **el/la miembro** *member*, **el/la modelo** *model*, **el/la soldado** *soldier*, **el/la piloto** *pilot, racing driver*.

---

[22] **Varón** is a polite word for *male*. **Macho** is used for animals and, pejoratively, for the type of man who tries to dominate women.
[23] **Las vacas** = *cows*. *Cattle* is **el ganado vacuno**. **El ganado** includes cows, horses, sheep, donkeys and pigs, and can be made specific with adjectives like **caballar** (horses), **lanar** (sheep), **menor** (sheep, goats, pigs), etc. These terms are rather technical in style.

-a no change
> el artista—la artista *artist*
> el belga—la belga *Belgian*

-í no change
> el iraní—la iraní *Iranian*
> el marroquí—la marroquí *Moroccan*

-e usually no change, but a few change -e to -a (although the invariable forms are common and are more formal in style) :

> el estudiante—la estudiante *student*
> el amante—la amante *lover*
> el principiante—la principianta *beginner*

-ón > -ona
> el preguntón—la preguntona *inquisitive person*
> el campeón—la campeona *champion*
> el león—la leona *lioness*

Some words denoting professions tend to be invariable in formal language, especially in Spain, but they may form their feminine with -a in informal speech, although usage is at present in flux. The formal form is safer and is felt to be more respectful:

masculine	*formal/informal fem.*
el jefe *boss*	la jefe/la jefa
el juez *judge*	la juez/la jueza
el médico *doctor*	la médico/la médica
el primer ministro *prime minister*	la primer ministro/la primera ministra
el arquitecto *architect*	la arquitecto/la arquitecta
el sargento *sergeant*	la sargento/la sargenta

PLURAL OF NOUNS

The plural of Spanish nouns is formed as follows:

■ Nouns ending in an unstressed vowel or in stressed **e** add -s:

la **casa** *house*	las **casas** *houses*
el **libro** *book*	los **libros** *books*
el **puente** *bridge*	los **puentes** *bridges*
la **tribu** *tribe*	las **tribus** *tribes*
el **café** *coffee*	los **cafés** *coffees*
el **té** *tea*	los **tés** *teas*

■ Nouns ending in a stressed vowel other than -e add -es:

el **iraní** *Iranian*	los **iraníes** *Iranians*
el **marroquí** *Moroccan*	los **marroquíes** *Moroccans*
el **tabú** *taboo*	los **tabúes** *taboos*

Exceptions:

el **menú** *menu*	los **menús** *menus*
el **papá** *father*	los **papás** *fathers*
el **sofá** *sofa*	los **sofás** *sofas*
el **tisú** *paper tissue*	los **tisús** *tissues*
la **mamá** *mother*	las **mamás** *mothers*

There is a growing tendency in informal spoken language to make the plural of all nouns ending in a stressed vowel by simply adding -s.

■ Nouns ending in a consonant add -es:

el **inglés** *Englishman*	los **ingleses** *Englishmen*
la **nación** *nation*	las **naciones** *nations*
la **red** *net/network*	las **redes** *nets/networks*

As the examples show, an accent written on a vowel disappears after -es is added, unless the vowel is **í** or **ú**:

el baúl *trunk (for storage)*   **los baúles** *trunks*
el país *country*   **los países** *countries*

Nouns whose singular ends in **-en** require an accent on the second vowel from last in the plural to show that the stress has not shifted:

la imagen *image*   **las imágenes** *images*
el origen *origin*   **los orígenes** *origins*
la virgen *virgen*   **las vírgenes** *virgins*

■ Many recent foreign borrowings add **-s** in the plural even though they end with a consonant:

el bit *bit* (in computing)   **los bits** *bits*
el iceberg *iceberg*   **los icebergs** *the icebergs*
el show *show*   **los shows** *shows*

■ The following do not change in the plural:

(a) Nouns whose singular ends in an *unstressed* vowel + **-s**:

la crisis *crisis*   **las crisis** *crises*
el lunes *Monday*   **los lunes** *Mondays*
el miércoles *Wednesday*   **los miércoles**
    Wednesdays
la tesis *thesis*   **las tesis** *theses*

(b) Nouns ending in **-x**:

el fax *fax*   **los fax** *faxes*

(c) A few foreign words which must be learned separately:

el déficit *deficit*   **los déficit** *deficits*
el láser *laser*   **los láser** *lasers*

■ In the case of compound nouns consisting of two nouns, only the first noun is pluralized:

el año luz *light year*   **los años luz** *light*
    years

el hombre rana *frogman*	**los hombres rana** *frogmen*
el perro guía *guide-dog*	**los perros guía** *guide-dogs*
la ciudad estado *city-state*	**las ciudades estado** *city-states*
la idea clave *key idea*	**las ideas clave** *key ideas*

One important exception is **el país miembro**—**los países miembros** *member country/member countries*.

■ The following plurals are irregular:

Three nouns show a shift in the position of the accent:

el carácter *character*	**los caracteres** *characters*
el espécimen *specimen*	**los especímenes** *specimens*
el régimen *regimes*	**los regímenes** *regimes*

The plural of the word **lord** *lord* (British title) is **los lores** *lords*.

COLLECTIVE NOUNS

Collective Nouns (see Glossary) are treated as singular, whereas familiar English often treats them as plural.

La minoría votó por el partido nacionalista *The minority voted for the nationalist party*

La mayoría es cristiana *The majority are christian*

El público se está irritando *The audience are/is getting irritated*

El pueblo está descontento *The people are discontented*

La policía es . . . *The police are . . .*

This applies even to collective numerals (see p.196 for more details):

> **Un billón de pesetas fue invertido** *A billion[24] pesetas were invested*
> **La primera treintena** *the first thirty or so*

However, plural agreement is optionally possible when a singular collective noun and a plural non-collective noun are joined by **de**:

> **Una treintena de personas perdieron** (or **perdió**) **la vida**
> **La mayoría de los indígenas son católicos** *The majority of the natives are Catholics*

---

[24] A million million in Spain. The American billion (1000 million) is much used in Latin America.

Personal Pronouns

Forms of pronouns *104*
Use of subject pronouns *107*
Formal and informal modes of address (tú, vos, usted(es), vosotros/as) *108*
Object pronouns (me, te, lo/la/le, nos, os, los/las/les) *109*
Order and position of object pronouns *113*
Redundant pronouns *117*
Emphasis of pronouns *118*
It's me, it's us, etc. *118*

FORMS OF PERSONAL PRONOUNS

Spanish Personal Pronouns can take different forms depending on Person (1st, 2nd or 3rd), Number (singular or plural) and grammatical function (Subject, Prepositional or Object). In the case of second-person pronouns, there are also different forms depending on the degree of familiarity.

SUBJECT PRONOUNS

yo	*I*
tú	*you* (familiar)
vos	*you* (familiar, Argentina and Central America; see below)
usted	*you* (formal)
él	*he/it*

ella	*she/it*
ello	*it* (neuter gender, explained on p.145)
nosotros	*we* (masculine or masc. and feminine mixed)
nosotras	*we* (feminine only)
vosotros	*you* (familiar, masculine or masc. and feminine mixed. Spain only)
vosotras	*you* (familiar, feminine only. Spain only)
ustedes	*you* (plural. Only formal use in Spain, both formal and familiar in Latin America)
ellos	*they* (masculine or masc. and feminine mixed)
ellas	*they* (feminine only)

Nosotros *we* (object form **nos**) is used to refer to male persons or to males and females mixed. **Nosotras** is used by females when referring to themselves and other females. See below for **vosotros/vosotras**.

OBJECT PRONOUNS

me	*me*
te	*you* (for **tú** or **vos**)
lo	*him/it/you* (**usted**) masculine Direct Object only
la	*her/it/you* (**usted**) feminine Direct Object only
le	*her/it/you* (**usted**) masculine or feminine Indirect Object
nos	*us*
os	*you* informal plural, Spain only
los	*them/you* (**ustedes**) masculine or mixed masc. and fem. Direct Object
las	*them* feminine Direct Object
les	*them/you* (**ustedes**) masculine or feminine Indirect Objects only

> **se**   3rd-person reflexive pronoun, singular or
>   plural, discussed on pp.66 ff

Masculine plural pronouns are always used for groups
of people or objects when at least one of them is masculine: **hay dos profesores y treinta profesoras. *Los* he
contado** *there are two male teachers and thirty female. I
counted them.*

Le and **les** become **se** whenever they precede **lo, la, los**
or **las**: see p.114 for details.

Usted and **ustedes** take third-person object pronouns,
so **yo la vi ayer** can mean *I saw her/it yesterday* or *I saw
you yesterday*. Adding **a usted** or **a ustedes** removes any
ambiguity in this case and also makes the form even more
formal and polite—**yo las vi a ustedes** *I saw you*
(plural)—but it is rarely necessary to do this since context
normally makes the meaning clear.

PREPOSITIONAL FORMS OF PERSONAL PRONOUNS

Only the first and second-person singular Personal
Pronouns and the so-called 'reflexive' pronoun **se** have
special forms, used after most prepositions:

> **de/a/por mí**[25] *of/to/by me*
> **para/contra ti** (no accent!) *for/against you*
> **de sí mismo/de sí misma** *of himself/of herself*

When the preposition is **con** a special form is used:

> **conmigo** *with me*: **ven conmigo** *come with me*
> **contigo** *with you*: **fue contigo** *he/she went with you*
> **consigo** *with himself/herself/yourself/themselves/
> yourselves*: **llevan el dinero consigo** *they're
> carrying the money on them(selves)*

For the rest of the pronouns the ordinary subject forms
[25] The accent distinguishes it from **mi** *my*.

are used: **contra él/ella/usted** *against him/her/you,* **de nosotros/vosotros/ustedes/ellos/ellas** *of us/you/them,* **con ellos/ustedes** *with them/you.*

The ordinary subject forms **yo** and **tú** are also used after **entre** *between* (**entre tú y yo** *between you and me*), **según** *according to* (**según tú** *according to you*), **excepto**, **menos** and **salvo** *except* (i.e. **excepto tú, menos yo** *except you, except me*), **hasta** when it means *even* (and not *as far as* or *up to*), and **incluso** *even.*

SUBJECT PRONOUNS

These pronouns are required only in special circumstances since Spanish verbs already include their subject pronouns in the ending: **fumo** means *I smoke, I'm smoking,* **fuiste** means *you went.* **Yo fumo** means *I* (and not someone else) *smoke,* **tú fuiste** means *you* (and not someone else) *went.* The pronouns must therefore not be used unnecessarily: '**¿Sabes lo que le ha pasado a Ana? Ella se ha roto el brazo*' *Do you know what's happened to Ana? She's broken her arm* does not make good sense in Spanish because it wrongly stresses the *she;* the **ella** must be deleted. The subject pronouns are used

■ When there is a switch from one pronoun to another, as in

> **Yo estoy aquí todo el día trabajando mientras que tú no haces nada** *I'm here all day working while **you** do nothing*
> **Te confundiste. Yo soy Juan. Él es Antonio** *You made a mistake. I'm Juan. He's Antonio*

Sometimes the switch is implied rather than explicit **yo sé la respuesta** *I know the answer* (implies *but you don't/he doesn't, etc.*).

■ When the subject pronoun stands in isolation (i.e. without a verb):

——¿**Quién va con Pedro?** ——**Yo** *'Who's going with Pedro?' 'Me'*

——¿**Quién fue el primero?** ——**Tú y ella** *'Who was first?' 'You and her'*

■ In the case of all pronouns except **yo**, **tú** and **se**, after prepositions (see above).

■ In the case of **usted** and **ustedes**, from time to time in order to be emphatically polite:

> **No se olvide usted de que tiene que estar aquí mañana a las ocho en punto** *Please don't forget that you must be here tomorrow at eight o'clock sharp*

FORMAL AND INFORMAL MODES OF ADDRESS

■ **Tú** (and the corresponding object and prepositional forms **te** and **ti**) is used to address anyone with whom one is on first-name terms, e.g. relatives, friends, colleagues, children, and also animals. The only exception to the rule about first names might be employees with whom one is not on familiar terms: **Antonia, haga el favor de preparar la cena** *Antonia, please prepare dinner* (speaking to a cook or maid).

Spanish **tú** is used much more widely than French **vous** or German **Sie**: Spaniards under about forty use it even to total strangers of their own age or younger, but it should not be used to older strangers or persons in authority. Latin Americans are generally less ready to use **tú** than Spaniards.

■ **Vos** (object form **te**, possessive adjective **tu**, prepositional form **vos**) is used instead of **tú** in many parts of Latin America, but the only places where this usage is accepted as correct by all social groups are Argentina and most of Central America (but not Mexico). **Vos** tends to be considered 'unrefined' elsewhere in Latin America (if it is used at all), and it is not heard in Spain.

■ **Vosotros** (and the object form **os**) is used only in Spain to address more than one person when one normally addresses them individually as **tú**. Two or more females are addressed as **vosotras**. Latin Americans use **ustedes** (see below).

■ **Usted** (object forms **lo/la/le**) is used everywhere to address strangers, especially older strangers, and persons in authority. It is always used for people with whom one is not on first-name terms. The verb is always in the third-person singular.

Ustedes (object forms **los/las/les**) is used in Latin America to address two or more people, regardless of one's relationship with them. Latin-Americans use it for small children and even for animals. In Spain it is used to address two persons whom one normally addresses individually as **usted**. The verb is always in the third-person plural.

OBJECT PRONOUNS

The object forms have two basic functions:

(a) To denote the Direct Object (see Glossary) of an action

> **Me criticaron** *They criticized me*
> **Me llamó** *He/she/you called me*
> **Te admiran** *They admire you*
> **No lo sé** *I don't know it*
> **Nos persiguen** *They're persecuting us*,
> **Él os respeta** (Lat. Am. **Él los/las respeta**) *He respects you* (plural)

(b) To denote the Indirect Object (see Glossary) of an action

> **Le dicen** *They say to him/her/you*
> **Usted les mandó una carta** *You sent a letter to them*
> **Dame algo** *Give me something*
> **Dile** *Tell him/her*
> **Nos dice** *He says to us*
> **Os envían** *They send to you* (i.e. **a vosotros**)
> **Les da dinero** *He gives money to them* (or *to you* = **a ustedes**)

It should be noted that the term *Indirect Object* includes not only the meaning *to* . . . but also *from* after verbs meaning removal or taking off/away from, and in some cases it can be translated *for*:

> **Me compró una camisa** *He bought a shirt off me* (or *for me*)
> **Les confiscaron el dinero que llevaban** *They confiscated (i.e. took off them) the money they were carrying*
> **Me robaron cien dólares** *They stole $100 from me*
> **Te escribiré el ensayo** *I'll write the essay for you*

Object Pronouns are also used to show the person affected by something done to his/her body or to some intimate possession:

> **Me sacó una muela** *He took one of my teeth out*
> **Te vas a romper una uña** *You're going to break a finger-nail*
> **Le has manchado la falda** *You've stained her skirt*

The third-person pronouns used for the Indirect Object are unusual in that they differ from the corresponding Third-Person Direct Object Pronouns:

3rd-Person Direct Object Forms

Lo vieron *They saw him/it/you* (**usted**)
La vieron *They saw her/it/you* (**usted**)
Los vieron *They saw them/you* (masculine)
Las vieron *They saw them/you* (feminine)

3rd-Person Indirect Object Forms

Le dijeron *They said to him/her/you*
Les dijeron *They said to them/you*
Le torcieron el brazo *They twisted his/her/your arm*
Le/les have no separate feminine form.

FURTHER REMARKS ON THE USE OF *LE* AND *LES*

The relationship between **le/les** and **lo/la/los/las** is rather complicated, since **le** and **les** are quite often used as *Direct* Object pronouns as well as for Indirect Objects. This happens:

■ In Central and Northern Spain, and in the standard written language of Spain, when the pronoun refers to a *human male* and is singular:

> **Le vimos** *We saw **him*** (elsewhere **lo vimos**)
> **Lo vimos** *We saw it*

Le is usual among the 'best' speakers in Spain (academics, schoolteachers, newsreaders, editors of quality publications, most writers), but the Academy in fact prefers **lo vimos** for both *we saw him* and *we saw it*. The **lo** construction is slowly spreading in Spain and is easier for beginners to remember. In Northern Spain one constantly also hears **le/les** used for human female direct objects (i.e. instead of **la**), but this is not approved usage.

Use of **les** for plural human direct objects is also very common in speech in central and northern Spain and is seen in writing in Spain, but it is not approved by the

Academy and other authorities; **los/las** should be used:
los vi ayer *I saw them (masc.) yesterday*, **las vi ayer** *I saw them (fem.) yesterday*.

■ With the following common verbs: (the list is not exhaustive)

> **creer** *to believe* (when its object is human): **yo le creo** *I believe him/her*
> **disgustar** *to displease*
> **gustar** *to please*: **les gusta** *they like it*
> **importar** *to matter to . . .*
> **interesar** *to interest*
> **llenar** when it means *fulfill* (British *fulfil*) in sentences like **ser ama de casa no le llena** *being a housewife doesn't fulfill her*. Compare **lo/la llena** *he fills it up*.
> **pegar** *to beat*: **su marido le pega mucho** *her husband beats her a lot*

■ **Le/les** are also preferred for third-person *human* direct objects in a number of other constructions, and in most parts of the Spanish-speaking world, although this topic is rather advanced for a grammar of this type. The most common cases are:

> (a) Optionally (but usually) after Impersonal **se**:
>
> **Se le** (or **lo**) **reconoció** *He was recognized*
>
> (b) Optionally when the direct object is **usted(es)** (but **lo/las/los/las** are also correct). Latin-American speakers from some regions may, for example, say
>
> **Perdone, señor, no quería molestar*le*** *Excuse me, sir, I didn't want to bother you*

even though they would use **lo** in other contexts.

> (c) Often when the subject of the verb is non-human and non-animal. Compare

> ***Le* espera una catástrofe** *A catastrophe awaits
> her*

and

> ***La* espera su hermana** *Her sister is waiting for her*

Usage fluctuates in some of these cases, especially in Latin America. Colombians especially tend to prefer **lo/la/los/las** where others may use **le**.

ORDER AND POSITION OF OBJECT PRONOUNS

When two or more object pronouns appear in a sentence there are strict rules governing their order and their position in relation to the verb.

The order of object pronouns is:

se	te	me	le lo/la
os	nos	les los/las	

In other words, **se** (discussed on p.66 ff) always comes first, **te/os** always precedes all the rest, **me/nos** always precedes any pronoun beginning with **l**, and **le/les** precedes **lo/la/los/las** (and then becomes **se** as explained after the examples).

This order applies whether the pronouns appear before the verb or as suffixes:

> **Te lo dijo** *He told it to you*
> **Os la entregaron** *They delivered it to you*, Lat.
> Am. **Se lo entregaron**
> **No te me pongas difícil** *Don't get difficult 'on me'*
> **Me lo enseñó** *He showed it to me*
> **Nos los enviaron** *They sent them to us*
> **Se te dijo** *It was said to you* (see p.73)
> **Se lo comuniqué a usted** *I informed you*
> **Quiero regalártelo** *I want to present it to
> you/make a present of it to you*

No pueden dárnoslo *They can't give it to us*

Note: Whenever **le** or **les** immediately precede **lo, la, los** or **las**, **le/les** become **se**. This is the so-called 'rule of two l's': two Spanish object pronouns beginning with **l** can *never* stand side-by-side:

> **Se lo dije** (never *"*le lo dije*'*) *I told him/her/you/them*
> **Se los dieron** (never *"*les los dieron*'*) *They gave them to him/her/you/them*

The overworked pronoun **se** can therefore (among other things) stand for **a él** *to him*, **a ella** *to her*, **a usted** *to you*, **a ellos** *to them* (masc.), **a ellas** *to them* (fem.) and **a ustedes** *to you* (plural). Usually context makes the meaning clear, but if real ambiguity arises one adds one of the phrases just listed:

> **Se lo dije a ella** *I told **her***
> **Se lo quité a ellos** *I took it off/from **them*** (masc.)
> **Se lo daré a ustedes** *I'll give it to **you***

These additional phrases should not be used unless emphasis or clarity are absolutely essential.

Familiar Latin-American speech very frequently shows that **se** stands for **les** and not **le** by adding **-s** to the Direct Object pronoun: **se** *los* **dije** = **se lo dije a ellos/ellas/ustedes** *I told it to them/you.* This is not accepted in written Spanish and is not heard in Spain.

POSITION OF OBJECT PRONOUNS

Object Personal Pronouns are placed:

■ *Before* all finite verb forms (i.e. forms other than the Gerund and Infinitive) *except* the positive Imperative. The pronouns appear in the order given above. No word can come between the pronouns and the verb:

> **Me lo deben** *They/you owe it to me*

Yo no la conozco *I don't know her*
Te lo has olvidado *You've forgotten it* (**olvidarse**
= *to forget*)
Siempre la recordaremos *We'll always remember
her*
No me lo tires *Don't throw it away for me*
No nos lo digan *Don't tell it to us*

■ *Attached to positive* Imperatives in the order given
above:

Dímelo *Tell it to me*
Contestadme (Lat. Am. **Contéstenme**) *Answer
me* (plural)
Dénselo a ella *Give* (plural) *it to her* (see p.114 for
se)

The position of the stress does not change, so a written
accent is required when the stress falls more than two syllables from the end of the word formed after the pronouns
are added: **organizo** *I organize*, **organízamelo** *organize it
for me*.

■ *Attached to* Infinitives and Gerunds in the order given
above:

Sería una buena idea vendérnoslo *It would be a
good idea to sell it to us*
No creo que sea posible explicárselo *I don't
think it's possible to explain it to him* (**selo** for
***'lelo'**)
Está pintándomelo *He's painting it for me*
Me llamó pidiéndome dinero *He called me ask-
ing for money*

As the examples show, a written accent may be required
to show that the stress has not shifted.

However, if the Infinitive or the Gerund is preceded by
a Finite Verb (see Glossary), pronouns may be optionally
put in front of the latter:

No puede decírmelo/No me lo puede decir *He
can't tell it to me*
**Queríamos guardártelo/Te lo queríamos
guardar** *We wanted to keep it for you*
Voy a hacerlo/Lo voy a hacer *I'm going to do it*
Estaba esperándonos/Nos estaba esperando
She/he was waiting for us
Iba diciéndoselo/Se lo iba diciendo *He was
going along saying it to himself/to her/to them,
etc.*

The second of these constructions is more usual in
everyday language, but it is not possible with all verbs.
The best advice for beginners is to use it only with the following verbs:

Verbs followed by Infinitive

acabar de *to have just . . .*
conseguir *to manage to*
deber *must*
empezar a *to begin to*
ir a *to be going to*
parecer *to seem to*
poder *to be able*
preferir *to prefer to*
querer *to want*
saber *to know how to*
soler *to habitually . . .*
tener que *to have to*
tratar de *to try to*
volver a *to . . . again* (**volvió a hacerlo/lo volvió a
hacer** *he did it again*)

Verbs followed by Gerund

andar: anda contándoselo a todo el mundo or
se lo anda contando . . . *he goes around telling
everyone*

    estar: está haciéndolo or **lo está haciendo** *he's doing it*
    seguir: sigue haciéndolo or **lo sigue haciendo** *he's still doing it*

In cases of doubt the suffixed construction is always correct, but it is slightly more formal. The non-suffixed construction should not be used if any word comes between the finite verb and the Infinitive or Gerund: **intentó muchas veces verla** *he often tried to see her*, not ***la intentó muchas veces ver*. The suffixed forms should also be used with the Imperative: **vuelve a llamarlos** *call them again*, **ve a verlos** *go and see them*.

REDUNDANT PRONOUNS

Spanish often apparently unnecessarily uses Personal Pronouns when the thing or person is also referred to by a noun in the sentence.

This happens:

■ When the Direct Object noun precedes the verb:

    Los libros te *los* mando por correo *I'll send you the books by post* (cf. **te mando los libros por correo**)

■ When the sentence contains a noun that is the Indirect Object:

    ***Se* lo diré a tu padre** *I'll tell your father* (not ***lo diré a tu padre*)
    Esto *les* parecía bien a sus colegas *This seemed OK to his colleagues*
    ***Le* robaron mil dólares a Miguel** *They stole 1000 dollars from Miguel*

However, a redundant pronoun is not used when a *Direct* Object comes after the verb. It should be remembered that the presence of the preposition **a** *to* does not necessarily show that the noun is the Indirect Object, since **a** also precedes human *direct* objects in Spanish (see p.157):

> **Vi a Miguel** *I saw Miguel* (not *"lo vi a Miguel"*, which, however, is normal in relaxed styles in Argentina and common in spoken Latin-American Spanish elsewhere)
> **La policía seguía a los ladrones** *The police were following the thieves*

EMPHASIS OF PERSONAL PRONOUNS

Subject Pronouns are emphasized simply by using the subject pronoun, since, as is explained on p.107, a Finite Verb in Spanish already contains its subject pronoun:

> **Lo sé** *I know it*
> **Yo lo sé** *I know it (but he doesn't, etc.)*

Object pronouns, direct and indirect, are emphasized by adding **a mí, a ti, a él/ella/usted, a nosotros/as, a vosotros/as** or **a ellos/ellas/ustedes**:

> **A mí nunca me dicen nada** *They never tell **me** anything*
> **A ella sí que la admiro** *I do admire **her*** (emphatic use of **sí**)
> **A ustedes sí los vi** *I did see **you***

TRANSLATING *IT'S ME, IT'S YOU*, ETC.

> **Soy yo** *It's me;* **Eres tú/Es usted** *It's you*
> **Son ellos** *It's them*
> **Son ustedes los que hacen más ruido** *You (plural) are the ones who make most noise*
> **Somos nosotras las que estamos más disgustadas** *It's we women who are most fed up*

| Indefinite Pronouns

This chapter discusses a series of miscellaneous pronouns that unlike the Personal Pronouns do not refer to specific individuals,

El que, la que, los que, las que

These mean *the one(s) that* or *the one(s) who/those that/who*. If the verb is in the subjunctive, the idea of **anyone who** is strengthened:

> **El que dice eso es tonto** *The person/man who says that is stupid*
> **El que diga eso . . . Anyone** *who says that . . .*
> **La que dijo eso** *The girl/woman who said that*
> **Los que vinieron ayer** *the ones who came yesterday*

El que is not always an indefinite pronoun since it can refer to specific persons or objects:

> **Antonio es el que lleva la boina azul** *Antonio's the one wearing the blue beret*
> **Esta cerveza es la que menos me gusta** *This beer's the one I like least*

For other uses of **el que**, see the Index.

Quien/quienes (no accent)

Quien may replace **el que/la que** and **quienes** may replace **los que/las que**, but only when they refer to humans:

Quienes/los que piensen así *Those who think/anyone who thinks like that . . .*
No te fíes nunca de quien no dice la verdad *Never trust the person who doesn't tell the truth*

For other uses of **quien/quienes** and also of **quién/quiénes** see the Index.

El de, la de, los de, las de

These mean *the one(s) belonging to*, or *the one(s) from*:

El coche de María es más grande que el de Antonio *Marías's car is bigger than Antonio's*
Las de allí son mejores que las de aquí *The ones (fem.) from there are better than the ones from here*

Lo que, lo de

These are neuter equivalents of **el que, el de**. They are required when they do not refer to a specific noun:

Lo que me irrita *What/the thing that irritates me*
Le sorprendió lo que dijo Ana *What Ana said surprised him*
Lo de Gabriel es increíble *That business of/about Gabriel is incredible*

Alguien

This invariable word is equivalent to *someone* or, in questions, *anyone* (but in negative sentences **nadie** is required; see p.154):

Alguien entró *Someone came in*
Vi a alguien en la calle *I saw someone in the street*

¿Conoces a alguien que sepa ruso? *Do you know anyone who knows Russian?*

Algo

This invariable word translates *something* or, in questions, *anything* (but **nada** is required in negative sentences; see p.154):

Me recuerda algo *It reminds me of something*
¿Tienes algo para mi dolor de cabeza? *Have you got anything for my headache?*

Alguno

This can be used either as a pronoun or an adjective.

As an adjective it appears before plural nouns with the meaning *some but not others*:

En algunos casos . . . *In some cases*
Algunas mariposas tienen alas muy bonitas
Some butterflies have very pretty wings

It can also be used as an adjective before singular nouns that do not refer to quantities or substances, in which case it roughly translates *one or other, the odd . . . , one or two . . .* When it comes directly before a singular *masculine* noun it loses its final vowel:

En algún momento de mi vida . . . *At some time or other in my life*
¿Has encontrado alguna falta? *Have you found some mistake/any mistakes?*

Alguno is *not* used before non-countable nouns or quantities of objects when the meaning is 'an unspecified amount of':

Necesito pan *I want some bread*
Trajo agua *He brought some water*

> **Tengo que comprar flores** *I've got to buy some flowers*

Used as a pronoun, **alguno** *some of them, the odd . . . , some people, some things*

> **De vez en cuando salía con alguna de sus amigas** *Now and again she went out with the odd girlfriend/with some girlfriend or other*
> **Algunos dicen que . . .** *Some people say that . . .*

For further remarks on the Spanish equivalent of the English 'some' see the chapter on 'Translation Traps'.

Cualquier(a)

This word can also function as an adjective or pronoun. As an adjective it means *any* in the sense of *it doesn't matter which*. When it comes directly before a noun it loses its final -**a**:

> **en cualquier caso . . .** *in any case . . .*
> **cualquiera que sea la respuesta . . .** *whatever the reply*

It can be put after the noun, in which case it may sound faintly pejorative:

> **Podríamos ir a un cine cualquiera para pasar el rato** *We could go to any cinema to kill time*

As a pronoun it is often followed by **de** and means *any of*:

> **Puedes usar cualquiera de estas dos habitaciones** *You can use any/either of these two rooms*

The plural is **cualesquiera**:

> **cualesquiera que sean sus razones . . .** *whatever his reasons* (also **sean cuáles sean sus razones**)

Uno

This corresponds to the English impersonal pronoun *one*:

> **Si uno tiene que pagar dos veces más, no vale
> la pena** *If one has to pay twice as much, it isn't
> worth it*

A female speaker referring to herself would say **una**.

In everyday language **tú** tends to replace **uno** in this
kind of sentence:

> **Si tienes que pagar dos veces más, no vale la
> pena** *If you have to pay twice as much, it isn't
> worth it*

Uno (or **tú**) must be used to form an impersonal form of
a verb that already has **se:**

> **A veces uno tiene que contentarse con lo que
> tiene** *Sometimes one has to put up with what
> one has* (never *'se tiene que contentarse'*
> since a verb cannot have two **se**'s)

| Relative Pronouns

These introduce Relative Clauses (see Glossary). There are several possibilities in Spanish, but the most frequent solutions are:

When no preposition precedes:	**que**
When a preposition precedes:	**el que** (people or things)
	quien/quienes (people)
	el cual (see below)
whose	**cuyo**

El que, el cual and **cuyo** agree in number and gender with the noun or pronoun that they refer to:

	Singular	*Plural*
Masculine	**el que, el cual, cuyo**	**los que, los cuales, cuyos**
Feminine	**la que, la cual, cuya**	**las que, las cuales, cuyas**

Quien has a plural, **quienes**, but no separate feminine form.

■ No preposition:

> **el perro que mordió a mi hermana** *the dog that bit my sister*
>
> **la mujer que vi ayer** *the woman that/whom I saw yesterday*
>
> **la carta que recibí de mi nieto** *the letter that I got from my grandson*

■ With preposition

el bolígrafo[26] **con el que lo escribí** *the ball-point pen that I wrote it with*

los novelistas a los que/a quienes me refiero *the novelists I'm referring to*

la mujer con la que/con quien se casó *the woman he got married to*

■ Familiar English usually omits a relative pronoun that is the Direct Object of a verb or is accompanied by a Preposition, but Spanish never does this:

el libro *que* leí *the book I read*

el cine *al que* fuimos *the cinema we went to*

■ English constantly puts prepositions at the end of relative clauses. This is *never* possible in Spanish:

la mesa encima de la que había dejado el plato *the table he'd left the plate on* (Spanish must say *the table on which he had left the plate*)

los pronombres de los que estoy hablando *the pronouns I'm talking about*

■ El cual

This is a substitute for **el que,** but it is less used nowadays as it tends to sound rather heavy in familiar styles:

muchachos y muchachas, algunos de los cuales llevaban sombrero *boys and girls, some of whom were wearing hats*

los puntos a los cuales/a los que me he referido *the points that I have referred to*

■ Cuyo

This word means *whose*. It agrees in number and gender with the thing possessed, not with the possessor:

---

[26] See the preface for a selection of Latin-American words for *ballpoint pen*.

la señora cuyo bolso encontré en el metro[27] *the lady whose bag I found in the subway/underground*

Tolstoy, cuyas novelas figuran entre las más leídas del mundo *Tolstoy, whose novels figure among the most widely read in the world*

---

[27] **El metro = el subte** in Argentina.

| Adjectives

Spanish adjectives (with rare exceptions) agree in number, and a majority also agree in gender, with the noun or pronoun they modify: **un edificio blanco** *a white building* (masc.), **una casa blanca** *a white house* (fem.), **tres edificios blancos/tres casas blancas** *three white buildings/three white houses*, etc.

FORMATION OF PLURAL OF ADJECTIVES

■ Add -s to an unstressed vowel:

> **grande—grandes** *big*
> **roja—rojas** *red* (fem.)

■ Add -es to a consonant or to a stressed vowel:

> **individual—individuales** *individual*
> **iraquí—iraquíes**[28] *Iraqi*

-z is changed to c if -es is added:

> **feroz—feroces** *ferocious*
> **feliz—felices** *happy*

FORMATION OF THE FEMININE OF ADJECTIVES:

■ Adjectives ending in -o: the -o changes to -a

[28] Familiar speech often simply adds -s to adjectives ending in a stressed vowel, but formal styles require -es.

	Masculine	Feminine	
Singular	bueno	buena	good
Plural	buenos	buenas	

	Masculine	Feminine	
Singular	fantástico	fantástica	fantastic
Plural	fantásticos	fantásticas	

■ Adjectives ending in any vowel other than -o have no separate feminine:

Masc.or Fem. Singular	Masc. or Fem. Plural	
inherente	inherentes	inherent
grande	grandes	big
indígena	indígenas	native
hindú	hindúes	Hindu[29]

Exceptions: Adjectives ending in -ote, -ete:

	Masculine	Feminine	
Singular	grandote	grandota	huge
Plural	grandotes	grandotas	

Adjectives ending in consonants have no separate feminine forms:

Singular	Plural	
natural	naturales	natural
feliz	felices	happy
gris	grises	gray/(Brit. grey)

But the following exceptions must be noted:

■ Adjectives ending in -és:

	Masculine	Feminine	
Singular	francés	francesa	French
Plural	franceses	francesas	

[29] Or, in Latin America, (Asian) *Indian*, since **indio** is always taken to mean Amerindian in the Americas.

Exception:

cortés	cortés	*courteous*
corteses	corteses	

■ Adjectives ending in **-n** or **-or**:

	Masculine	*Feminine*	
Singular	chiquitín	chiquitina	*tiny*
Plural	chiquitines	chiquitinas	
Singular	revelador	reveladora	*revealing*
Plural	reveladores	reveladoras	

But comparative adjectives ending in **-or** have no separate feminine form:

Singular	*Plural*	
mejor	mejores	*better*
anterior	anteriores	*former/preceding*
exterior	exteriores	*outer/exterior*
inferior	inferiores	*lower/inferior*
interior	interiores	*inner/interior*
mayor	mayores	*greater*
menor	menores	*smaller*
superior	superiores	*upper/superior*
peor	peores	*worse*
posterior	posteriores	*later/subsequent*
ulterior	ulteriores	*ulterior/further.*

The following two adjectives also have no separate feminine forms:

Singular	*Plural*	
marrón	marrones	*brown*
afín	afines	*related by affinity*

■ **español** and **andaluz**:

	Masculine	*Feminine*	
Singular	español	española	*Spanish*
Plural	españoles	españolas	

Singular	**andaluz**	**andaluza**	*Andalusian*
Plural	**andaluces**	**andaluzas**	

INVARIABLE ADJECTIVES

A small number of adjectives are invariable (at least in literature and careful speech), i.e. they have no separate plural or feminine form, e.g. **las camisas rosa** *pink shirts*, **los rayos ultravioleta** *ultraviolet rays*. The following are the most common:

alerta	*alert*, optional plural **alertas**
ardiendo	*burning*
escarlata	*scarlet*
hembra	*female* (**los ratones hembra** *female mice*)
hirviendo	*boiling*
macho	*male* (**las ratas macho** *male rats*)
malva	*mauve*
modelo	*model* (i.e. *exemplary*)
naranja	*orange*
tabú	*taboo*
violeta	*violet*

Two-word color adjectives of the form *navy blue*, *deep brown*, *signal red* are also invariable:

> **los ojos verde oscuro** *dark green eyes*
> **los zapatos azul marino** *navy blue shoes*
> **las corbatas azul claro** *light blue ties*

In the case of adjectives joined by a hyphen, only the second element agrees:

> **las negociaciones anglo-francesas** *Anglo-French negotiations*

SHORT FORMS OF ADJECTIVES

Grande *big* becomes **gran** immediately before any singular noun: **un gran libro** *a big/great book*, but **dos grandes libros** *two big books*.

The following lose their final **-o** before a singular *masculine* noun:

bueno *good*	**un buen momento** *a good moment*
malo *bad*	**un mal ejemplo** *a bad example*
tercero *third*	**el tercer día** *the third day*
primero *first*	**el primer año** *the first year*

The adjective/pronouns **alguno** *some* and **ninguno** *none/no* also lose their final vowel before a singular *masculine* noun, and **cualquiera** *any* loses its vowel before any singular noun. They should be sought in the index.

Santo *saint* becomes **san** before the names of male saints not beginning with **Do-** or **To-**: **San José** *St Joseph*, but **Santo Domingo**, **Santo Toribio**. It is not abbreviated when it means *holy*: **el Santo Padre** *the Holy Father*.

AGREEMENT OF ADJECTIVES

Adjectives agree in number and, when possible, in gender with the noun or pronoun they refer to. Mixed groups of feminine and masculine nouns are treated as masculine:

> **tres profesores españoles** *three Spanish teachers* (males, or males and females)
> **tres profesoras españolas** *three female Spanish teachers*

Exceptions to this rule are:

■ Adjectives placed before nouns, which usually agree only with the first noun:

> **su notoria inteligencia y perspicacia** *his well-known intelligence and clear-sightedness*

■ Adjectives used as adverbs are always in the masculine singular form:

> **Estamos fatal** *We're feeling awful/We're in a real mess*
> **María habla muy claro** *Maria speaks very clearly*

■ Adjectives that do not refer to any specific noun or pronoun. These are always masculine singular in form:

> **Eso es fantástico** *That's fantastic*
> **Es muy bueno lo que has hecho** *What you've done is really good*

COMPARISON OF ADJECTIVES

■ The Comparative (see Glossary) is formed by using **más** *more* or **menos** *less*. *Than* is **que**:

> **Eres más grande que yo** *You're bigger than me*
> **El terremoto fue más violento que el anterior**
> *The earthquake was more violent than the previous one*
> **Esta silla está menos sucia que la otra** *This seat is less dirty than the other*

There are four special forms which replace **más** + the adjective:

bueno *good*	**mejor** *better*
grande *big*	**mayor** (or **más grande**) *bigger/greater*
malo *bad*	**peor** *worse*
pequeño *small*	**menor** (or **más pequeño**) *smaller*

These must not be used with **más**: **ella es mejor actriz que su hermana** *she's a better actress than her sister.*

Mayor and **menor** usually mean *greater* and *lesser* rather than *bigger* and *smaller*, but **mayor** is also used of physical size: **esta aula es mayor/más grande que la otra** *this lecture room is bigger than the other* (**más grande** is more usual in everyday language).

■ **Más de** or **menos de** must be used before numbers or quantities:

> **Su hijo tiene más de cuarenta años** *His son is more than forty*
>
> **No traigas menos de un kilo** *Don't bring less than a kilo*

The correct number and gender of **del que** (**del/de la/de los/de las que**) must be used if the **que** precedes a verb phrase:

> **Pone más azúcar del que le recomienda el médico** *He puts in more sugar than the doctor recommends him*
>
> **Siempre le da más flores de las que ella se espera** *He always gives her more flowers than she expects*

The form **de lo que** must be used if there is no noun with which **el que** could agree:

> **Es menos tonta de lo que parece** *She's less stupid than she looks*
>
> **más de lo que tú piensas** . . . *more than you think* . . .

■ *As . . . as* is expressed by **tan . . . como** (*not* *'*tan que*').

> **Una jirafa es tan alta como un elefante** *A giraffe is as tall as an elephant*
>
> **Este problema no es tan complicado como el anterior** *This problem isn't as complicated as the one before*

■ *The more . . . the more, the less . . . the less*

The standard formula, normal in speech in Spain, is
cuanto más . . . más or **cuanto menos . . . menos**.
Cuanto is often replaced by **mientras** in Latin-American
speech or, in Mexico and some other places, by **entre**:

> **Cuanto más trabajas, más/menos te dan** *The
> more you work, the more/the less they give you*

■ The Superlative (see Glossary) is usually expressed by
using a definite article with the Comparative:

> **Tú eres *el* más fuerte** *You're* (masculine) *the
> strongest*
> **Eres *la* mujer menos sincera que he conocido**
> *You're the least sincere woman I've met/known*

The definite article is omitted:
(1) When a possessive (e.g. **mi, tu, su, nuestro,** etc.)
precedes: **fue nuestro peor momento** *it was our worst
moment,* **es mi mejor amigo** *he's my best friend.* The article is retained if **de** follows: **ésta ha sido la peor de mis
películas** *this was the worst of my films.*
(2) When the adjective does not refer to any specific
noun: **sería menos complicado dejarlo como es** *it
would be less/least complicated to leave it as it is*
(3) After **el que** *the one who*:

> **Ana fue la que más colorada se puso** *Ana
> was the one who blushed most*
> **Éste es el que menos estropeado está** *This is
> the one that's least spoilt*

THE SUFFIX -*ÍSIMO*

The suffix -**ísimo** (fem. -**ísima**, plural -**ísimos/ísimas**)
strongly intensifies the meaning of an adjective: **es
grande** *it's big,* **es grandísimo** *it's enormous.*

It is added after removing a final vowel (if there is one):

duro *hard*   **durísimo** *extremely hard*
fácil *easy*   **facilísimo** *extremely easy*

Adjectives whose masculine singular end in **-go, -co** or **-z** require spelling changes:

rico *rich*   **riquísimo** *tremendously rich*[30]
vago *vague/lazy*   **vaguísimo** *very vague/bone
                                   idle*
feliz *happy*   **felicísimo** *really happy*

POSITION OF ADJECTIVES

The question of whether a Spanish adjective appears before a noun, as in **un trágico incidente** or after, as in **un incidente trágico** (both translatable as *a tragic incident*) is one of the subtler points of the language. Hard and fast rules are difficult to formulate, but the following guidelines should help to train the ear of beginners.

An adjective *follows* the noun:

■ If it is used for the purposes of contrast. Sometimes the other term in the contrast is missing, but if a contrast is implied, the adjective must follow the noun:

Quiero comprar una camisa *azul* I *want to buy a
blue shirt* (i.e. and not a red/green one, etc.
Implied contrast)
Debiste casarte con una mujer *paciente* You
should have married a patient woman
El pan *blanco* **cuesta más** *White bread costs
more* (i.e. contrasted with others)

---

[30] **Rico** with **estar** means *tastes good*: **el pastel está muy rico** *the cake's delicious.*

■ If it is a scientific, technical or other adjective that is not meant to express any emotional or subjective impression:

> **la fusión nuclear** *nuclear fusion*
> **un programa gráfico** *a graphics program/programme*
> **la física cuántica** *quantum physics*
> **la vida extraterrestre** *extra-terrestrial life*
> **un líquido caliente** *a hot liquid*

■ With very rare exceptions, if it denotes religion, ideology or place of origin:

> **un niño católico** *a Catholic child*
> **unas actitudes democráticas** *democratic attitudes*
> **un libro francés** *a French book*

An adjective *precedes* the noun:

■ If it is an adjective used so often with a specific noun that it virtually forms a set phrase. Swear-words also fall into the this class:

> **el feroz león africano** *the fierce African lion*
> **la árida meseta castellana** *the arid Castilian plain*
> **los majestuosos Andes** *the majestic Andes*
> **mi adorada esposa** *my beloved wife*
> **este maldito sacacorchos** *this damned corkscrew*

■ If it is one of the following common adjectives:

> **ambos** *both*
> **llamado** *so-called*
> **mero** *mere*
> **mucho** *a lot of*
> **otro** *another*
> **pleno** *total, mid-*
> **poco** *little/few*
> **tanto** *so much*

The following adjectives *may* precede the noun, and usually do in emotional, poetic or high-flown styles:

■ Any adjective denoting the speaker's emotional reaction to something:

> **un triste incidente** *a sad incident*
> **un feliz encuentro** *a happy encounter*
> **un sensacional descubrimiento** *a sensational discovery*

■ Adjectives describing shape, color, size, appearance. These especially tend to precede the noun in poetic or emotional styles:

> **la enorme mole del Everest** *the enormous mass of mount Everest*
> **una remota galaxia** *a remote galaxy*
> **la blanca luna** *the white moon*

■ **Grande** and **pequeño** usually precede the noun, although **grande** tends to follow when it is necessary to restrict its meaning to *big/large* rather than *great*:

> **un pequeño problema** *a slight problem*
> **un gran poeta** *a great poet*
> **un gran libro** *a big/great book*
> **un libro grande** *a big book*

Demonstrative Pronouns & Adjectives

These are words that translate *this, these, that, those*. Spanish differs from English in having two words for *that/those*, one resembling the old English *yonder* in that it points to distant things.

	masculine	feminine	
singular	**este**	**esta**	*this, this one*
plural	**estos**	**estas**	*these, these ones*
	(neuter form **esto**: see below)		
singular	**ese**	**esa**	*that, that one*
plural	**esos**	**esas**	*those, those ones*
	(neuter form **eso**: see below)		
singular	**aquel**	**aquella**	*that, that one* (far)
plural	**aquellos**	**aquellas**	*those, those ones* (far)
	(neuter form **aquello**: see p.140)		

When these are used as pronouns, i.e. when they mean *this one, those ones*, etc., they may be written with an accent. According to a ruling made by the Royal Spanish Academy in 1959, the accent can be omitted except in those very rare cases where confusion could arise, as in **esta llama** *this flame* and **ésta llama** *this woman is calling*, or **este vale** *this receipt/IOU*, and **éste vale** *this one is okay*. This ruling of the Academy has not met with universal approval and many of the best publishers and most ordinary people always put an accent on the pronouns. In this book the accent is always written on the pronoun forms. The accent must *never* be written on a demonstrative *adjective*: **un libro como ése** or (according to the Academy) **un libro como ese** *a book like that one* (pronoun) is correct, but **'éste libro'* for **este libro** *this book* (adjective) looks very bad. The neuter forms **esto, eso,** and **aquello** are *never* written with an accent.

Difference between *ese* and *aquel*

Aquel and **ese** must be used correctly when a contrast is made between *there* and *further over there*:

> **Ponlo en el estante. No en ése sino en aquél**
> *Put it on the shelf. Not that one but that one over there*

If no such contrast is involved, either **aquel** or **ese** may be used for things that are far from the speaker. **Aquel** is also often used for things that are in the distant past.

> **¿Ven ustedes esas/aquellas montañas?** *Do you see those mountains (over there)?*
> **en aquella/esa época** *at that time* (**aquella** if we are talking of a remote past)

The former . . . the latter

The difference between **ese** and **aquel** is often exploited to mean *the former, the latter,* **aquel** meaning *the former*:

> **Había dos grandes grupos políticos, los Conservadores y los Liberales, aquéllos de tendencias clericales y éstos enconados enemigos de la Iglesia** *There were two large political groups, the Conservatives and the Liberals, the former clerical in tendency and the latter bitter enemies of the Church*

Use of the Neuter Demonstrative Pronouns

These are **esto** *this*, **eso** *that* and **aquello** *that*; **eso** can usually replace **aquello**. These refer to no noun in particular:

> **Eso es horrible** *That's horrible*
>
> **No quiero hablar de eso/aquello** *I don't want to talk about that* (**aquello** suggests something further in the past)

The following patterns should be noted:

> **Éste es *un* problema** *This one* (male or masculine object) *is a problem*
>
> **Esto es *un* problema** *This* (i.e. business, matter) *is a problem*
>
> **Éste es *el* problema** *This is the problem*

| Possessives

There are two sets of possessive adjectives. The Short Forms can function only as adjectives and appear only directly before a noun phrase; these words translate the English *my, your, his, her, its,* etc. The Long Forms function as adjectives or pronouns and translate the English *mine, yours, ours, theirs,* etc. They cannot appear directly before a noun phrase.

THE SHORT FORMS

	Singular	Plural	
	mi	**mis**	*my*
	tu	**tus**	*your* (= **de ti**)
	su	**sus**	*his, her, its*
			your (= **de usted**)
masc.	**nuestro**	**nuestros**	*our*
fem.	**nuestra**	**nuestras**	
masc.	**vuestro**	**vuestros**	*your* (= **de vosotros**)
fem.	**vuestra**	**vuestras**	
	su	**sus**	*their*
			your (= **de ustedes**)

These agree in number and, where possible, in gender, *with the thing possessed,* not with the possessor:

mi hijo *my son*	**mis hijos** *my sons/my children*
tu agenda *your diary*	**tus agendas** *your diaries*
su lápiz *his/her/your/ their pencil*	**sus lápices** *his/her/your/ their pencils*

nuestro coche *our car*	**nuestros coches** *our cars*
nuestra hija *our daughter*	**nuestras hijas** *our daughters*
vuestro amigo *your friend*	**vuestros amigos** *your friends*
vuestra mano *your hand*	**vuestras manos** *your hands*

Vuestro is used only in Spain: **su** replaces it in Latin America.

Su/sus has so many possible meanings that ambiguity occasionally arises. The identity of the possessor can be clarified by adding **de él, de ella, de usted, de ustedes, de ellos** or **de ellas** as required: **su casa de usted y no la de él** *your house, not his*. However, context nearly always makes such clarification unnecessary.

REPLACEMENT OF POSSESSIVE ADJECTIVES BY THE DEFINITE ARTICLE

Spanish Possessive Adjectives differ from their English counterparts in one major respect: they are replaced by the Definite Article when the sentence makes the identity of the possessor clear. This happens when:

■ An Indirect Object pronoun also refers to the possessor, as is normal when an action is done to someone's body or to some intimate possession:

> **Me estrechó la mano** *He/she shook my hand*
> **Le cortaron el pelo** *They cut his hair*
> **Me dejé el dinero en casa** *I've left my money at home*
> **Quítate la blusa** *take off your blouse*
> **Nos aparcó el coche** *He parked our car for us*

■ When the meaning of the sentence makes it obvious

who the possessor is (this replacement is optional, but usual):

> **María levantó la mano** *Maria raised her hand*
> **Mario puso la cartera en el maletín** *Mario put his notebook/wallet in his briefcase*
> **Dame la mano** *Give me your hand*

LONG FORMS

All of these forms agree in number and gender:

	singular	*plural*	
masculine	**mío**	**míos**	*mine*
feminine	**mía**	**mías**	
masculine	**tuyo**	**tuyos**	*yours (= **de ti**)*
feminine	**tuya**	**tuyas**	
masculine	**suyo**	**suyos**	*his/hers/its/*
feminine	**suya**	**suyas**	*(yours = **de usted** & **de ustedes**)/theirs*
masculine	**nuestro**	**nuestros**	*ours*
feminine	**nuestra**	**nuestras**	
masculine	**vuestro**	**vuestros**	*yours (= **de vosotros/de vosotras**)*
feminine	**vuestra**	**vuestras**	

Vuestro is replaced by **suyo** in Latin America.

The long forms are used:

■ To translate *a . . . of mine, a . . . of yours*, etc.

> **un amigo mío** *a friend of mine*
> **una tía nuestra** *an aunt of ours*
> **una carta suya** *a letter of his/hers/yours/theirs*

■ To translate *mine, yours*, etc.

> **Este saco es mío** *This jacket is mine* (Spain **esta chaqueta es mía**)
> **Esta casa es nuestra** *This house is ours*

The Definite Article is used (a) when the thing possessed is the Subject or Object of a verb, (b) if the possessive is preceded by a preposition:

> **De los tres dibujos yo prefiero el tuyo** *Of the three drawing I prefer yours*
> **La mía está abajo** *Mine is downstairs* (refers to some feminine object)
> **Estamos hablando del suyo** *We're talking about his/hers/yours/theirs* (refers to some masculine object)

The definite article is not used after the verb **ser** when the thing referred to is owned by the person involved, e.g. **ese reloj es mío** *that watch is mine*. The article is used when the thing referred to does not literally belong to the person involved: **ese asiento debe de ser el tuyo** *that seat must be yours*.

USE OF POSSESSIVES AFTER PREPOSITIONS AND PREPOSITIONAL PHRASES

Colloquial language in Latin-America tends to use long forms of possessives after prepositional phrases, i.e. **delante mío** for **delante de mí** *in front of me*, **detrás nuestro** for **detrás de nosotros/nosotras** *behind us*. This is avoided in standard Spanish and is frowned upon in Spain: the prepositional forms of pronouns should be used (see p.106). However, the possessive construction appears even in the best authors in Argentina.

Neuter Pronouns and Articles

Spanish has a series of words of neuter gender, so called because they do not refer to any specific masculine or feminine noun.

■ **Esto** *this*, **eso** *that*, **aquello** *that* see p.140.

■ **Ello**

Ello is most frequently used after prepositions. It translates *it* when this word does not refer to any specific noun or pronoun. Compare

> **No sé nada de él** *I don't know anything about him/it* (i.e. some male person or some masculine noun)

and

> **No sé nada de ello** *I don't know anything about it* (the situation or problem in general)

■ **Lo**

Lo has various uses. It may be

  (a) a third-person masculine Direct Object personal pronoun as in **lo admiro** *I admire him/it:* see p.111.

  (b) the Direct Object counterpart of **ello**. This is discussed in the next section.

  (c) the neuter article, discussed after the next section.

■ **Lo** as a neuter third-person pronoun

This is the Direct Object form of **ello** and it is used to translate *it* when this does not refer to any noun or pronoun:

> **Su padre había muerto, pero él no lo sabía todavía** *His father had died but he didn't know (it) yet*

Lo is usually required after **ser** and **estar** when these refer back to something already mentioned in the sentence:

> **Dicen que es tonta, pero no lo es** *They say she's stupid, but she isn't*
>
> **Parece que estoy contento pero no lo estoy** *It looks as if I'm pleased, but I'm not*

For the use of **lo** with **hay** *there is/are*, see p.81.

■ **Lo** used to make abstract nouns from adjectives

Lo + a masculine singular adjective usually corresponds to an English phrase consisting of adjective + *thing*:

> **Lo increíble fue que** *The incredible thing was . . .*
>
> **lo más importante . . .** *the most important thing*
>
> **Lo mejor sería no mencionarlo** *The best thing to do would be not to mention it*

■ **Lo** + adverbs or adjectives to translate *how . . .* + adjective or adverb

Lo + an adverb, or **lo** + an adjective that agrees in number and gender, conveniently translates *how* after words implying admiration, blame, surprise, knowledge, etc.

> **Me sorprende lo bien que lo hizo** *I'm surprised at how well he did it*
>
> **Mira lo blancas que están estas sábanas** *Look how white these sheets are*
>
> **Ahora me doy cuenta de lo difícil que es** *Now I realize how difficult it is*

The word **cuán** is occasionally used instead in literary styles, but it is very rare in spoken Spanish:

> **Ahora me doy cuenta de cuán difícil es**

■ **Lo más** or **lo menos** + adverb can be used to translate the idea of *as . . . possible*:

> **Hágalo lo mejor posible** *Do it as well as possible*
> **Lo comió lo más deprisa que pudo** *He ate it as fast as he could*

Adverbs

ADVERBS FORMED FROM ADJECTIVES

The usual way of forming an adverb from an adjective is by adding the suffix **-mente** to the singular form of an adjective (to the feminine form if it has one):

igual *equal*	**igualmente** *equally/likewise*
fantástico *fantastic*	**fantásticamente** *fantastically*

If the adjective has an accent, this remains unchanged:

increíble *incredible*	**increíblemente** *incredibly*
esporádico *sporadic*	**esporádicamente** *sporadically*

■ If two adverbs ending in **-mente** are joined by **y/e** *and*, **o/u** *or*, **ni** *nor/and not*, **pero/sino** *but*, the first drops the suffix **-mente**:

> **Se puede justificar económica y (p)sicológicamente** *It can be justified economically and psychologically*
>
> **Contestó irónica pero inteligentemente** *She/he replied ironically but intelligently*

■ Adverbs ending in **-mente** are used sparingly, rarely more than one to a sentence. One adverb ending in **-mente** should not be used to modify another.

> **Se defendieron con un valor increíble** *They defended themselves incredibly bravely* (not ***'increíblemente valientemente'**)

■ There are alternative ways of expressing an adverbial idea, and these are preferred if the original sounds clumsy:

inteligentemente—con inteligencia *intelligently*
decididamente—de una manera decidida *decid-
    edly*
increíblemente—de forma increíble *incredibly*
rápidamente—deprisa *quickly*
etc.

OTHER ADVERBS

A large number of Spanish adverbs are independent
words not formed from adjectives. These must be learned
separately:

abajo *downstairs/down*
arriba *upstairs/up*
(a)dentro *inside*
(a)fuera *outside*
adelante *forward*
atrás *back*
adrede *on purpose*
ahora *now*
apenas *scarcely*
así *thus*
bien *well*
despacio *slowly*
igual *in the same way*
mal *badly*
mañana *tomorrow*
mucho *much/a lot*
poco *not much*
etc.

Even more numerous are adverbial phrases formed
from a preposition + a noun; these must be learned separately. The following are typical:

a contrapelo *unwillingly*

> **a gritos** *while shouting*
> **a mano** *by hand*
> **a menudo** *often*
> **a oscuras** *in the dark*
> **a propósito** *on purpose*
> **a ratos** *occasionally*
> **a veces** *sometimes*
> **con ganas** *eagerly*
> **de noche/de día** *by night/day*
> **en balde/en vano** *pointlessly/for nothing*
> **en cambio** *on the other hand*

RECIÉN

The adverb **recién** deserves special mention. It means
just, only in Latin America: **llegó recién** *he's just arrived*
(= **acaba de llegar**), **recién entonces** (colloquial usage)
only then (= **sólo entonces**). In Spain it means *recently,*
newly and appears only in combination with participles :
recién pintado *just painted/recently painted*.

ADJECTIVES AS ADVERBS

Some adjectives may be used as adverbs, in which case
they are invariably masculine singular:

> **Trabaja muy duro** *He works very hard*
> **Hable claro** *Speak clearly*
> **Estamos fatal** *We're feeling dreadful/We're in a*
> *dreadful mess*

■ Very often normal adjectives can replace adverbs when
the adjective really applies to the subject of the verb and
not to the verb itself. The result is not always easily trans-

lated. The adjective agrees in number and gender with the subject of the verb:

> **Andaban cansados y tristes** *They were walking along (looking) tired and sad*
> **Vivían amargados** *They led bitter lives*
> **Me miró asustada** *She looked at me in alarm*

COMPARATIVE AND SUPERLATIVE OF ADVERBS

The comparative of adverbs is formed by using **más** *more* or **menos** *less*. **Que** is *than*:

> **fácilmente** *easily*   **más fácilmente** more easily
> **a menudo** *often*   **más a menudo** more often

The only irregular forms are

> **bien** *well*—**mejor** *better*
> **mal** *badly*—**peor** *worse*
> **mucho**—*much* **más** *more*
> **poco**—*little* **menos**—*less*

These latter forms do not agree in number when they are adverbs. Compare **son mejores** *they're better* (adjective) and **están mejor** *they're better off/in better condition* (adverb).

■ The superlative of adverbs is usually formed with **el que** or **quien**:

> **Ella es la que lo hará más fácilmente** *She's the one who will do it most/more easily*
> **Antonio es quien mejor canta** *Antonio sings best*
> **Tú eres el que más sabe de todo esto** *You know most about all this*

ADVERBS OF PLACE

The following are particularly frequent:

aquí *here*	**ahí** *(just) there* **allí** *there*
allá *there*	**acá** *here*
(a)dentro *inside*	**(a)fuera** *outside*
abajo *down/downstairs*	**arriba** *up/upstairs*
adelante *forward*	**atrás** *backwards/back*
delante *in front*	**detrás** *behind*

Aquí is the equivalent of *here*. **Ahí** means *just there (close by you)* and **allí** indicates somewhere further away; the distinction should be maintained.

Allá and **acá** are less common in Spain but they are obligatory everywhere when they follow **más**:

> **un poquito más allá/acá** *a bit more that/this way*

Acá replaces **aquí** in many regions of Latin America, especially in Argentina and neighbouring countries.

■ The forms **adentro, afuera** are, in the standard language, generally used only to express motion, and the forms **dentro** and **fuera** are used to indicate static position:

> **Fue adentro** *He went inside* (motion)
> **Estaba dentro/fuera** *He was inside/outside* (static position)

But this distinction is lost in Latin America, where the forms beginning with **a-** are generally used for static position and motion too: **estaba adentro/afuera**

The prepositional phrases are **dentro de** and **fuera de**:

> **dentro/fuera de la casa** *inside/outside the house*

However, the forms **adentro de, afuera de** are commonly heard in Latin America and are accepted in writing in Argentina.

Prepositional phrases are discussed at p.159 ff.

POSITION OF ADVERBS

■ When an adverb or adverbial phrase modifies a verb it generally follows the latter:

> **Canta bien** *He sings well*
> **Hablaba a gritos** *He was talking at the top of his voice*
> **El presidente consiguió también que se modificara la ley** *The President also managed to get the law modified*

■ When an adverb modifies a Modal Verb (see Glossary) plus a participle or Infinitive, the adverb should not be inserted between the modal and the non-finite form:

> **Lo ha hecho siempre/Siempre lo ha hecho** *He's always done it* (never *'**lo ha siempre hecho**')
> **Por fin voy a verla/Voy a verla por fin** *I'm finally going to see her*

■ When an adverb modifies a whole phrase and not just the verb, it usually precedes the whole phrase (as in English):

> **Normalmente viene a las tres** *Normally he comes at three*

Negation

■ The following are the words most commonly used to make negative statements:

apenas	*hardly, scarcely*
nada	*nothing*
nadie	*no one*
ni	*nor, not even*
ninguno	*none*
no	*not*
nunca or **jamás**	*never*

■ Negating a verb

The basic patterns are as follows. Note that if a negative word *follows* a verb, the verb must also be *preceded* by a negative word: this is the so-called double negative construction:

Positive	Negative
Vamos *We're going*	**No vamos** *We aren't going*
Lo han comprado *They've bought it*	**No lo han comprado** *They haven't bought it*
Tengo algo *I have something*	**No tengo nada** *I don't have anything*
Conozco a alguien *I know someone*	**No conozco a nadie** *I don't know anyone*
Ana o María *Ana or Maria*	**ni Ana ni María** *neither Ana nor Maria*
Vino con él o con ella *He came with him or with her*	**No vino ni con él ni con ella** *He didn't come with him or with her* (i.e. with neither of them)

algún día *some day*　　　　**ningún día** *no day*
Lo/le vi con alguna chica　　**No lo/le vi con ninguna**
　I saw him with some girl　　　**chica** *I didn't see him with*
　　　　　　　　　　　　　　　any girl
Siempre llueve *It always rains*　**No llueve nunca** *It never*
　　　　　　　　　　　　　　　rains (or **nunca llueve**)

■ Negatives may be combined:

> **Apenas conoce a nadie** *He hardly knows anyone*
> **Nunca sale con nadie** *He never goes out with*
> *anyone*
> **Nadie compra nada** *No one buys anything*
> **No te he visto nunca en ninguna parte con**
> **ninguna de ellas** *I've never seen you anywhere*
> *with any of those girls/women*

■ Spanish negative words are also used in comparisons,
where English uses *anyone, anything, ever*:

> **Está más guapa que nunca** *She's more attractive*
> *than ever*
> **Se acuesta antes que nadie** *He goes to bed*
> *before anyone else*
> **Es más impresionante que nada que yo haya**
> **visto hasta ahora** *It's more impressive than any-*
> *thing I've seen up until now*

■ **Ni**, or **ni siquiera** translate *not . . . even*

> **Ni (siquiera) pienses en llamarme** *Don't even*
> *think about calling me*
> **Ni siquiera se acordó del cumpleaños de su**
> **mujer** *He didn't even remember his wife's birthday*

■ **Ninguno** may be used as an adjective or a pronoun. Its
forms are:

	Singular	Plural
Masculine	**ninguno**	**ningunos**
Feminine	**ninguna**	**ningunas**

But when it comes before a singular masculine noun it loses its final **-o**:

> **Ningún presidente americano se atrevería a decir eso** *No American President would dare to say that*
>
> **Ninguna mujer inteligente defiende el machismo** *No intelligent woman defends machismo*
>
> **¿Libros? No tengo ninguno** *Books? I haven't got a single one*

■ **Nomás** is much used in Latin America (but not in Spain) to mean *just, barely*

> **Los vimos en la entrada nomás** *We saw them right in the entrance* (Spain **en la misma entrada**)
>
> **Te llamaré nomás llegue a casa** *I'll call you as soon as I get home* (Spain **nada más llegue . . .**, **en cuanto llegue . . .**)

■ No words should be inserted between the auxiliary verb **haber** and the Past Participle in Compound tenses:

> **No lo he hecho nunca** *I've never done it* (not *'**no lo he nunca hecho**')

| Personal *A*

In Spanish, certain kinds of noun and pronoun must be preceded by **a** when they are the **Direct Object** of a verb. This happens:

■ When the Direct Object represents a *known* human being or animal:

> **Vi a Antonio** *I saw Antonio*
> **Admiro a ese profesor** *I admire that teacher*
> **Llama al camarero**[31] *Call the waiter*
> **Conozco a alguien que sabe chino** *I know some-one who knows Chinese*
> **Arrestaron al narcotraficante** *They arrested the drug-pusher*
> **Criticaron al gobierno** *They criticized the government* (collective noun standing for known human beings)
> **Voy a lavar al perro** *I'm going to wash the dog*

Compare **voy a lavar el coche** *I'm going to wash the car*— never *'... **al coche**' since the car is non-human. In the case of an unknown human being or animal, **a** is usually omitted; the more impersonal the object the less likely is the use of **a**:

> **Vi (a) un hombre en la calle** *I saw a man in the road*
> **Odio las serpientes** *I hate snakes*

■ In those cases in which word order does not make it clear which is the object and which is the subject of the

---

[31] **Camarero** = **el mesero** in much of Latin America.

verb. This usually happens in Relative Clauses where the word order is usually Verb-Subject:

> **una medida que afecta al problema** *a measure that affects the problem* (since . . . **que afecta el problema** could mean either . . . *that affects the problem* or . . . *that the problem affects*)

> **Se llamaba al director "Maxi"** *people called the director Maxi* (Impersonal **se**. The **a** avoids confusion with . . . **se llamaba Maxi** *the director's name was Maxi*)

Prepositions

Alphabetical list of Spanish prepositions and
their use *160*
Preposition finder (English–Spanish) *183*

Prepositions—words like *in, of, on, through, to, underneath, without*—stand in front of nouns or pronouns and relate them in various ways to the rest of the sentence: **en España** *in Spain*, **de María** *of María*, **encima de la mesa** *on (top) of the table*, etc.

■ Prepositions can also stand in front of verbs: *without looking, by shouting*. In English the verb form used in this case is the *-ing* form, but in Spanish the form used is always the Infinitive: **sin ver** *without seeing*, **(cansado) de hablar** *(tired) of talking*. Prepositions do not appear before a Gerund. A rare exception is **en** + Gerund, as in **en llegando** 'on arriving', but this construction is old-fashioned and is nowadays expressed by **al** + Infinitive, e.g. **al llegar a Madrid** *on arriving in Madrid*.

■ The prepositions **a** 'to' and **de** 'of' combine with the masculine singular Definite Article **el** to form **al** 'to the' and **del** 'of the'. No other combinations of these prepositions are used: compare **a él** 'to *him*' and **de él** 'of *him*'. The combined form is not used when the **el** is part of a proper name: **a El Ferrol** 'to El Ferrol', **de El Cairo** 'from Cairo'.

■ Prepositional phrases consist of more than one word, of which one is always a preposition. They function like prepositions: **a causa de** *because of*, **detrás de** *behind*. The more common of these are included with the simple prepositions in the following list.

ALPHABETICAL LIST OF SPANISH PREPOSITIONS AND THEIR USE

There are minor local variations between Spain and Latin America with respect to prepositional usage. These variations are more numerous in colloquial speech than in written language.

Prepositional usage is often dictated by apparently arbitrary rules and frequently does not correspond between languages: compare English *to dream of someone*, Spanish **soñar *con* alguien** (literally '*to dream with someone*'), or English *to try to*, Spanish **tratar *de*** (literally '*to try of*').

a[32] *to* (after words denoting motion or giving, sending, showing, beginning, etc.)

>**Vamos a Caracas** *We're going to Caracas*
>**Volaron a Roma** *They flew to Rome*
>**Le dio cien dólares a su hijo** *He gave 100 dollars to his son*
>**Envíe esta carta al Ministerio** *Send this letter to the Ministry*
>**Voy a verla** *I'm going to see her*
>**Empezó a llorar** *He/she began to cry*
>**un viaje a la luna** *a journey to the moon*
>**un homenaje al rey** *a homage to the King*

at, but usually only when it means *towards*:

>**Apuntaba al blanco** *He was aiming at the target*
>**Tiraban piedras a la policía** *They were throwing stones at the police*

---

[32] The preposition ***a*** is also used in Spanish before human or animal direct objects: **vio a Miguel/a su hermana** *He saw Miguel/his sister*. This is discussed on p.157.

When the English word *at* means *in* or *close to* a place, as in *at the bus-stop*, *at the table*, *at Cambridge*, the Spanish translation is **en** (q.v.), although the following exceptions should be noted:

> **a la salida/entrada** *at the exit/entrance*
> **a la mesa** *at table* (cf. **en la/una** *mesa* at *the/a table*)
> **a mi espalda/derecha/izquierda** *at my back/right/left*
> **a pie de página** *at the foot of the page*

at, before numbers and in several set phrases

> **a las seis** *at six o'clock*
> **a las ocho y media** *at eight-thirty*
> **a doscientos kilómetros por hora** *at 200 km per hour*
> **a treinta kilómetros** *at a distance of thirty km*
> **a los treinta años** *at the age of thirty*
> **al mismo tiempo** *at the same time*
> **al amanecer** *at dawn*

by, in the manner of, in set phrases indicating the manner in which something is done

> **a mano, a pie, a caballo** *by hand, by/in pencil, by horse/on horseback*
> **escribir a máquina** *to type*
> **a empujones** *by pushing*
> **arroz a la catalana** *rice cooked Catalan-style*
> **vestido a la inglesa** *dressed in the English style*

in, in set phrases

> **al sol/a la sombra** *in the sun/shade*
> **a lo lejos** *in the distance*

on, in set phrases

> **a la derecha/izquierda** *on the right/left*
> **a la llegada de** *on the arrival of*

al día siguiente *on the next day*
al salir de casa *on leaving home*
estar a dieta *to be on a diet*

onto after verbs of motion

El gato saltó a la mesa *The cat jumped onto the table*

into after verbs of motion

Se tiró al agua *He dived into the water*
Entró corriendo al cuarto *He ran into the room* (Spain . . . *en* el cuarto)

after in set phrases

Se cansa a los dos minutos *He gets tired after two minutes*
a los dos días de hacerlo *two days after doing it*

per

tres veces a la semana *three times per/a week*
cinco mil dólares al mes *$5,000 per/a month*

of, like, after words meaning *taste, smell, sound like, look like*

Sabe a ajo *It tastes of garlic*
Huele a pescado *It smells of fish*
un olor/sabor a vino *a smell/taste of wine*
Suena a mentira *It sounds like a lie*
Se parece a su madre *He looks like his mother*

from, away from, off (after words meaning *steal, take away from, buy, hear*)

Le compró un coche a su hermano *He bought a car off his brother*
Les roban dinero a los turistas *They steal money from the tourists*
Se lo oí decir a Miguel *I heard it from Miguel*

a bordo de *on board of*

a cambio de *in exchange for*

a causa de *because of*

> **a causa del ruido/calor** *because of the noise/heat*

a costa de *at the cost of*

a diferencia de *unlike*

> **a diferencia de algunos de sus amigos** *unlike some of his friends*

a espaldas de *behind the back of*

a excepción de *with the exception of*

a falta de *for lack of/for want of*

a favor de *in favor* (Brit. *favour*) *of*

a fin de *with the aim of*

a finales/a fines de *towards the end of*

> **a finales de junio** *towards the end of June*

a fuerza de *by dint of*

a juicio de *in the opinion of*

a mediados de *towards the middle of*

> **a mediados de julio** *in mid-July*

a modo de *in the manner of*

además de *as well as*

a la hora de *at the moment of*

a lo largo de *throughout/along*

> **a lo largo del río** *along (the length of) the river*
> **a lo largo del siglo** *throughout the century*

a partir de *starting from*

> **a partir de hoy** *from today*
> **a partir de ahora** *from now on*

a pesar de *despite, in spite of*

> **No me lo dio, a pesar de toda su generosidad**
> *He didn't give it to me, despite all his generosity*

a por (Spain only) same as **por** (q.v.) when the latter
means *in search of*

> **Voy a por el médico** *I'm going for the doctor/to
> fetch the doctor*

a principios de *towards the beginning of*

a prueba de . . . *proof*

> **a prueba de bomba** *bomb-proof*

a punto de *on the verge of*

> **Estaba a punto de decirlo** *He was on the verge of
> saying it*

a raíz de (literary) *immediately after/as an immediate result
of*

> **a raíz de la Guerra Civil** *immediately after the
> Civil War*

a riesgo de *at the risk of*

a través de *through/across*

> **a través del llano** *across the plain*

a vista de *in the sight/presence of*

a voluntad de *at the discretion of*

> **El servicio es a voluntad del cliente** *The service
> charge is at the customer's discretion*

acerca de *about* (= *on the subject of*)

> **Me preguntó qué pensaba acerca de todo eso** *He
> asked me what I thought of/about all that*

además de *as well as*

al alcance de *within reach of*

al cabo de *at the end of*

> **al cabo de una semana** *after a week/at the end of a week*

al contrario de *contrary to*

al corriente de *informed about/up to date with*

> **No estoy al corriente de todo lo que ha pasado** *I'm not up to date with everything that's happened*

al estilo de *in the style of*

al frente de *at the head/forefront of*

al lado de *next to*

> **Se sentó al lado de su jefe** *He sat next to his boss*

al nivel de *at the level of*

al tanto de = **al corriente de**

alrededor de *around*

> **un viaje alrededor del mundo** *a journey round the world*
> **alrededor de mil** *around/about 1,000*

ante *in the presence of, faced with*

> **ante este problema** *faced with this problem*
> **ante el juez** *in the presence of/before the judge*

In literary styles it may be an equivalent of **delante de** *in front of* (q.v.).

antes de *before* (time)

> **Tienen que terminarlo antes de las doce** *They've got to finish it before 12 o'clock*

Compare **antes** *que rather than*: **cualquier cosa antes que tener que asistir a una de esas reuniones** *anything rather than have to go to one of those meetings.*

bajo *beneath, under*

Debajo de (q.v.) is the usual Spanish translation of *underneath*, although **bajo** is used in literary language to mean our *beneath* with words like **el cielo** *sky*, **el sol** *sun*, **el techo** *roof*: **bajo un cielo azul** *beneath a sky of blue*. **Bajo** is also required with social and political systems, with temperatures and in some set phrases:

> **debajo de la cama** *under the bed*
> **bajo un régimen totalitario** *under a totalitarian regime*
> **bajo cero** *below zero*
> **bajo órdenes** *under orders*
> **Estás bajo aviso** *You've been warned* (lit. 'You're under a warning')
> **bajo la condición de que** . . . *on condition that* . . .

cerca de *near*

> **Vivo cerca del puente** *I live near the bridge*

con *with*. The following special forms should be noted:

> **con + mí = conmigo** *with me*
> **con + ti = contigo** *with you*
> **con + sí = consigo** *with himself/herself/yourself, with themselves/yourselves*

> **Vine con mi tía** *I came with my aunt*
> **con amor** *with love, lovingly*
> **Vamos contigo** *We're going with you*
> **Lo abrió con el destornillador** *He opened it with the screwdriver*
> **Es muy cariñoso con ellos** *He's very affectionate with/towards them*

Está enojada (Spain **enfadada**) **con usted** *She's angry with you*

despite (same meaning as **a pesar de**)

Con todos sus esfuerzos, no lo consiguió
Despite all his efforts he didn't achieve it
Con ser su amigo, no habla bien de él *Despite being his friend, he doesn't speak well of him*

if after an Infinitive (this construction is not particularly common)

Con trabajar un poquito más, aprobará el examen *If he works a little more, he'll pass the examination*

into, against, to, when some idea of a collision or mutual encounter is involved

El autobús chocó con (or **contra**) **un árbol** *The bus ran into a tree*
Me encontré con el jefe *I ran into/unexpectedly met the boss*
Se ve con ella todos los días *He sees/meets her* (US *meets with her*) *every day*
Yo me escribo con ella *I write to her regularly/correspond with her*

with . . . in in phrases that mention the contents of some vessel or receptacle

un camión con frutas *a truck/lorry loaded with fruit*
una botella con agua *a bottle with water in it*

con motivo de *on the occasion of*

con motivo del quinto aniversario de . . . *on the occasion of the fifth anniversary of*

con objeto de *with the object/intention of*

con relación a *in respect of/in relation to*

con respecto a *with respect/reference to/in comparison to*

The spelling of the word **el respeto** *respect* (shown to someone) should be noted.

contra *against*

> **Escribió un artículo contra el uso de las drogas**
> *He wrote an article against the use of drugs*
> **Se apoyó contra un árbol** *He leaned against a tree*

Adverbially, the phrase **en contra** is used: **votar en contra** *to vote against*.

de *of* (i.e. *belonging to* or *made of*). English may join nouns to form compound nouns where **de** is normally used in Spanish:

> **el Banco de España** *The Bank of Spain*
> **los zapatos de Antonio** *Antonio's shoes*
> **el ama de casa** *the housewife*
> **un talonario de cheques** *a checkbook* (British cheque-book)
> **la sopa de legumbres** *the vegetable soup*
> **la base de datos** *the database*
> **un chaleco de cuero** *a leather jacket*
> **Murió de paludismo** *He died of/from malaria*

from

> **una carta de mi madre** *a letter from my mother*
> **Es de Almería** *He comes from Almería* (**viene de**
> ... means *he's coming from* ...)
> **Hemos llegado ahora de Madrid** *We've just arrived from Madrid*
> **a partir de ahora** *starting from now*
> **la carretera que va de Madrid a Valencia** *the road that goes from Madrid to Valencia*

See also **desde**, which also means *from*.

off/down from

> **Se bajaron del autobús** *They got off the bus*
> **Bájate de ahí** *Come down from there*

by after verbs meaning *pull*, *take by*, *seize*

> **Me tiraba de la oreja** *He/she used to pull me by my ear*
> **Iban cogidos de la mano** *They were walking hand-in-hand*

measuring, costing, old, before quantities, years, etc.

> **una soga de cinco metros** *a rope measuring five meters/metres* (i.e. *five meters long*)
> **el menú de dos mil pesetas** *the 2,000 peseta menu*
> **un niño de tres años** *a three-year old child*
> **Tiene cien metros de largo/profundo** *It's 100 meters/metres long/deep*

about in the sense of *concerning*, after verbs meaning *speak*, *complain*, etc.

> **Me niego a hablar de eso** *I refuse to talk about that*
> **Se quejó de la mala comida** *He complained about the bad food*
> **Le informaron de lo que pasaba** *They informed him about what was happening*

like, as, in phrases referring to condition or state

> **trabajar de profesor/guía** *to work as a teacher/guide*
> **Vas de marqués por la vida** *You give yourself airs and graces* (literally *you go through life like a marquis*)

> **Se vistió de payaso** *He dressed up as a clown*
> **estar de broma** *to be joking, to be fooling about*

This use can also be translated as *for* or *on* in some phrases:

> **Se va de viaje** *He's going on a journey*
> **Se fueron de fin de semana** *They've gone away for the weekend*

in, after Superlative expressions

> **El mejor restaurante de España** *the best restaurant in Spain*

with to show the cause of some event

> **Saltaba de alegría** *They were jumping with joy*
> **Enfermó** (Latin America **se enfermó**) **de bronquitis** *He fell ill with bronchitis*

if before Infinitives

> **De ser verdad, provocará un escándalo** *If it's true, it'll cause a scandal*

than in the expression **más/menos de** *more/less than*, when a quantity follows (see p.133) and also before clauses (see p.133)

De also appears in many adverbial phrases, e.g.

> **de broma** *as a joke*
> **de golpe/de repente** *suddenly*
> **de maravilla** *fantastically well*
> **de nuevo** *again*
> **de paso** *on the way through*

The use of **de** before **que** is discussed on p.233.

de acuerdo con *in accordance with*

> **de acuerdo con el Código Penal** *in accordance with the Penal Code*

de parte de *on the part of, on behalf of*

—**¿Puedo hablar con Antonio?—Claro. ¿De parte de quién?** *'Can I speak to Antonio?' 'Of course. Who's speaking/Who shall I say is speaking?'*

de regreso a *on returning to*

debajo de *underneath*

> **debajo de la mesa** *underneath the table*

Latin Americans often say **abajo de,** but this is not used in Spain.

delante de *in front of*

> **No quiero decirlo delante de ella** *I don't want to say it in front of her*

dentro de *inside*

> **dentro de la casa** *inside the house*

Latin Americans often say **adentro de,** a form not accepted in Spain.

in, i.e. before deadline

> **Llegarán dentro de veinte minutos** *They'll arrive in twenty minutes*

Latin Americans often say **. . . en veinte minutos.**

desde *from* (a place), when some kind of motion is implied or distance is stressed

> **Se veía desde lejos** *It was visible from a distance*
> **Desde aquí hay más de cien kilómetros** *It's more than 100 km from here*
> **Han venido desde Barcelona** *They've come **all the way** from Barcelona* (cf. **. . . de Barcelona** *. . . from Barcelona*)

There is some overlap in meaning in this case with **de.**

since in time phrases

> **desde entonces** *since then*
> **desde marzo** *since March*
> **Desde niño siempre he creído en Dios** *I've always believed in God since I was a child*

For the phrase **desde hace**, as in **desde hace tres años** *for three years*, see pp.206–7.

después de *after (time)*

detrás de *behind*

durante *during*

> **durante el siglo veinte** *during the twentieth century*

for in expressions of time

> **Durante varios días no hablaste de otra cosa** *You talked of nothing else for several days*
> **durante varias horas** *for several hours*

For other ways of expressing *for **n** days/minutes*, see p. 205 ff.

en This word combines the meanings of *in*, *into*, *on*, and *at*. Spanish-speakers often have difficulty in distinguishing between these English words.

on
> **El plato está en la mesa** *The plate's on the table* (or **encima de**[33])
> **Lo vi en la televisión** *I saw it on television*
> **Flotaba en el agua** *It was floating on/in the water*
> **en la luna** *on the moon*

in
> **Está en el maletero de tu coche** *It's in the trunk/(British boot) of your car*

---

[33] **Encima de** is the clearest and most usual way of expressing *on top of* a flat surface.

Nací en Caracas *I was born in Caracas*
en el campo *in the countryside*
en 1999/verano/abril/español *in
    1999/summer/April/Spanish*
en la mañana/tarde/noche *in the morning/after-
    noon/by night* (this is Latin-American Spanish:
    Spain uses **por** with these nouns)

In time phrases of the sort *he'll be here in five minutes*,
dentro de is more usual than **en** (at least in Spain): **lle-
gará dentro de cinco minutos.**

into   **Entró corriendo en la habitación** *He ran into the
          room* (**entrar** is followed by **en** in Spain, usually in
          Latin America by **a**)
          **Introduzca una moneda de cien pesetas en la
          ranura** *Put a 100-peseta coin into the slot*

at   with nouns denoting place, when motion is not
          implied

          Estudié en Cambridge *I studied at Cambridge*
          en la parada del autobús *at the bus-stop*
          Me senté en una mesa del bar *I sat down at a
              table in the bar*
          en el semáforo *at the traffic-lights*
          en la puerta *at the door*

En is also used with certain festivals and special days

          en Navidad *at Christmas*
          en los fines de semana *at weekends*

at, by in estimates of quantity, value, price, quality or
        characteristics

          La casa fue valorada en doscientos mil dólares
          The house was valued at 200,000 dollars
          Me tienen en poca estima *They hold a low opin-
          ion of me*

¿En cuánto lo estiman? *How much do they estimate that it's worth?*

Ha bajado en un diez por ciento *It's gone down by ten per cent*

La reconocí en la manera de hablar *I recognized her by her way of speaking*

en busca de *in search of*

en caso de *in case of*

en caso de incendio *in case of fire*

en contra de *in opposition to*

en cuanto a *as for . . . /concerning*

en cuanto a los demás . . . *as far as the rest are concerned . . .*

en forma de *in the shape of*

en lugar de *instead of* (+ noun, pronoun or infinitive)

en medio de *in the middle of*

en medio de la calle *in the middle of the street*

en torno a *around (the subject of)/concerning*

en vez de *instead of* (+ Infinitive)

en vista de *in view of*

en vista de lo ocurrido *in view of what's happened*

encima de *on top of*

El libro está encima de la mesa *The book's on the table*
See also **en**, **sobre**

enfrente de *opposite*

La comisaría está enfrente del museo *The police-station is opposite the museum*

entre *between*

> **entre tú y yo** *between you and me* (note that the
> prepositional forms of **tú** and **yo**—**ti** and **mí**—are
> not used when two pronouns follow **entre**)
> **entre los dos pinos** *between the two pinetrees*

among, through

> **El sol se veía apenas entre las nubes** *The sun
> was barely visible among/through the clouds*
> **Encontraron la sortija entre la hierba** *They found
> the ring among/in the grass*
> **Recuerdo haberla visto entre la gente que
> estaba en la fiesta** *I recall seeing her among the
> people that were at the party*

what with

> **Entre una cosa y otra, se me ha ido el día** *What
> with one thing and another my day has gone*

The phrases **entre semana** *on weekdays* and **entre sí**
among themselves or *to himself/herself/themselves* (as in **decía
entre sí** *he said to himself*) should be noted.

excepto *except*

Prepositional forms of pronouns are not used with this
word.

> **Vinieron todos, excepto Antonio** *They all came,
> except Antonio*
> **Excepto tú y yo** *except you and me*

frente a *opposite*

> **Aparcaron frente a la comisaría** *They parked in
> front of the police-station*

in contrast with

> **Frente a otros miembros de su partido, atacó la
> política de la nacionalización** *In contrast with*

> other members of his party, he attacked the pol-
> icy of nationalization

fuera de *outside*

> **fuera de la casa** *outside the house*

Latin Americans often say **afuera de**, a form not accepted in Spain.

hacia *towards*

> **El cometa viaja hacia el sol** *The comet is travel-
> ing* (British *travelling*) *towards the Sun*
> **Se volvió hacia ella** *He turned towards her*
> **su actitud hacia sus padres** *his attitude towards
> his parents*

around (i.e. *approximately*) in time phrases

> **hacia mil novecientos** *around 1900*

hasta *as far as, until*

> **Caminaron hasta la estación** *They walked as far
> as the station*
> **Las obras continuarán hasta octubre** *The work
> will continue until October*
> **hasta mañana** *until tomorrow*
> **hasta luego** *good-bye/see you later* (lit. *until then*)

From Colombia northwards **hasta** can also mean *not
until . . . not before . . .* :

> **Terminamos hasta ayer** (= **no terminamos hasta
> ayer**) *We didn't finish until yesterday*

junto a *next to, by*

> **Estuvo esperando junto a la puerta** *He waited
> by/next to the door*

lejos de *far from*

> **lejos de aquí** *far from here*

mas allá de *beyond*

> **más allá del mar** *beyond/on the other side of the sea*

mediante *by means of*

> **Intentaron solucionar el problema mediante una serie de medidas económicas** *They tried to solve the problem by a series of economic measures*

This word is rather literary, **con** being more usual in everyday language.

no obstante (literary) *notwithstanding* (same as **a pesar de**)

para *for*

This preposition must be carefully distinguished from **por**, which is also sometimes translatable as *for*.

> **Este dinero es para ti** *This money is for you*
> **Necesitamos habitaciones para ocho personas** *We need rooms for eight people*
> **¿Tienen ustedes algo para el dolor de muelas?** *Do you have something for toothache?*
> **¿Para qué lo hiciste?** *What did you do it for?*

to (when it means *in order to*) followed by Infinitive

> **Pon más ajo para darle más sabor** *Put in more garlic to give it more flavor/*(Brit. *flavour*)
> **Se fue de vacaciones para descansar** *He went away on vacation/holiday to rest*
> **Tiene suficiente dinero para vivir** *He's got enough money to live*

by in time phrases

> **Lo necesito para mañana** *I need it by tomorrow*
> **Para entonces ya no servirá** *It'll be no use by then*

for in expressions meaning *to need **for** n days*, etc.

> **Necesito el coche para dos días** *I need the car for two days*

on the point of (with Infinitive. Latin Americans use **por**)

> **Está para/por llover** *It's about to rain*

in . . . view

> **Para ella, él era el más atractivo de todos** *In her view, he was the most attractive of all*
> **Para mí que eso suena falso** *In my view, that sounds false*

towards after positive emotions (i.e. love, affection), in combination with **con**

> **el cariño que tenía para con sus hijos** *the affection he had for his children*

por   Various meanings

Although the English translation may sometimes be *for*, its meaning is not the same as **para** and the two words must be carefully distinguished.

As a result of, because of, for (when it means *because of*)

> **Tuvimos que cerrar las ventanas por los mosquitos** *We had to shut the windows because of the mosquitoes*
> **Muchas gracias por todo lo que has hecho** *Many thanks for* (i.e. *because of*) *all you have done*
> **Lo hice por ti** *I did it because of you/for your sake* (compare **lo hice para ti** *I did/made it for* (i.e. *to give to*) *you*
> **Te lo mereces por no decir la verdad** *You deserve it for not telling the truth*
> **La admiro por su generosidad** *I admire her for* (i.e. *because of*) *her generosity*

Lo hago por dinero *I do it for money* (i.e. *because of*)

Llegamos tarde por la nieve *We arrived late because of the snow*

words meaning *in return for*

Te dan doscientas pesetas por libra esterlina *They give you 200 pesetas to the pound*

Cambió el coche por otro *He changed his car for another*

per   **dos mil kilómetros por hora** *2,000 km an/per hour*

dos pares de zapatos por persona *two pairs of shoes per person*

The preposition **a** is used for time: **dos veces al día** *twice per day/a day*

for in the sense of substitution *for*

Me tomó por español *He took me for* (i.e. *confused me with*) *a Spaniard*

Hazlo por mí *Do it for* (i.e. *instead of*) *me*

for meaning *in support of*

Estamos luchando por la libertad *We're fighting for freedom*

No estoy por la pornografía *I don't support pornography*

Se esforzó mucho por su hijo *He made a great effort for his son*

for in the meaning *to the value of*

una camisa de seda por cien dólares *a 100-dollar silk shirt*

una factura por dos millones de pesos *a bill for two million pesos*

Podrás venderlo por un millón *You'll be able to sell it for a million* *for* in the meaning *in search of*. In this case European Spanish regularly uses **a por**:

> **Tendré que ir (a) por gasolina** *I'll have to go for (i.e. to get) some gas/petrol*
>
> **Ir por lana y volver trasquilado** *To go for wool and come back shorn* (proverb used when a plan misfires)

by to indicate *by* whom or what something is done

> **Esta novela fue escrita por Juan Goytisolo** *This novel was written by Juan Goytisolo*
>
> **La iglesia fue destruida por un terremoto** *The cathedral was destroyed by an earthquake*

by = by means of

> **Los motores diesel funcionan por compresión** *Diesel engines work by compression*
>
> **Funciona por electricidad** *It works on/by electricity*
>
> **Más por chiripa que por otra cosa** *More by fluke than by anything else*
>
> **Consiguió el empleo por enchufe** *He got the job through connections/by influence*
>
> **por avión** *by plane* (but **en tren, en coche, en bicicleta**)
>
> **por teléfono/fax** *by phone/fax*

however in phrases of the type *however hard you work, however tall he is*

> **Por muy alto que seas, no lo alcanzarás** *You won't reach it, however tall you are*
>
> **Por más deprisa que andemos, no llegaremos a tiempo** *However fast we walk, we won't get there in time*

in, around when referring to places or time. In this case it implies approximate location or time

Vivo por aquí *I live round here*
por ahí *somewhere around there*
por enero *around January*

along, through, via after words indicating motion

Andábamos por la calle *We were walking along the street*
Pasaron por San Pedro *They passed through San Pedro*
a Madrid por Segovia *to Madrid via Segovia*

to before an Infinitive, in the sense of *in order to*.
This overlaps in meaning with the much more frequent **para**. **Por** is used only when there is a personal or subjective motive, and *para* is usually optionally possible as well:

He venido por estar contigo *I've come to be with you* (i.e. *because I **want** to be with you*)
Yo haría cualquier cosa por conseguir ese empleo *I'd do anything to get that job*

por debajo de *under* (with figures, quantities)

muy por debajo de las cifras del año anterior *well below last year's figures*

salvo = **excepto,** and like the latter word it does not take prepositional forms of pronouns: **salvo/excepto tú** *except you*.

según *according to*

según el parte meteorológico *according to the weather forecast*
según tú *according to you* (note that the prepositional forms of pronouns—**mí, ti**—are not used after this preposition)

depending on

según la cantidad que pongas *depending on the quantity you put in*

según la persona con la que hables *depending on the person you talk to*

sin *without*

Lo hice sin ayuda *I did it without help*
sin dudar *without hesitating*
sin nada/nadie *without anything/anyone* (Spanish says *without nothing/no one*)

sobre *on top of*

There is some overlap between this use of **sobre** and **encima de** and **en**. **Sobre** is more specific than **en** in that its spatial meaning is clearly *on top of*, and it is somewhat more literary than **encima de**, which is the usual translation of *on top of*:

sobre/encima de/en la mesa *on (top of) the table*

over with verbs like *fly, pass*

El avión voló sobre la ciudad *The plane flew over the city*
Pasó sobre mi cabeza *It passed over my head*

around (i.e. *roughly*) before times and quantities

sobre las tres *around three o'clock*
Tenía sobre cinco metros de largo *it was about 5 meters/metres long*

over, i.e. *more than, above*, with numbers

un aumento sobre el año pasado *an increase over last year*
veinte grados sobre cero *20 degrees above zero*

about in the meaning *on the subject of*

un programa sobre problemas ecológicos *a program/*(British *programme*) *about ecological problems*
hablar sobre . . . . *to talk on the subject of . . .*

on, over, above in the meaning of *overlooking*

> **una casa sobre el mar** *a house on/overlooking
> the sea*
> **el castillo que está construido sobre la ciudad**
> *the castle that is built overlooking the city*

over in the sense of superiority *over*

> **sobre todo** *above all*
> **la superioridad sobre** *superiority over . . .*

tras *after*

This word is literary and is replaced in everyday language
by **detrás de** (space) or **después de** (time).

> **tras (después de) la victoria de los conser-
> vadores** *after the victory of the conservatives*
> **tras (detrás de) la puerta** *behind the door*
> **año tras año** *year after year* (set phrase)

PREPOSITION FINDER (ENGLISH-SPANISH)

This list gives the Spanish equivalents of the more common English prepositions. The Spanish words should be
checked in the preceding alphabetical list:

about	= *on the subject of* **sobre, de, acerca de** = *roughly* **sobre, alrededor de** = *all over* **por**
above	**encima de, sobre**
according to	**según, de acuerdo con**
across	**a través de, por**
after	time **después de** place **detrás de**

among(st)	**entre**
(a)round	as in *walk round the tree* **alrededor de**
	= *approximately* **sobre, alrededor de**
as far back as	(= *since*) **desde**
at	place (no motion involved) **en**
	place (motion at, towards) **a, contra**
	time **a**
	with numbers **a, en**
before	time **antes de**
	place **delante de** (= *in front of*)
below	place **debajo de**
	numbers **bajo**; = *inferior to* **por debajo de**
beneath	**debajo de, bajo**
beside	**al lado de**
	= *as well as* **además de**
between	**entre**
by	= *done by* **por**
	time **para**
	= *near to* **junto a, al lado de**
	= *by transport* **por, en**
	= *by night* **por**
	= *by doing*, see Gerund,. p.52
by means of	**mediante, por**
during	**durante**
except	**excepto, salvo**
for	= *made/bought/designed/intended for* **para**
	= *as a result of, because of* **por**
	= *on behalf of* **por**
	= *instead of* **por, en lugar de**
	= *in search of* **(a) por**
	time (i.e. *for n days*) **durante, por**; see also p.205.

	= *in exchange for* **a cambio de**
	= *for a quantity, price* **por**
from	**desde, de**
	time **desde, a partir de**
in	time and place **en**
	after superlatives **de**
	= *within* a certain time **dentro de**
in front of	**delante de, ante**
inside	**dentro de, en**
into	**en**
of	**de**
on	**encima de, sobre, en**
	a after verbs of motion
	= *on doing something* **al** + Infinitive
on behalf of	**de parte de**
onto	**a**
out of	place **de**
	motive, reason for **por**
	number **sobre**
outside	**fuera de**
over	= *above* **sobre, encima de**
	= *across* **a través de**
	motive (e.g. *fall out over*) **por**
	number **sobre, encima de**
per	*per day, week* **a**
	per person **por**
since	**desde**
through	= *across* **a través de, entre**
	= *thanks to* **por**
	= *by means of* **mediante, por**

to	place **a**
	purpose (=*in order to*) **para**; **a** after verbs of motion
	after **bastante** *enough* **para**
towards	**hacia**
	= *emotion towards* **hacia, para con**
under	= *underneath* **debajo de**
	under *regime, orders* **bajo**
	with figures **por debajo de**
underneath	**debajo de**
upon	see *on*
via	**por**
with	**con**
	emotions *with* (= *arising from*) **de, con**
without	**sin**

| Conjunctions

These are words like *and*, *but*, *so*, used for joining words, phrases or clauses.

■ como

This word has several meanings:

(1) With the subjunctive, *if*: see p.41.

(2) To introduce Relative Clauses after words describing manner:

> **la manera como** . . . *the way that* . . .

(3) To mean *seeing that/as/since*. In this case it must come at the head of the phrase:

> **Como se nos hacía tarde, decidimos dejarlo para el día siguiente** *As/since it was getting late, we decided to leave it for the next day*

In this context **ya que** or **puesto que**, which both mean *seeing that* . . . can also be used.

Cómo (note accent) means *how* and is discussed on p. 202.

■ ni *nor, not even*. See p. 155.

■ o *or*

It is written and pronounced **u** before words beginning with and **o** sound:

> **sociedades u organizaciones** *societies or organizations*
>
> **mujeres u hombres** *men or women*

■ pero, sino

Spanish has two words for *but*. **Sino** is used in constructions that mean *not A but B*, and especially in the formula

no sólo . . . sino *not only . . . but*:

> **Esto no es vino, sino agua** *This isn't water but wine/This isn't water. It's wine*
> **no sólo en España, sino en Latinoamérica también** *not only in Spain but in Latin America too*

It sometimes means *except*:

> **No se podía hacer otra cosa sino disculparse** *There was nothing else to be done except/but to say sorry*
> **No podía ser sino un mensaje de sus tíos** *It could be nothing else except/but a message from his aunt and uncle*

The form **sino que** must be used when the words introduce a verb phrase:

> **No sólo hablaba alemán, sino que sabía otras cinco lenguas también** *He not only spoke German but he knew five other languages as well*

In other cases *but* is translated **pero**, which differs from **sino** in that it does not suggest incompatibility or replacement, but merely a limiting of meaning.

> **Ana no sabe francés, pero sí sabe escribir a máquina** *Ana doesn't know French, but she can type*
> **Te daré cincuenta dólares, pero no te voy a dar un regalo también** *I'll give you fifty dollars, but I'm not going to give you a present as well*
> **Es inteligente pero perezoso** *He's intelligent but lazy*

■ **porque** *because*

Porque means *because* and it must be distinguished in pronunciation and spelling from **por qué** *why*: Compare **yo comprendo, porque me lo explicaste** *I understand,* *because you explained it to me*, and **yo comprendo por qué me lo explicaste** *I understand why you explained it to me*.

The phrase **no porque** requires the subjunctive:

> **Lo hizo no porque realmente quisiera hacerlo sino porque se sentía presionado** *He did it not because he really wanted to, but because he felt pressured*

■ **puesto que, ya que** *since (= because)*

> **No ha sido posible terminarlo, ya que/puesto que no hay dinero** *It hasn't been possible to finish it, since there's no money*

■ **pues**

This may mean *because* when it is used as a conjunction, but this usage is literary, like the English *for* and it is not heard in spoken Spanish:

> **Se le entendía poco, pues** (i.e. **porque**) **hablaba muy bajo** *One could understand very little of what he said, for he spoke in a very low voice*

In everyday language it is very common in the meaning *in that case*: **si no te gusta, pues vete** *if you don't like, well, in that case go away*.

■ **que**

This word has numerous functions other than as a conjunction, and they must be clearly distinguished.

(1) It may be a Relative Pronoun, as in **la mujer que compró las flores** *the woman who bought the flowers*.

(2) It means *than* in comparisons: **eres más alto que yo** *you're taller than me*.

(3) **Qué** (note accent) is a separate word and translates *what* in direct and indirect questions: **no sé qué hacer** *I don't know what to do*.

The conjunction **que** introduces clauses in the same way as the English *that*:

>**El plomero**[34] **dice que viene esta tarde** *The plumber says he's coming this afternoon/evening*

Unlike its English counterpart, it is not omitted (at least in normal styles): **creo que es verdad** *I think it's true*.

See the chapter on Translation Traps for the phrase **de que**. See p.39 for imperatives phrases like **que venga** *tell him to come/let him come*.

■ **y** *and*

Pronounced as though it were written *i*: **mexicanos y norteamericanos** *Mexicans and Americans*. It is written and pronounced **e** before any word beginning with an **i** sound:

>**la agricultura e industria peruanas** *Peruvian agriculture and industry*
>**Vinieron Mario e Iris** *Mario and Iris came*
>**musulmanes e hindúes** *Muslims and Hindus*

but

>**carbón y hierro** *coal and iron* (because **hierro** begins with a *y* sound)

---

[34] The word for *plumber* in Spain is **el fontanero**.

Numbers, Time, Quantities

CARDINAL NUMBERS

1 un/uno/una
2 dos
3 tres
4 cuatro
5 cinco
6 seis
7 siete
8 ocho
9 nueve
10 diez
11 once
12 doce
13 trece
14 catorce
15 quince
16 dieciséis
17 diecisiete
18 dieciocho
19 diecinueve
20 veinte
21 veintiún/veintiuno/veintiuna
22 veintidós
23 veintitrés
24 veinticuatro
25 veinticinco
26 veintiséis

27 veintisiete
28 veintiocho
29 veintinueve
30 treinta
31 treinta y un/uno/una
32 treinta y dos
33 treinta y tres
34 treinta y cuatro
35 treinta y cinco
36 treinta y seis
37 treinta y siete
38 treinta y ocho
39 treinta y nueve
40 cuarenta
41 cuarenta y un/uno/una
50 cincuenta
60 sesenta
70 setenta
80 ochenta
90 noventa
100 cien/ciento
101 ciento un/uno/una
102 ciento dos
200 doscientos/doscientas
210 doscientos diez/doscientas diez
300 trescientos/trescientas
400 cuatrocientos/cuatrocientas
500 quinientos/quinientas
600 seiscientos/seiscientas
700 setecientos/setecientas
800 ochocientos/ochocientas
900 novecientos/novecientas
1.000 mil
1.050 mil cincuenta
1999 mil novecientos noventa y nueve
2.000 dos mil

66.000 sesenta y seis mil
1.000.000 un millón
1.000.000.000 an American billion: **mil millones**
1.000.000.000.000 a million millions: **un billón**[35]

■ Thousands are separated by periods/full-stops—**10.000** = **diez mil** *10,000*—and decimals are separated by commas: **10,25 = diez coma veinticinco** = *ten point two five*. But Mexico uses our system—10,000; 10.25, etc.

■ 16 through 29 are written as one word.

■ **Mil** is not pluralized in numbers—**cinco mil** *5000*. It is, however, pluralized when it is used as a noun: **los miles de personas que creen eso** *the thousands of people who believe that*. When used thus **mil** is a masculine noun.

■ **Uno** becomes **un** before a masculine noun, **una** before a feminine noun:

> **Hay treinta y un libros** *There are thirty-one books*
> **Hay treinta y una cartas** *There are thirty-one letters*

but

> **¿Cuántos libros hay? Treinta y uno** *How many books are there? Thirty-one*

■ **Ciento** *one hundred* is used when another number follows—**ciento trece** *113*—but **cien** is used in all other cases: **hay más de cien** *there are more than 100*, **cien hombres** *100 men*.

However, **ciento** is used in percentages: **el quince por ciento** *15%*

[35] In Spain **un billón** is a million million, although for Latin-Americans it is often the same as the US billion (a thousand million). It is a good idea to get this point straight before discussing prices or the national debt!.

■ The hundreds (i.e. 100, 200, 300, 400, 500, 600, 700, 800 and 900) are written as one word and the suffixed form **-cientos** agrees in number with the thing counted:

> **doscient*as* mujeres/mesas** *200 women/tables* (fem.)
> **quinient*os* quince hombres/dólares** *515 men/dollars* (masc.)

The irregular forms **quinientos/as** *500*, **setecientos/as** *700*, and **novecientos/as** *900* should be noted.

■ **Millón** and **billón** are nouns, whereas other numbers are adjectives. They therefore required **de** before the thing counted: **ha costado un millón/billón de dólares** *it cost a million/billion dollars*, but **ha costado un millón tres mil dólares** *it cost one million three thousand dollars*

■ Telephone numbers are said by tens whenever possible, and one begins either by hundreds or by a single digit when there is an odd number of figures:

> **ocho treinta y siete veintidós quince** *837 2215*
> or **ochocientos treinta y siete veintidós quince**

Cero is used for *zero*:

> **cero quince cuarenta veintiséis** *015 4026*

ORDINAL NUMBERS

Ordinal Numbers higher than ten are rather a mouthful in Spanish and they are usually avoided in all but formal styles. One says **el quince aniversario** rather than **el decimoquinto aniversario** *the 15th anniversary*, or **el capítulo veintiséis** *chapter 26/the 26th chapter*. The higher the number, the rarer the ordinal form. For this reason only ordinal numbers up to 20th and a few other common forms are given here.

The forms ending in **-avo** should strictly speaking be

used only for fractions—**diez quinceavos** *ten fifteenths*. But they are very commonly used in Latin America to form the higher ordinal numbers, although this is not usually accepted in Spain.

primer(o)	*first*	
segundo	*second*	
tercer(o)	*third*	
cuarto	*fourth*	
quinto	*fifth*	
sexto	*sixth*	
séptimo/sétimo	*seventh*	
octavo	*eighth*	
noveno	*ninth*	
décimo	*tenth*	
undécimo	*eleventh*	**onceavo**
duodécimo	*twelfth*	**doceavo**
decimotercero	*thirteenth*	**treceavo**
decimocuarto	*fourteenth*	**catorceavo**
decimoquinto	*fifteenth*	**quinceavo**
decimosexto	*sixteenth*	**dieciseisavo**
decimoséptimo	*seventeenth*	**diecisieteavo**
decimoctavo	*eighteenth*	**dieciochavo**
decimonoveno	*nineteenth*	**diecinueveavo**
vigésimo	*twentieth*	**veinteavo**
centésimo	*hundredth*	**centavo**
milésimo	*thousandth*	

■ All these are normal adjectives and agree in number and gender:

> **los treinta primeros hombres** *the first thirty men*
> **la segunda calle a la derecha** *the second street on the right*

■ **Primero** and **tercero** lose their final vowel before a singular masculine noun: **el primer/tercer día** *the* *first/third day*, but **la primera/tercera semana** *the first/third week*.

APPROXIMATE NUMBERS

Approximate numbers are formed by adding **-ena** to the cardinal number after removing any final vowel. These numbers exist for 10, 15, the tens 20 through 50 and for 100. They are in common use, although **docena** *dozen* is not used as much as in English:

una decena	*about ten* (note irregular form)
una quincena	*about fifteen*
una veintena	*about twenty, a score*
una treintena	*about thirty*
una centena	*about a hundred* (note irregular form)

Note special form **un millar** *about a thousand*.

Like all collective nouns, these are normally grammatically *singular*: **la primera treintena** *the first thirty or so*, **ha venido una veintena** *about twenty have come*. When **de** + a plural noun follows, either agreement is possible: **una treintena de estudiantes se quedaron/se quedó en el aula** *about thirty students remained in the lecture hall*.

FRACTIONS

The following special words exist:

> **1/2 una mitad**
> **1/3 un tercio**
> **2/3 dos tercios**, etc.

For higher fractions the masculine ordinal number is used, although the feminine form is also found:

1/4 **un cuarto**
1/5 **un quinto**
3/7 **tres séptimos**
7/10 **siete décimos**
tres millonésimos/as *three millionths*

In non-mathematical language the word **parte** is added for values over *half*: **la tercera parte** *a third*, **la quinta parte** *a fifth*.

As was mentioned earlier, decimals are expressed with a comma (although Mexico follows our system):

3,75 = **tres coma setenta y cinco**

■ The main arithmetical signs are:

+ **más**	**: dividido por** or **entre**
− **menos**	× **(multiplicado) por**
² **al cuadrado**	% **por ciento**

Dos más ocho son diez $2 + 8 = 10$
Ocho dividido por dos (or **ocho entre dos**) **son cuatro** $8:2 = 4$
Tres multiplicado por cinco son quince $3 \times 5 = 15$
Nueve son tres al cuadrado $9 = 3^2$
el treinta por ciento 30%

TIME

¿Qué hora es? (Lat. Am. often **¿Qué horas son?**) *What's the time?*, **¿Qué hora tiene?** *What time do you have?/What's the time, please?*

Es la una	*it's one o'clock*
Es la una y cinco	*five past/five after one*
Son . . .	*It's . . .*
las dos	*two o'clock*
las once	*eleven o'clock*

las tres y cuarto	*three fifteen*
las cuatro y veinticinco	*four twenty-five*
(also in Lat. Am. **las cuatro con veinticinco minutos**)	
las cinco y media	*five thirty*
las seis menos veinte	*twenty before/to six*
las siete menos cuarto	*a quarter before/to seven*
las ocho menos diez	*ten minutes before/to eight*
las nueve en punto	*nine o'clock exactly*
Son menos diez/y diez	*It's ten to/ten past*
Son pasadas las cinco	*It's past five o'clock*
Es medianoche	*It's midnight*
Es mediodía	*It's mid-day*
las siete de la tarde	*seven p.m.*[36]
las tres de la madrugada[37]	*three a.m.*

■ The twenty-four hour clock is much used for timetables and in official documents: **a las quince veinticinco** *at fifteen twenty-five, at three thirty-five p.m.*

■ **Por la mañana, por la tarde** *in the afternoon/evening,* **por la noche** *at night* (Latin Americans may use **en** or **a** for **por**). **Mañana por la mañana** *Tomorrow morning.*

---

[36] **La tarde** stretches from about 1p.m. to about 8 p.m. and therefore includes both our afternoon and evening.

[37] **La madrugada** is the hours between midnight and 6 a.m. **La mañana** corresponds to our *morning* and can also be used instead of *la madrugada.*

PREPOSITIONS ETC. WITH TIMES OF DAY

a *at*

> **Te veo a las ocho** *I'll see you at eight o'clock*

para *by*

> **Tienes que estar allí para las siete** *You have to be there by seven*

a partir de *from*

> **Las llamadas telefónicas cuestan menos a partir de la una** *Phone calls cost less from/after one o'clock*

al cabo de *after* (i.e. *at the end of*)

> **Al cabo de unos instantes se dio cuenta de que** *After a few moments she realized that . . .*

sobre/a eso de *about*

> **Llegaremos sobre/a eso de las ocho** *We'll arrive around eight*

hasta *until*

> **hasta las cinco** *until five o'clock*

a más tardar *at the latest*

> **Hay que llegar a las tres a más tardar**

DAYS, MONTHS, SEASONS

Days of the week

lunes *Monday*
martes *Tuesday*
miércoles *Wednesday*
jueves *Thursday*
viernes *Friday*

Months and seasons

enero *January*
febrero *February*
marzo *March*
abril *April*
mayo *May*

Days of the week	Months and seasons
sábado *Saturday*	**junio** *June*
domingo *Sunday*	**julio** *July*
	agosto *August*
hoy *today*	**se(p)tiembre** *September*
ayer *yesterday*	**octubre** *October*
anteayer *the day before yesterday*	**noviembre** *November*
mañana *tomorrow*	**diciembre** *December*
pasado mañana *the day after tomorrow*	**la primavera** *spring*
	el verano *summer*
al día siguiente *the following day*	**el otoño** *autumn/fall*
	el invierno *winter*

Days and months are all masculine and are usually written with a small letter, as are the seasons.

PREPOSITIONS WITH DAYS, MONTHS, SEASONS, ETC.

■ **En** is used for *in* in most cases:

> **en abril** *in April*
> **en el mes de agosto** *in the month of August*
> **en mil novecientos noventa y nueve** *in 1999*
> **en el siglo veinte** *in the twentieth century*
> **en los años ochenta** *in the eighties*

■ With days of the week no preposition is used:

> **Llegaron el martes** *They arrived on Tuesday*
> **Está cerrado los lunes** *It's closed on Mondays*

THE DATE

> **¿A cuántos estamos?** *What's the date?*
> **El once de febrero** *February 11*

No preposition is used and the cardinal numbers are used:

> **Llegué a Managua el quince de enero** *I arrived at Managua on January 15*
> **Llegaremos el primero** (sometimes also **el uno**) **de mayo** *We'll arrive on May 1*

AGE

> **¿Cuántos años tienes?** *How old are you?*
> **¿Qué tiempo tiene?** *How old's the baby?* (if it's possibly less than one)
> **¿Qué edad tiene?** *What's his/her age?*
> **Tengo cuarenta y ocho años** *I'm 48*
> **Mañana cumplo treinta años** *I'm thirty tomorrow*
> **El cumpleaños** *birthday*

MEASUREMENTS

> **¿Cuánto mides?** *How tall are you?*
> **¿Cuánto tiene de largo/longitud?** *How long is it?*
> **¿Cuánto mide?** *How high is it?*
> **¿Cuánto tiene de profundidad?** *How deep is it?*
> **Tiene cien metros de largo/alto/ancho/profundi-dad** *It's 100 meters/metres long/high/wide/deep*
> **¿Qué número calzas?** *What size shoes do you take?*
> **Mi talla es la cuarenta** *My size is 40* (European system used for dresses, suits)[38]

---

[38] 40 Continental European = 14 British, 12 American. There is much scope for confusion since all three systems are in use in the Spanish-speaking world. Mexico generally uses the American system and Spain the European.

Questions

■ It is often possible in informal styles to turn a simple statement into a question simply by changing the intonation:

> **Tu mamá lo sabe** *Your mother knows*
> **¿Tu mamá lo sabe?** *Does your mother know?* (rising intonation)

■ Alternatively, the order of the verb and its subject can be reversed:

> **¿Lo sabe tu mamá?** *Does your mother know?*
> **¿Conoce Antonio a mi suegro?** *Does Antonio know my father-in-law?*

■ Spanish has a series of words that correspond to our question words:

> **¿cómo?** *how?*
> **¿cuál?/¿cuáles?** *which?*
> **¿cuándo?** *when?*
> **¿dónde?** *where?*
> **¿para qué?** *what for?*
> **¿por qué?** *why?* (contrast with **porque** *because*)
> **¿qué?** *what?/which?*
> **¿quién?/¿quiénes?** *who?*

These question words must be written with an accent and are pronounced as stressed words. This is the case in both Direct and Indirect Questions:

> **¿Cuándo viene?** *When's he coming?* (Direct Question)
> **No sé cuándo viene** *I don't know when he's coming* (Indirect Question)

After these words the verb is put before the subject:

> **¿Cómo van ustedes a Miami?** *How are you going to Miami?*[39]
>
> **¿Por qué dice eso tu jefe?** *Why does your boss say that?*

Who? must be translated by **quiénes** if we are certain that more than one person is involved:

> **¿Quién lo hizo?** *Who did it?*
>
> **¿Quiénes lo hicieron?** *Which persons did it?*

■ Translating *what?*

When the English word is followed by nothing, the Spanish word is **qué**:

> **Tenemos que hacer algo, pero no sabemos qué**
> *We have to do something, but we don't know what*

The English *what + to be* is translated **cuál + ser**, except when *what is?* really means *what is the definition of?* or *how many?*

> **¿Cuál fue la solución que él propuso?** *What was the solution that he suggested?*
>
> **¿Cuál es su profesión?** *What's your profession?*

but

> **¿Qué hora es?** *What's the time?*
>
> **¿Qué es un agujero negro?** *What is (the definition of) a Black Hole?*

When the English *what* precedes a verb other than **ser** it is translated **lo que**, but before an Infinitive by **qué**:

> **No sé lo que quieres** *I don't know what you want*

---

[39] Cubans may use ordinary word order here—**¿Cómo ustedes van . . . ?**, etc.

> **No sé qué decirles** *I don't know what to say to them*

When *what* stands before a noun, it is translated **qué**:

> **Dinero? ¿Qué dinero?** *Money? What money?*
> **No sé en qué canal es** *I don't know what/which channel it's on*

Many Latin-Americans use **cuál** in such sentences, e.g. **¿A cuáles libros te refieres?** for **¿A qué libros te refieres?** *what books are you referring to?*, but this is not done in Spain and is not the case in every Latin-American country.

■ Translating *which?*

When *which* stands alone, it is translated **cuál**, plural **cuáles** (although **quién**, plural **quienes** is more appropriate for human beings):

> **He leído alguno de estos libros, pero no recuerdo cuál** *I've read one or other of these books, but I can't remember which*

Which of? is **cuál de**, plural **cuáles de**. When *which* is an abbreviated form of *which of them* **cuál/cuáles** must also be used:

> **Puedes elegir tres de estos. ¿Cuáles prefieres?** *You can choose three of these. Which (ones of them) do you prefer?*

When *which* can be replaced by *what* it should be translated **qué**. See the previous section for examples.

For n Days/Weeks, Ago, Since and Similar Expressions

■ *for n days, weeks, etc.*

The most frequently used construction in everyday Spanish uses the regular verb **llevar**[40]. Note that Spanish uses the Present or the Imperfect tense where English uses the Perfect or Pluperfect tenses:

> *Llevo* **seis años estudiando español** *I have been studying Spanish for six years*
>
> *Llevaba* **seis años estudiando español** *I had been studying Spanish for six years*
>
> **Lleva años aquí** *He/she's been here for years*
>
> **Llevas varios días enfadado** *You've been angry for several days*
>
> **Llevábamos tres horas esperando** *We had been waiting for three hours*

The following constructions with **hacer** are more formal:

> **Estudio español desde hace seis años** *I have been studying Spanish for six years*

or

> **Hace seis años que estudio español**
>
> **Yo estudiaba español desde hacía seis años** *I had been studying Spanish for six years*

[40] Use of **tener**, e.g. **tengo seis años aquí** *I've been here six years*, is common in Latin America, but not in Spain.

or

Hacía seis años que yo estudiaba español

English-speakers are easily misled into thinking that a sentence like *he estado* **tres meses en Nueva York** *I was in New York for three months* means the same as **llevo tres meses en Nueva York** *I've been in New York for three months.* The former implies that the speaker has now left the city, whereas the latter clearly indicates that his/her stay is still continuing.

When the period of time is clearly finished, **durante** may be used:

> **La estuvo mirando durante tres minutos** *He gazed at her for three minutes*
> **Victoria reinó durante casi cuarenta años** *Victoria reigned for nearly forty years*

In some cases no preposition is used:

> **Estuve tres días en Barcelona** *I was in Barcelona (for) three days*

■ *Ago*

The usual construction uses **hacer**:

> **La vi hace tres días/Hace tres días que la vi** *I saw her three days ago*

■ *Since*

The use of the Present and Imperfect tenses should be noted:

> *Vivo* **aquí desde abril** *I've been living here since April*
> **Mi madre** *vive* **con mi tía desde que murió mi padre** *My mother's been living with my aunt since my father died*
> *Vivíamos* **allí desde el año anterior** *We had been living there since the year before*

Spaniards may use the Perfect and Pluperfect tenses in these sentences, but the Present or Imperfect are usually required by Latin-Americans. If the sentence is negated, the Perfect tense is used, or the Preterit in those regions (much of Latin America) where the Perfect is little used:

> **No la he visto/No la vi desde el domingo** *I haven't seen her since Sunday*

■ *The first time that . . .* , etc.

Use of the Spanish Present and Imperfect tenses should be noted in these sentences:

> **Es la primera vez que *oigo* mencionar su nombre** *It is the first time I have heard his name mentioned*
> **Era la primera vez que *entraban* en ese edificio** *It was the first time they had entered that building*

Affective Suffixes

'Affective' suffixes are suffixes like **-ito**, **-illo**, **-ón**, **-azo** that add various emotional overtones to a noun, adjective or adverb. In general, foreign learners should avoid using them until they are very fluent in the language, since they can sound silly or even insulting if misused. They are less frequent in some places than in others: Mexicans and Central Americans sprinkle their speech with diminutive suffixes, in Argentina and Spain they are less common (but still much used), and in some places diminutive forms are considered more appropriate in women's speech than men's.

DIMINUTIVE SUFFIXES

The main Diminutive Suffixes are **-ito**, **-ecito** (or **-ico** in some regions), **-illo**, **-ecillo**. Other suffixes like **-uelo**, **-iño**, **-ín** are also encountered, the latter two being regional in use

They are used:

■ To make one's speech especially friendly or affectionate

For this reason they are much used when talking to little children, but they are also often used between strangers in order to make the tone friendly. Compare

> **¿Le pongo un poco de sal?** *Shall I put some salt on it for you?* (neutral tone)
> **¿Le pongo un poquito de sal?** (same thing but more friendly)

> **Eres un comilón** (or **comelón**) *You eat a lot*
> **Eres un comiloncillo** *You sure like your food!* (more friendly)

Ahora se lo traigo *I'll bring it to you now*
Ahorita se lo traigo (same but more friendly).

Ahorita is especially common in Mexico, but
Spaniards say **ahora mismo**)

■ To convey the idea of smallness, usually with some feel-
ing of affection:

La casa tiene un jardincito *The house has a little
backyard/garden*
¡Mira los pajaritos! *Look at the little birds!*
un cafetín *a little café*

■ Sometimes, especially in the case of **-illo**, to add a sarcastic tone:

¡Qué listillo eres! *Aren't you smart! What a know-
all you are!* (sarcastic: **listo** = *clever*)
señorito (roughly) *a spoilt son from a rich family*
miedica *cowardly/'chicken'*

Sometimes diminutive suffixes simply change the original meaning without any emotional overtones:

el palo *a stick*   **el palillo** *a toothpick*
la tesis *thesis*   **la tesina** *dissertation*
la ventana *window*   **la ventanilla** *vehicle window*

AUGMENTATIVE SUFFIXES

The main Augmentative Suffixes are **-ón**, **-azo** and **-ote**.
As their name suggests, they indicate increased size or
intensity, often (especially in the first two cases) with
some overtone of excess or unpleasantness:

mandón *bossy*
aburridón *really boring* (**aburrido** = *boring*)
dramón *a big melodrama* (sarcastic, cf. **el drama**
drama)

un **vinazo** *a really strong, heavy wine* (**el vino** = *wine*)
la **palabrota** *swearword* (**la palabra** = *word*)
grandote *enormous* (**grande** = *big*)

PEJORATIVE SUFFIXES

-ajo, -uco, -ucho, -astro are also sometimes added to nouns and adjectives to add an idea of unpleasantness:

el **hotelucho** *flophouse/dump of a hotel*
la **palabreja** *peculiar, horrible word*
la **casuca**, la **casucha** *hovel/dingy house* (**la casa** = *house*)

| Word Order

Word order in questions is mentioned on p.203. Word order with adverbs is mentioned on p.153. Other useful points to remember are:

■ Spanish is unlike English in that it puts a Verb and an Object (if there is one) before the Subject rather than separate them by many intervening words. Spanish does not like to leave verb phrases dangling at the end of the sentence far from their subject. The position of the verbs in italics should be noted in these sentences:

> *Rompió* la ventana el vecino que siempre lleva el sombrero amarillo *The neighbor/*(Brit. *neighbour) who always wears the yellow hat broke the window*
>
> *Ganó* el partido el equipo que más se había entrenado antes *The team that had trained most before won the match*
>
> Me fui porque me *revienta* tener que esperar varias horas en la parada del autobús *I left because having to wait several hours at the bus-stop gets on my nerves*

The preceding rule is almost always applied in Subordinate and Relative Clauses. The verb is usually not left at the end of the sentence:

> Esa es la moto que me vendió Alfredo *That's the motor-bike that Alfredo sold me* (lit. *that sold me Alfredo*)
>
> Quedará prohibido cuando entre en vigor la nueva ley *It'll be prohibited when the new law*

        comes into effect (lit. *comes into effect the new law*)

■ After adverbs and adverbial phrases, the verb is often put before the subject:

> **Si bien *dice* el refrán que "ojos que no ven, corazón que no llora"** . . . *If the proverb is right* (literally *if well says the proverb that* . . .) *that 'what the eye doesn't see, the heart doesn't weep about'* . . .
>
> **Con la noche *llegan* a su fin las actividades del día** *At nightfall the day's activities come to an end*

■ An English preposition can appear at the end of a sentence, but Spanish prepositions *always* stand before the noun or pronoun that they refer to:

> **La chica a la que di el dinero** *The girl I gave the money to* . . .
>
> **Las escaleras por las que subieron** *The stairs they went up*
>
> **alguien con quien salir** . . . *someone to go out with* . . .

■ No word ever comes between Object Pronouns and their verb:

> ***Me lo* diste ayer** *You gave it to me yesterday*
>
> ***Me* has defendido siempre** *You've always defended me*

■ There is a tendency, especially in colloquial speech, to put the most urgent information first. This is required in some contexts, e.g. **¡viene la policía!** *the police are coming!*, but normal word order would also be correct in the following sentences:

> **Dinero tiene, pero no es un millonario** *He's got money, but he's no millionaire* (literally *money he's got* . . .)

Invitada está, pero no sé si viene *She's invited—but I don't know if she'll come* (literally *invited she is . . .*)

Todos esos detalles ya me los explicaste ayer *You already explained all those details to me yesterday*

In the last example the Direct Object (**todos estos detalles**) is echoed or resumed by **los**, as explained on p.117.

| Pronunciation

The descriptions given in this section are approximate: it is not possible to give an exact picture in writing of the pronunciation of a foreign language. An attempted representation of the pronunciation is shown between square brackets, e.g. [elpérro] = **el perro** *dog*: the letters in the square brackets should be given their normal Spanish pronunciation, although a few special signs are used, explained below. Where two pronunciations are shown, the Latin-American version is first.

VOWELS

Spanish vowels are neither numerous nor complicated, but none of them is exactly like any English vowel sound. They are all *short* and do not vary in length or quality, whether stressed or not; compare the English pronunciation of *panorama*, which has three different *a* sounds, and the Spanish **panorama**, which has only one kind of *a*.

	Approximate equivalents	
	American English	Southern British
a	*father* (but much shorter)	*father*(shortened), *cut*

The vowel must be as short as the *a* of *cat*.

e	*egg*	*egg*

Not like the *ay* of *day* (which is much too long and ends in a *y* sound), although the first part of this English diphthong is close to Spanish **e**. Spanish **e** is an equivalent of the French *e* in **un café**

i	*seen* but much shorter and with no trace of a *y* sound at the end	same
o	no exact equivalent? Not like the *o* of *note* (which is too long and ends in a *w* sound) but a very short version of the first part of this sound with rounded lips is good	*hot* (rounded)
u	*good*, but with rounded lips Not like *oo* of *food* (too long, lips not rounded and ends in a *w* sound)	same

Examples: **cama, teme, sin, somos, luz**.

English-speakers, American and British, must learn to pronounce adjacent vowels without a trace of a pause (glottal stop), *y, r* or *w* sound between them: **sea o no** *whether it is or not* is [seaonó], not 'sayer-ou-nou', **lo ha hecho** *he's done it* = [loaécho], not 'lo-wa-echou'.

Vowels are not slurred when they are unstressed. **Beca** *(study) grant* is [béka] and nothing like the English word *baker*. The sound of the English *a* in *above* or *e* in *the* does not exist in Spanish.

DIPHTHONGS

American and Southern British

ai, ay	*aisle*
au	*cow*, but with rounded lips
ei, ey	*day*
eu	like *e* in *egg* followed by *w* of *well*
ie, ye	*yes*
ia, ya	*y* of *yes* + Spanish **a**
iu	*y* of *yes* + Spanish **u**
oi, oy	*boy*

ou   *low* but with rounded lips

ua   *w* of *want* (with rounded lips) + Spanish **a**

ue   **went** with rounded lips

uy   Spanish **u** + *y* of *yes*

Examples: **hay** *there is/are*, **causa** *cause*, **ley** *law*, **Europa** *Europe*, **bien** *well*, **ya** *already*, **la viuda** *widow*, **no unió** *he did not join together* (pronounced [nounyó]), **Managua**, **bueno** *good*, **muy** *very*.

Words are run together whenever possible without pauses between them: **nos han dado una fortuna** = [nosandaðounafortúna] *they've given us a fortune.* When one word ends in a vowel and the next one begins with a vowel a diphthong is formed if possible and identical vowels are run together to form a very slightly longer vowel. English speakers must avoid inserting a pause or a *y* or *w*:

> **ha iniciado** [aynisyáðo]/[ayniθyáðo] *has initiated* (***ay*** as in English *eye*)
>
> **la apertura** [lapertúra] *the opening*
>
> **he indicado** [eyndikáðo] *I have indicated* (***ey*** as *ay* in English *day*)
>
> **he entrado** [entráðo] *I have entered*
>
> **si han dicho** [syandícho] *if they've said* (***sya*** like *cea* in English *oceanic*)
>
> **no implica** [noymplíka] *it doesn't imply*

TRIPHTHONGS

These arise when one of the above diphthongs is preceded or followed by a *y* sound or a *w* sound:

American and British English

uai, uay *wise*, but with rounded lips
uei, uey *ways*, but with rounded lips

iai   *yike*
iei   *Yates*

Examples: **continuáis** *you continue*, **Paraguay**, **continuéis** *you continue* (Subjunctive form), **buey** *ox*, **y aire** [yáy-re] *and air*.

CONSONANTS

p, **t**, **k** and **ch** are pronounced as in American and British English except that no puff of breath follows them. A piece of tissue paper hung two inches from the lips should barely move when one says the Spanish words **pipa** *pipe*, **tú** *you*, **kilo** *kilogram*, **chacha** *housemaid* (familiar style, Spain)

t is always pronounced with the tongue against the front teeth and not as in English with the tongue on the ridge of gum behind the front teeth.

c is pronounced as Spanish **k** before **a**, **o** and **u**: **cama** *bed*, **cosa** *thing*, **el cura** *the priest*.

Before **e** and **i** it is pronounced the same as Spanish z, i.e. as *c* in *rice* in Latin America and [θ] (like the *th* of *think*) in Spain: **cinco** [sínko]/[θínko] *five*, **central** [sentrál]/[θentrál] *central*.

b and **v** are pronounced in nearly every position as [ß], a sound that does not exist in English. It is technically known as a voiced bilabial fricative and is made by holding the lips as for *b* and murmuring through them; it should be possible to produce the sound as long as you have breath. The sound of English *v* in *vat* does not exist in Spanish: the pairs of words **tuvo/tubo** [túßo] *he had/tube*, **iba/IVA** [íßa] *he was going/Value Added Tax*, **lavase/la base** [laßáse] *he washed/the base* sound exactly the same in Spanish.

The same two letters are pronounced like the *b* of *big*

only when they come after **n** (even between words) or when they occur after a pause): **son buenos** [sombwénos] *they're good*, **en Bolivia** [embolíßya] *in Bolivia*, **ambos** [ámbos] *both*. Note that **n** is pronounced **m** before **b** and **v**.

d is pronounced [δ] in nearly every position, i.e. like the English *th* in *this*, *then*: **lado** [láδo] *size*, **los dados** [losdáδos] *the dice*, **libertad** [lißertáδ] *freedom*. **d** is, however, pronounced like the *d* of *dog* (but with the tongue against the front teeth) after **n** and **l** and after a pause: **han dicho** [andícho] *they've said*, **cuando** [kwándo] *when*, **falda** [fálda] *skirt*, **sal de mar** [saldemár] *sea salt*.

f is pronounced as in English.

g is pronounced like Spanish **j** before **e** and **i**: see notes on **j**. It is pronounced [γ] in nearly every other position, a sound that does not exist in English. It is technically known as a voiced velar fricative and is made by holding the mouth as for the *g* in *ago* and gently releasing air through the throat while murmuring; it should be possible to keep the sound up as long as you have breath: **hago** [áγo] *I do*, **laguna** [laγúna] *pond*, **Paraguay** [paraγwáy].
    The same letter is pronounced like the English *g* of *go* only after **n** and at the beginning of a word after a pause: **son grandes** [songrándes] *they're big*, **sin ganas** [singánas] *without enthusiasm/appetite*, **tengo** [téngo] *I have*. The **n** must be pronounced like the *ng* of *bring* when **g** follows it.
    The combination **gue** and **gui** are pronounced as the Spanish **g** of **hago** plus **e** or **i**; the silent **u** merely shows that the **g** is not pronounced like Spanish **j**: **pague** [páγe] *pay*, **la guirnalda** [laγirnálda] *wreath*. In the combinations **güe** and **güi** the **u** is pronounced like *w*, cf. **desagüe** [desáγwe] *drain*, **nicaragüense** [nikaraγwénse] *Nicaraguan*.

h is always silent. Compare the pairs **asta/hasta**
spear/until, **ha/a** *has/to*, **hecho/echo** *done/I throw out*,
which are each pronounced identically. The rule in
Spanish is the reverse of English: in Spanish *not* dropping
one's aitches tends to sound illiterate.

j is pronounced in Spain and most of Argentina like the *ch*
in Scottish *loch* (phonetic sign [χ]). In most of the rest of
Latin America it is soft like the *h* in English *hat*. **G** is pronounced like **j** before **e** and **i**: **rojo** [rróχo] *red*, **ajo** [áχo]
garlic, **jarra** [χárra] *jar*, **general** [χenerál] *general*, **gente**
[χénte] *people*, **rígido** [rríχiδo] *rigid*.

l is always pronounced like the *l* in Southern British or
Southern Irish *leaf*. It is not pronounced like the *l* in the
English *cold*. Americans and Scots tend to use the latter
kind of *l* even at the beginning of words like *leaf*, so they
must take care over the Spanish sound: **lobo** *wolf*, **sal** *salt*,
natural, **gol** *goal* (in soccer).

ll varies from region to region. The correct pronunciation
in standard Spanish does not correspond to anything in
English: it is a palatal **l**, i.e. **l** pronounced with the tongue
spread flat against the roof of the mouth. Many English-
speakers pronounce it like the *li* in *million*, but this is the
Spanish sound **li** in words like **alianza** *alliance*, **exilio**
exile: the two words **polio** *polio* and **pollo** *chicken* sound
quite different. The best solution for English speakers is to
pronounce it always like the *y* of *yacht*—as millions of
Spanish speakers do. This may sound slovenly to some
speakers, but it is much better than the *li* of *million*. In
most of the Argentina and Uruguay it is pronounced like
the *s* of *pleasure*.

m is pronounced as in English, or sometimes like **n**
when it occurs at the end of a word, as in
referéndum.

n is pronounced as in English before a vowel or **d, t**, another **n**, or when nothing follows it: **no**, **Londres** *London*, **antes** *before*, **innato** *innate*, **son** *they are*.

Before all other consonants it is pronounced with the mouth in the same position as for the following consonant, i.e.

before **k, j, g** and **c** when pronounced **k**, like *ng* in *song*: **con kilos** *with kilos*, **sin gusto** *without taste*, **lengua** *tongue/language*, **en Colombia**, **banco** *bank/bench*;

before **m, b, p, v**, like the *m* in *mouse*: **en Madrid**, **han bajado** *they've got down*, **en París**, **han visto** *they've seen*;

before **ll, y** and **ch**, like **ñ** (see below): **en llamas** *in flames*, **en Yepes**, **ancho** *wide*, **en Chile**;

before **f** it is pronounced with the tongue and lips in the position for pronouncing **f**: **son fuertes** *they're strong*, **en frente** *opposite*.

ñ is difficult for Americans and Britons. It is a palatal *n*, i.e. an *n* pronounced with the tongue flat against the roof of the mouth. It is not the same as the *ni* in *onion*, which is the Spanish **ni** in words like **Sonia**, **milenio** *millennium*. Students should try their pronunciation of the two words **huraño** [uráño] *shy/unsociable* and **uranio** [urányo] *uranium* on a native Spanish-speaker: if the difference of meaning is clear, all is well.

q is found only in the combination **que** and **qui**, which are pronounced [ke] and [ki]. See **k** (first item in list of consonants) for details: **parque** *park*, **quiso** *he wanted*

r between vowels and at the end of words is rather like the *d* in the American English *soda* or the *r* in Scottish English *carry*: i.e. a single flap of the tongue against the gum ridge. It is not like the *r* in American or British *red*, *rose*. **R** is never dropped, as it is in southern British English in words like *cart*, and it is never pronounced with the tongue curled back, as it is in the USA in words like *far*.

Examples **Carlos, bar, cara** *face*, **mero** *mere*, **decir** *to say*.

At the beginning of a word and after **n, l** and **s** it is rolled like Spanish **rr**, e.g. in **Roma, alrededor** *around*, **honra** *honour*, **Israel**.

rr is a rolled **r** (three taps of the tongue). It is important to distinguish between **caro** *dear* and **carro** *car/cart*, **pero** *but* and **perro** *dog*.

s is pronounced like *s* in *hiss*, not as in *rose*.

w is found only in foreign words, where it is pronounced like Spanish **v/b** (see above): **kiwi** [kíßi] *kiwi fruit*, **Kuwait** [kußáyt].

x is the same as in English in Latin America, but in Spain it is often pronounced *s* before a consonant: **explicar** [eksplikár]/[esplikár] *explain*, but **taxi** [táksi].

y is like y in *yacht*. In Argentina it is like the *s* in *pleasure*.

z is always pronounced the same as the Spanish **c** when the latter occurs before **e** and **i**, i.e. like *ss* in *hiss* in Latin America and [θ] (as *th* in *think*) in Spain: **haz** [as]/[aθ] *do*, **las veces** [lasßéses]/[lasßéθes] *the times*.

STRESS (see Glossary)

The position of stress in a Spanish word is often variable and can change the meaning. See the section on Writing Accents (p.222) for details.

Spelling and Punctuation

This chapter presupposes a knowledge of Spanish pronunciation (explained in the previous chapter).

THE ALPHABET

The Spanish alphabet has the following letters:

a **a**	g **ge**	m **eme**	r **erre/ere**	y **i griega**
b **be**	h **hache**	n **ene**	s **ese**	z **zeta**
c **ce**	i **i**	ñ **eñe**	t **te**	
d **de**	j **jota**	o **o**	u **u**	
e **e**	k **ka**	p **pe**	v **uve**	
f **efe**	l **ele**	q **cu**	w **uve doble**	

Letters of the alphabet are all feminine: **la a, una ce**.

Ch and **ll** were counted as separate letters of the alphabet until the Association of Academies of Spanish decided
to introduce normal alphabetical order in April 1994. As a
result alphabetical order in dictionaries and directories
printed before that date will differ from ours, e.g. **chato**
came after **cubrir**, **llama** after **luz**.

WRITING ACCENTS

There are three written accents in Spanish: the acute
accent, the dieresis and the **tilde**.

The dieresis occurs only in the combinations **güe** and

güe, where it shows that the **u** is not silent as in **nicaragüense** *Nicaraguan*, **el pingüino** *the penguin*.

The **tilde** appears only over **ñ**, and forms an entirely different letter, described on p.220.

■ The acute accent is used for three purposes:

(a) Occasionally to distinguish two words that are spelt the same, e.g. **sólo** *only* and **solo** *alone*.

(b) On question words: **¿cuándo vienes?** *when are you coming?*, **no sabe qué hacer** *he doesn't know what to do*. See p.202 for details.

(c) To show where the stress falls in unpredictably stressed words

This latter function is very important, since the position of stress in a Spanish word is crucial for the meaning: compare **hablo** *I speak* and **habló** *he spoke*.

An accent must be written on the stressed vowel:

(1) Whenever the stress falls more than two full vowels[41] from the end:

> **rápido** *fast*
> **las imágenes** *images*
> **dígamelo** *say it to me*
> **fácilmente** *easily*
> **cámbiate** *change your clothes* (third full vowel from end)

(2) Whenever the word ends in a vowel or **n** or **s** and the stress falls on the final vowel:

> **habló** *he spoke*
> **iraní** *Iranian*
> **cambié** *I changed*

---

[41] By 'full vowel' is meant **a**, **e** and **o** and also **i** when it is pronounced as in **sin** and not like *y* as in **Colombia**, and **u** when it is pronounced as in **uno** and not like *w* as in **continuo**.

la nación *the nation*
francés *French*

Compare the following words which are stressed on the last full vowel but one and therefore do not require an accent: **hablo** *I speak*, **cambio** *I change*, **dicen** *they say*, **la imagen** *the image*, **las naciones** *the nations*, **las series** *the series* (plural).

(3) When the word ends in a consonant other than **n** or **s** and it is *not* stressed on the last vowel:

el récord *the record* (in sport, etc.)
el revólver *the revolver*
fácil *easy*

Compare the following words which are stressed on the last vowel and therefore do not require an accent: **la libertad** *freedom*, **natural** *natural*, **el complot** *conspiracy/plot*.

■ Words of one syllable (i.e. having only one fully pronounced vowel) are not written with an accent:

fui [fwi] *I was*[42]
fue [fwe] *he was*
vio [byo] *he saw*
dio [dyo] *he gave*
la fe *faith*

The only exceptions are accents written to distinguish one word from another: see list below.

Words like **fió** *he entrusted*, **crié** *I bred/raised* have two syllables (i.e. the **i** is pronounced separately).

■ The following words are distinguished by an accent:

aun *even*   **aún** *still/yet*[43]

---

[42] **fui, fue, vio** and **dio** were written with an accent until 1959.
[43] **Aun** should be pronounced as one syllable [awn] (aw like *ow* in *how*) and **aún** as two [a-ún].

de *of*	**dé** Present Subjunctive of **dar** *to give*
el *the*	**él** *he*
este *this*	**éste** *this one* (see p.138)
ese/aquel *that*	**ése/aquél** *that one* (see p.138)
mas *but* (poetic)	**más** *more*
mi *my*	**mí** *me* (after prepositions)
se pronoun	**sé** *I know*
si *if*	**sí** *yes*; *himself/herself/ yourself/themselves*, etc.
solo *alone*	**sólo** *only*
te *you*	**té** *tea*
tu *your*	**tú** *you*

DIPHTHONGS AND TRIPHTHONGS: SPELLING AND ACCENT RULES

■ Diphthongs consist of a *y* or *w* sound preceded or followed by a vowel. The pronunciation of the following diphthongs is shown on p.215:

> **au ua ai/ay ia/ya**
> **eu ue ei/ey ie/ye**
> **iu**
> **ou uo oi/oy io/yo**

The sound *y* is always written **y** at the end of words:

> **rey** *king*
> **doy** *I give*

The sound *y* is written either **y** or **hi** at the beginning of words:

> **el yate** *yacht*
> **la hierba** or **la yerba** *grass*

The sound *w* is always written **hu** at the beginning of a word or when it comes between vowels:

> **la huerta** [lawérta] *orchard*
> **ahuecar** [awekár] *to hollow out*

When the combinations of vowel plus **i** or **u** represent two separate vowels and not a diphthong, the **i** or **u** is written with an accent (even if **h** intervenes):

> **dúo** *duo*
> **el búho** *the owl*
> **hacías** *you were doing*
> **prohíben** *they prohibit*
> **se reúnen** *they hold a meeting*

■ Triphthongs consist of one of the above Diphthongs preceded or followed by a *y sound* or a *w* sound:

> **actuáis** [aktwáys] *you act*
> **buey** [bwey] *ox*

Diphthongs and Triphthongs count as one full vowel for the purpose of finding the stress accent:

Regular stress	Irregular
hacia *towards*	**ha**cía *he made*
dio *he gave*	me **fí**o *I trust*
aire *air*	**aí**sla *he isolates*
sois *you* (**vosotros**) *are*	**prohí**be *he prohibits*

MISCELLANEOUS SPELLING RULES

The main traps set by the Spanish spelling system are:

■ **b** and **v** are pronounced the same, so words like **vello** *down* (i.e. very fine hair) and **bello** *beautiful* sound the same.

■ The sound **s** (as in English *hiss*) can be spelt three different ways in Latin America:

feroz *ferocious* [ferós]   **as** *ace* [as]   **haz** *do* [as]
hace *does* [áse]   **cinco** *five* [sínko]

The **z** and **c** in the above words are pronounced like *th* of *think* in central and northern Spain.

■ There is no certain way of predicting the spelling of the sound [χ] (like the *ch* in the Scottish *loch*). It is usually written **j** before **a, o, u** and **g** before **e** and **i**. But there are quite a few words in which the combination **je** occurs, e.g. **el viaje** *journey*, **el equipaje** *baggage*, **el paisaje** *country-side*, **Jesús** *Jesus*, **condujeron** *they drove*, etc.

■ **gue/güe** and **gui/güi**: see p.218.

■ **h** is a silent letter, so there is no difference in sound, for example, between **hecho** *done* and **echo** *I pour out*.

■ **que** and **qui**: the **u** is silent and the **q** is pronounced [k].

■ **r** and **rr**: see p.220

■ A number of alternative spellings exist, the most important of which are:

words beginning with **psic-** (the equivalent of our *psych-*) may be written **sic-**: **psicología** or **sicología** *psychology*, because the **p** is silent;

the words **septiembre** *September* and **séptimo** *seventh* can be spelt without the **p**;

words beginning with **ree-** may be spelt **re-**, e.g. **relegir** or **reelegir** *re-elect*.

In all cases the longer forms are more usual (at least in Spain).

PUNCTUATION

There are variations in punctuation rules depending on country and, to some extent, on publisher. Only the major differences between Spanish and English practice are mentioned.

■ A comma is used to separate decimals (but not in Mexico, which uses the same system as English):

12,75 doce coma setenta y cinco *12.75*

■ A period (British 'full stop') is used to separate thousands

1.000.000 un millón *a million*

Mexico uses our system.

■ In some publications double inverted commas (**las comillas**) are used to enclose quoted words, in others chevrons are used (« »):

Tuvieron problemas por "el fuerte carácter de la suegra" or ... **«por el fuerte carácter de la suegra»** *They had problems due to 'their mother-in-law's strong character'*

■ Question marks and exclamation marks must be written upside-down at the beginning of questions and exclamations as well as the right way up at the end:

Oye, ¿sabes qué hora es? *Listen, d'you know what time it is?*
Pero, ¡qué tonto! *But what a fool!*

As can be seen, the start of the question or exclamation does not always coincide with the start of the sentence.

A **raya** or double-length dash is used to mark off dialogue in novels and stories:

—Tengo un hijo tuyo —me dijo después—. Allí está.
Y apuntó con el dedo a un muchacho largo con los ojos azorados.
—¡Quítate el sombrero, para que te vea tu padre!

'*I've got a son of yours*', he said to me afterwards.
'*There he is.*'
    And he pointed to a tall boy with alarmed eyes.
    '*Take your hat off so your father can see you!*'

| Translation Traps

This section covers a number of important miscellaneous points that could not be neatly fitted in elsewhere in the book.

'afternoon'/'evening'
'American'/'Latin-American', 'Spanish-American'
'any'
aun and *aún*
'to become'
de que and *de*
'-ing' forms of English verbs
'to like'
'only'/'alone'
'some'
'Spanish'/'Castilian'
'would'
ya

Afternoon, evening

It is difficult to differentiate these words in Spanish, since **la tarde** runs from about 1 p.m. to after sunset and therefore includes our afternoon and evening. **La noche** begins around 8 or 9 p.m.

American, Latin-American, South American, Spanish-American

In Spain **americano** usually means the same as the English *American*. In Latin America the same word is usually taken to mean *Latin-American* and **norteamericano** is used for our *American*. The adjective **estadounidense** 'pertaining to the USA' is generally found only in newspaper styles.

América Latina or **Latinoamérica** is *Latin America* and is a preferred term since it stresses trans-national identity; the adjective is **latinoamericano**. However, these terms include Brazil, Haiti, Martinique and one or two other places that speak Latin-based languages, and there is no entirely satisfactory word for Spanish-speaking Latin America. **La América de habla española** *Spanish-speaking America* is long-winded, but **Hispanoamérica**, **hispanoamericano** strictly mean *Spanish-America(n)* and some people consider them unfair to the non-European or non-Spanish components of the populations.

América del sur, adjective **sudamericano** or **suramericano** (the latter frowned on by strict grammarians) means *South America* and does not include Central America or the Caribbean.

Any

This word is translated as follows:

(a) Before substances and countable nouns, in negative and interrogative sentences, no Spanish equivalent:

> **No tengo agua/flores** *I haven't got any water/flowers*
> **¿Hay?** *Is there any/Are there any?*
> **¿Hay americanos en tu clase?** *Are there any Americans in your class?*

(b) When it means *it doesn't matter which*: **cualquiera** (see p.122):

> **Puedes elegir cualquiera de ellos** *You can choose any of them*
> **en cualquier sitio y a cualquier hora** *in any place and at any time*

(c) In comparisons: **ninguno** (see p.155):

> **Ella es mejor que ninguno de los hombres**
> *She's better than any of the men*

(d) After **sin** *without*, no Spanish equivalent:

> **Ha venido sin dinero** *He's come without any
> money*

Aun and aún

Aun means *even*, as in **aun en ese caso no lo haría** *even
in that case I wouldn't do it*. **Incluso**[44] means the same
thing, and is nowadays more common.

Aún means the same as **todavía** *yet*: **todavía/aún no
han llegado** *they haven't arrived yet*.

To become

There are several ways of translating this word and words
similar to it in meaning (cf. *to get angry*, *to go red*, *to
turn nasty*):

(a) Use a Pronominal Verb if one exists, e.g. **alegrarse**
to become cheerful, **se cansó** *he/she got/became tired*.

(b) Use **ponerse** for short-lived changes of mood,
appearance: **no te pongas así** *don't get like that*, **esto se
pone difícil** *this is getting difficult*, **se puso colorada** *she
went red*.

(c) Use **volverse** for more permanent changes: **te has
vuelto muy reaccionario** *you've got very reactionary*, **se
volvió loco** *he went mad*.

(d) Use **convertirse en** for total changes of nature, cf.
English *to turn into*: **los alquimistas creían que el
plomo podía convertirse en oro** *alchemists thought lead
could become/turn into gold*.

---

[44] Many Latin Americans say **inclusive** for **incluso**.

(e) Use **hacerse** for conversions to a belief or changes of profession involving qualifications: **se hizo diseñador** *he became a designer.* **Hacerse** is also found in some set phrases with non-human subjects, e.g. **se ha hecho tarde** *it's got late.*

(f) Use **nombrar** for posts, offices, titles: **lo/le han nombrado Ministro de Asuntos Exteriores** *he's become the Minister for Foreign Affairs.*

de que and que

These both translate *that*: **dice que viene** *he says that he's coming,* **la idea de que viene . . .** *the idea that he's coming.*

De que must be used:

(a) After nouns, to show that what follows is a Subordinate Clause and not a Relative Clause. Compare **el argumento que él defiende es absurdo** *the argument that/which he's defending is absurd* (Relative Clause) and **el argumento de que la luna está hecha de queso es absurdo** *the argument that the Moon is made of cheese is absurd* (Subordinator). If the English word *which* could replace *that* in such sentences, **de que** cannot be used.

(b) Before clauses after prepositional phrases, verbs and adjectives that include **de**: Compare

> **antes de la salida del tren** *before the departure of the train*
> **antes de que salga el tren** *before the train leaves*
>
> **Estoy seguro de tu amor** *I'm sure of your love*
> **Estoy seguro de que me quieres** *I'm sure that you love me*
>
> **Se queja de que no la dejan dormir** *She complains that they don't let her sleep*

(c) **De que** must *not* be used after verbs meaning *to say, to think, to tell,* etc.

Dice que está enferma *She/he says that she's ill*
(*never* **'dice de que está enferma'*)

'*-ing*' forms of English verbs

This English verb form has many different uses, either as
an adjective, a noun, a participle or, sometimes, as a
gerund. The following are some of the most common
ways of translating the *-ing* form:

(a) When it is a noun it must be translated by the
Infinitive or by a suitable Spanish noun:

> *Smoking is forbidden* **Prohibido fumar**
> *I like dancing* **Me gusta bailar**
> *hunting and fishing* **la caza y la pesca**

In compounds like *driving wheel, fishing rod, diving suit,* the
-ing form is a noun and the translation must be learned
separately: **el volante, la caña de pescar, la escafan-
dra/el traje de buceo.**

(b) When it is an adjective it must be translated by an
adjective:

> *A boring film* **una película aburrida**
> *An overwhelming majority* **una mayoría abru-
> madora**
> *A worrying problem* **un problema preocupante**

(c) After a preposition it is translated by the Infinitive:

> *Do it without complaining* **Hazlo sin quejarte**

But when the subject of the *-ing* form is not the same as
the subject of the main verb, the Subjunctive or the
Indicative may be required. See p.29 ff for more details:

> *I entered without him seeing me* **Entré sin que él
> me viera**

(d) When the -*ing* form shows when or how an action is done, use the Spanish Gerund:

> *I realized it while walking down the street* **Me di cuenta andando por la calle**
> *He stood looking at me* **Se quedó mirándome**
> *You'll get nothing by shouting like that* **No conseguirás nada gritando así**

(e) For the phrase '*on . . . -ing*' use **al** plus the Infinitive:

> *on entering the room* **al entrar en el cuarto**

(f) To translate 'standing', 'sitting', 'leaning' or other bodily positions, use the Past Participle:

> *I was sitting on the beach* **Yo estaba sentado en la playa**
> *She was leaning against the tree* **Estaba apoyada contra el árbol**
> *He was crouching in the corner* **Estaba agazapado en el rincón**

(g) After many verbs, the -*ing* form must be translated by an Infinitive, often with a preposition:

> *Stop shouting* **Deja de gritar**
> *Start writing* **Empiece a escribir**

See the list of verbs that take the Infinitive on p.44 ff.

To like

Spanish uses the verb **gustar**, which means *to please*, so the English subject must become the object in Spanish:

> **Me gusta el vino** *Wine pleases me = I like wine*
> **No me gusta** *It doesn't please me = I don't like it*
> **¿Te/Le gusta bailar?** *Does dancing please you? = Do you like dancing?*

Le gusta trabajar aquí *Working here*
pleases/him/her = (S)he likes working
here
¿Te gusto? *Do I please you? = Do you like me?*
Me gustas *You please me = I like you*

Only and *alone*

Solo (agrees in number and gender: **sola, solos, solas**) is
an adjective meaning *alone*: **está sola** *she's on her own.*
Sólo (with accent) means *only*, and is the same as **sola-
mente**: **sólo sé español** *I only know Spanish.*

Some

This word may be translated in several different ways:

(a) Before substances and vague quantities of countable
nouns: no Spanish equivalent

Pon azúcar *Put in some sugar*
Compra pan/flores *Buy some bread/flowers*
Hay patatas (Lat. Am. **papas**) *There are some*
potatoes

(b) Before countable nouns when it means *a small number*: **unos/unas**:

Han venido unos ingleses *Some/a couple of*
English people have come

(c) When *some* means *certain*, i.e. *some but not others*:
alguno (discussed on p.121):

En algunos países está prohibido beber alcohol
In some countries drinking alcohol is forbidden
Algún día podré comprarlo *I'll be able to buy it*
some day

Spanish, Castilian

España is the country, and **español** is the adjective
Spanish. **El español** is not *the* language of Spain, since
Catalan, Basque and Galician also have official status and
several other languages are recognized locally. **El caste-
llano** *Castilian* is the official name for the language
described in this book, although Castilian-speakers often
call it **el español**, which may annoy speakers of the other
languages.

What and which

See p.p. 203–4.

Would

This usually forms the Conditional tense in English, in
which case it is translated by the Spanish Conditional
tense:

> *If we sold more, prices **would** be lower* **Si
> vendiéramos más, los precios serían más
> bajos**

But *would* is occasionally used in English narrative to
express habitual actions, in which case it must be translated by the Spanish Imperfect tense or by **soler** +
Infinitive:

> *Each day he **would** get up (= used to get up) at six
> and he'd feed the chickens* **Todos los días se
> levantaba a las seis y daba de comer a las
> gallinas**
> *He **would** (= used to) ring her every night before
> going to bed* **Solía llamarla todas las noches,
> antes de acostarse**

Ya

This constantly-used word basically means:

> *already* with a past tense: **ya ha llegado/ha llegado ya** *he's already arrived*;
>
> *right now* with a present tense or imperative: **ya vienen** *they're coming right now*, **¡dímelo ya!** *tell me right now!*;
>
> *for sure/soon* with a positive future tense: **no te preocupes: ya llegará** *don't worry, she'll come for sure/she'll be here soon*;
>
> *not . . . any more* with a negative present or future: **ya no vienen/vendrán** *they're not coming any more*.

Verb Forms

Conjugation of regular -ar verb *240*
Conjugation of regular -er verb *243*
Conjugation of regular -ir verb *246*
Spelling rules affecting all regular and irregular verbs *249*
Spanish verbs: hints and tips for learners *250*
Tables of irregular and radical changing verbs and of typical verbs affected by spelling changes *253*
List of irregular and radical-changing verbs and common verbs affected by spelling changes *302*

FORMS OF REGULAR VERBS

As the following tables show, one adds the appropriate endings to the stem, which is the form left after removing the **-ar**, **-er** or **-ir** of the Infinitive:

Infinitive	Stem	Examples
hablar	**habl-**	**hablas** *you speak*
beber	**beb-**	**bebíamos** *we were drinking*
vivir	**viv-**	**vivieron** *they lived*

Each tense has a separate set of endings, which differ for each of the three conjugations, although the endings of certain tenses (e.g. the Future and Conditional) are identical for all verbs, and the differences between the endings of the -ir and -er conjugations are not numerous.

CONJUGATION OF REGULAR VERB
HABLAR to speak

Infinitive	**hablar**
Gerund	**hablando**
Past Participle	**hablado**
Imperative	
Tú	**habla**
Vosotros/as	**hablad**
Usted	**hable**
Ustedes	**hablen**

INDICATIVE

Present		*Imperfect*	
hablo	**hablamos**	**hablaba**	**hablábamos**
hablas	**habláis**	**hablabas**	**hablabais**
habla	**hablan**	**hablaba**	**hablaban**

Preterit	
hablé	**hablamos**
hablaste	**hablasteis**
habló	**hablaron**

Present Continuous	*Imperfect Continuous*
estoy hablando	**estaba hablando**
etc.	*etc.*

Preterit Continuous
estuve hablando
etc.

See p.269 for the conjugation of **estar**.

Perfect
he hablado   **hemos hablado**
has hablado   **habéis hablado**
ha hablado   **han hablado**

Pluperfect
había hablado   **habíamos hablado**
habías hablado   **habíais hablado**
había hablado   **habían hablado**

Perfect Continuous   *Pluperfect Continuous*
he estado hablando   **había estado hablando**
etc.   *etc.*

Pretérito anterior
hube hablado   **hubimos hablado**
hubiste hablado   **hubisteis hablado**
hubo hablado   **hubieron hablado**

Future
hablaré   **hablaremos**
hablarás   **hablaréis**
hablará   **hablarán**

Future Perfect
habré hablado   **habremos hablado**
habrás hablado   **habréis hablado**
habrá hablado   **habrán hablado**

Future Continuous   *Future Perfect Continuous*
estaré hablando   **habré estado hablando**
etc.   *etc.*

Conditional
hablaría   **hablaríamos**
hablarías   **hablaríais**
hablaría   **hablarían**

Perfect Conditional
habría hablado   **habríamos hablado**
habrías hablado   **habríais hablado**
habría hablado   **habrían hablado**

The Perfect Conditional may also be formed with the **-ra**
Imperfect Subjunctive of **haber, e.g. hubiera hablado**, *etc.*

Conditional Continuous	*Perfect Conditional Continuous*
estaría hablando	**habría estado hablando**
etc.	*or* **hubiera estado hablando**
	etc.

SUBJUNCTIVE

Present Subjunctive *Present Subjunctive Continuous*

hable	**hablemos**	**esté hablando**
hables	**habléis**	*etc.*
hable	**hablen**	

Imperfect Subjunctives

-ra *form*		**-se** *form*	
hablara	**habláramos**	**hablase**	**hablásemos**
hablaras	**hablarais**	**hablases**	**hablaseis**
hablara	**hablaran**	**hablase**	**hablasen**

Imperfect Subjunctive Continuous
estuviera hablando *or* **estuviese hablando**
etc.   *etc.*

Perfect Subjunctive

haya hablado	**hayamos hablado**
hayas hablado	**hayáis hablado**
haya hablado	**hayan hablado**

Perfect Subjunctive Continuous
haya estado hablando
etc.

Pluperfect Subjunctive

hubiera hablado	**hubiéramos hablado**
hubieras hablado	**hubierais hablado**
hubiera hablado	**hubieran hablado**
or **hubiese hablado** *etc.*	

Perfect Subjunctive Continuous
haya estado hablando
etc.

Pluperfect Subjunctive Continuous
hubiera estado hablando
or **hubiese estado hablando**
etc.

Future Subjunctive

hablare	habláremos
hablares	hablareis
hablare	hablaren

CONJUGATION OF REGULAR VERB
BEBER *to drink*

Infinitive	**beber**
Gerund	**bebiendo**
Past Participle	**bebido**
Imperative	
Tú	**bebe**
Vosotros/as	**bebed**
Usted	**beba**
Ustedes	**beban**

INDICATIVE

Present

bebo	bebemos
bebes	bebéis
bebe	beben

Imperfect

bebía	bebíamos
bebías	bebíais
bebía	bebían

Preterit

bebí	bebimos
bebiste	bebisteis
bebió	bebieron

Present Continuous
estoy bebiendo
etc.

Imperfect Continuous
estaba bebiendo
etc.

Preterit Continuous
estuve bebiendo
etc.

Perfect
he bebido	**hemos bebido**
has bebido	**habéis bebido**
ha bebido	**han bebido**

Pluperfect
había bebido	**habíamos bebido**
habías bebido	**habíais bebido**
había bebido	**habían bebido**

Perfect Continuous
he estado bebiendo
etc.

Pluperfect Continuous
había estado bebiendo
etc.

Pretérito anterior
hube bebido	**hubimos bebido**
hubiste bebido	**hubisteis bebido**
hubo bebido	**hubieron bebido**

Future
beberé	**beberemos**
beberás	**beberéis**
beberá	**beberán**

Future Perfect
habré bebido	**habremos bebido**
habrás bebido	**habréis bebido**
habrá bebido	**habrán bebido**

Future Continuous
estaré bebiendo
etc.

Future Perfect Continuous
habré estado bebiendo
etc.

Conditional
bebería	**beberíamos**
beberías	**beberíais**
bebería	**beberían**

Perfect Conditional
habría bebido   **habríamos bebido**
habrías bebido   **habríais bebido**
habría bebido   **habrían bebido**

The Perfect Conditional may also be formed with the **-ra**
Imperfect Subjunctive of **haber,** *e.g.* **hubiera bebido,** *etc.*

Conditional Continuous   *Conditional Perfect Continuous*
estaría bebiendo   **habría estado bebiendo**
etc.   *or* **hubiera estado bebiendo,** *etc.*
                               etc.

SUBJUNCTIVE

Present Subjunctive   *Present Subjunctive Continuous*
beba   bebamos   **esté bebiendo**
bebas   bebáis   *etc.*
beba   beban

Imperfect Subjunctives
-ra *form*   **-se** *form*
bebiera   bebiéramos   **bebiese   bebiésemos**
bebieras   bebierais   **bebieses   bebieseis**
bebiera   bebieran   **bebiese   bebiesen**

Imperfect Continuous Subjunctive
estuviera bebiendo *or* **estuviese bebiendo**
etc.   *etc.*

Perfect Subjunctive
haya bebido   **hayamos bebido**
hayas bebido   **hayáis bebido**
haya bebido   **hayan bebido**

Pluperfect Subjunctive
hubiera bebido   **hubiéramos bebido**
hubieras bebido   **hubierais bebido**
hubiera bebido   **hubieran bebido**
or **hubiese bebido,** *etc.*

Perfect Subjunctive Continuous
haya estado bebiendo
etc.

Pluperfect Subjunctive Continuous
hubiera estado bebiendo
or **hubiese estado bebiendo**
etc.

Future Subjunctive

bebiere	**bebiéremos**
bebieres	**bebiereis**
bebiere	**bebieren**

CONJUGATION OF REGULAR VERB **VIVIR**
to live

■ *Only the endings marked with an asterisk differ from those of the* **-er** *conjugation.*

Infinitive	**vivir★**
Gerund	**viviendo**
Past Participle	**vivido**
Imperative	
Tú	**vive**
Vosotros/as	**vivid★**
Usted	**viva**
Ustedes	**vivan**

INDICATIVE

Present		*Imperfect*	
vivo	**vivimos★**	**vivía**	**vivíamos**
vives	**vivís★**	**vivías**	**vivíais**
vive	**viven**	**vivía**	**vivían**

Preterit	
viví	**vivimos**
viviste	**vivisteis**
vivió	**vivieron**

Present
estoy viviendo
etc.

Imperfect Continuous
estaba viviendo
etc.

Preterit Continuous
estuve viviendo
etc.

Perfect
he vivido
has vivido
ha vivido

hemos vivido
habéis vivido
han vivido

Pluperfect
había vivido
habías vivido
había vivido

habíamos vivido
habíais vivido
habían vivido

Perfect Continuous
he estado viviendo
etc.

Pluperfect Continuous
había estado viviendo
etc.

Pretérito anterior
hube vivido
hubiste vivido
hubo vivido

hubimos vivido
hubisteis vivido
hubieron vivido

Future
viviré★ **viviremos★**
vivirás★ **viviréis★**
vivirá★ **vivirán★**

Future Perfect
habré vivido
habrás vivido
habrá vivido

habremos vivido
habréis vivido
habrán vivido

Future Continuous
estaré viviendo
etc.

Future Perfect Continuous
habré estado viviendo
etc.

Conditional

viviría★	viviríamos★
vivirías★	viviríais★
viviría★	vivirían★

Conditional Perfect

habría vivido	habríamos vivido
habrías vivido	habríais vivido
habría vivido	habrían vivido

The Perfect Conditional may also be formed with the -ra *Imperfect Subjunctive of* **haber**, e.g. **hubiera vivido**, etc.

Conditional Continuous	*Conditional Perfect Continuous*
estaría viviendo	**habría estado viviendo**
etc.	*etc.*

SUBJUNCTIVE

Present Subjunctive

viva	vivamos
vivas	viváis
viva	vivan

Present Subjunctive Continuous
esté viviendo
etc.

Imperfect Subjunctives

-**ra** *form*		-**se** *form*	
viviera	viviéramos	viviese	viviésemos
vivieras	vivierais	vivieses	vivieseis
viviera	vivieran	viviese	viviesen

Imperfect Subjunctive Continuous
estuviera viviendo *or* **estuviese viviendo**
etc.   *etc.*

Perfect Subjunctive

haya vivido	hayamos vivido
hayas vivido	hayáis vivido
haya vivido	hayan vivido

Pluperfect Subjunctive
hubiera vivido   **hubiéramos vivido**
hubieras vivido   **hubierais vivido**
hubiera vivido   **hubieran vivido**
or **hubiese vivido** *etc.*

*Perfect Subjunctive Continuous Pluperfect Subjunctive
Continuous*

haya estado viviendo   **hubiera estado viviendo**
etc.   *or* **hubiese estado viviendo**
                            etc.

Future Subjunctive
viviere   **viviéremos**
vivieres   **viviereis**
viviere   **vivieren**

SPELLING RULES AFFECTING CONJUGATION OF ALL SPANISH VERBS

- Infinitive ends in -**car**   c > **qu** before **e** or **i**. See **sacar** (no.52)

- Infinitive ends in -**gar**   g > **gu** before **e** or **i**. See **pagar** (no. 34)

- Infinitive ends in -**zar**   z > **c** before **e** or **i**. See **rezar** (no. 49)

- Infinitive ends in -**guar**   dieresis needed on **u** before **e**. See **averiguar** (no.7)

- Infinitive ends in -**cer**: a few verbs are conjugated like **vencer** (no. 61), i.e. **c** > **z** before **a** or **o**: these include **ejercer** *to exercise*, **convencer** *to convince*, **mecer** *to rock/sway*. **Escocer** *to sting* and **torcer** *to twist* are conjugated like **cocer** *to cook* (no.12). The rest, which are the vast majority, are conjugated like **parecer** (no. 35) and show a slight irregularity: **c** > **zc** before **a, o**.

■ Infinitive ends in vowel + **-er** or vowel + **-ir**: a *y* sound is written **y** between vowels. See **poseer** (no. 40) and **construir** (no. 13) for examples.

■ Infinitive ends in **-cir**. Check verb in list.

■ Infinitive ends in -**ger** or -**gir**: **g > j** before **o** or **a**. See **proteger** (no. 43).

■ Infinitive ends in **-ñer, -ñir** or **-llir**: diphthong **ió** in Preterit > **ó**; diphthong **ie** in Preterit and in Imperfect Subjunctive > **e**. See **tañer** (no. 57).

SPANISH VERBS: HINTS AND TIPS FOR LEARNERS

The Spanish verb system is complicated, but there are a number of short cuts that will save learners time and effort.

■ Compound Tense Formation: all verbs

The Compound Tenses (see Glossary) of all verbs are formed with the verb **haber** and the Past Participle, formed as explained on p. 55.

The most frequently used compound tenses are:

> Perfect   **he hablado** / *have spoken, etc.*
> Pluperfect **había hablado** / *had spoken*
> Future   **habré hablado** / *will have spoken,*
> Conditional **habría** or **hubiera hablado** / *would have spoken*

The Past Participle is invariable in form in these tenses. The full conjugation of the irregular verb **haber** appears on p.271.

■ Imperfect Indicative: only three verbs are irregular:

ser *to be*: **era eras era éramos erais eran**
ir *to go*: **iba ibas iba íbamos ibais iban**
ver *to see*: **veía veías veía veíamos veíais veían**
(the *e* is unexpected)

In all other cases the endings of the Imperfect are added to the stem left after removing the -ar, -er or -ir of the Infinitive, e.g. **dar** *to give*: **daba, dabas, daba, dábamos, dabais, daban; tener** *to have*: **tenía, tenías, tenía, teníamos, teníais, tenían.**

■ Future and Conditional: with twelve exceptions, all verbs form their Future by adding **-é -ás -á -emos -éis -án** to their Infinitive, and all verbs form their Conditional by adding **-ía -ías -ía -íamos -íais -ían** to their Infinitive (the latter endings are the same as the endings of the Imperfect Indicative of -**er** verbs). The exceptions are the following verbs (and also any compound verbs based on them, e.g. **componer** *to compose*). The Future and Conditional endings are added to the slightly modified form of the Infinitive shown in bold italics:

caber *cabr-* to fit in	**querer** *querr-* to want
decir *dir-* to say	**saber** *sabr-* to know
haber *habr-* auxiliary verb	**salir** *saldr-* to leave
hacer *har-* to do/to make	**tener** *tendr-* to have
poder *podr-* to be able	**valer** *valdr-* to be worth
poner *pondr-* to put	**venir** *vendr-* to come

■ The Present Subjunctive can be formed for nearly all verbs by adding the following endings to the stem left after removing the -**o** of the first-person Present Indicative:

-ar verbs :	-e	-es	-e	-emos	-éis	-en
-er & -ir verbs:	-a	-as	-a	-amos	-áis	-an

Examples:

Infinitive	1st-person singular Present Indicative (stem in Italics)	Present Subjunctive
hablar *to speak*	*habl*o	**habl**e, etc.
comer *to eat*	*com*o	**com**a, etc.
vivir *to live*	*viv*o	**viv**a, etc.
contar *to tell*	*cuent*o	**cuent**e, etc.
perder *to lose*	*pierd*o	**pierd**a, etc.
pedir *to ask for*	*pid*o	**pid**a, etc.
hacer *to do*	*hag*o	**hag**a, etc.
tener *to have*	*teng*o	**teng**a, etc.

The main exceptions are the following verbs, which should be checked in the tables printed below:

> **dar** *to give* (unexpected accent in Subjunctive)
> **estar** *to be* (unexpected accents in Subjunctive)
> **haber**
> **ir** *to go*
> **morir** *to die* and **dormir** *to sleep*
> **saber** *to know*
> **sentir** *to feel* (and all verbs like it)
> **ser** *to be*

In the case of Radical-Changing verbs like **contar**, **mover**, **cerrar**, **perder** only the stressed vowel is altered: **cuente—contemos, pierda—perdamos**, etc.

■ The Imperfect Subjunctive of all verbs is predictable: the endings are added to the stem left after the ending of the third-person singular Preterit is removed (but this stem may require separate learning in the case of Radical-Changing and Irregular verbs):

Infinitive	3rd-person Preterit (stem in italics)	Imperfect Subjunctive
hablar *to speak*	**habl**ó *he spoke*	*habl*ara, *habl*ase, etc.
sentir *to feel*	**sin**tió *he felt*	*sint*iera, *sint*iese, etc.
estar *to be*	**estuv**o *he was*	*estuv*iera, *estuv*iese, etc.
tener *to have*	**tuv**o *he had/got*	*tuv*iera, *tuv*iese, etc.
decir *to say*	**dij**o *he said*	*dij*era, *dij*ese, etc.

Note the loss of **i** after **j** in words like **dijera/dijese, trajera/trajese, produjera/produjese.**

■ The Imperative

The **vosotros** Imperative (not used in Latin America) is always regularly formed by replacing the **-r** of the Infinitive by **-d: hablar—hablad, ir—id, ser—sed**, etc.

The **Usted** and **Ustedes** Imperative are always identical to the 3rd-person Present Subjunctive, singular and plural respectively, e.g. **hacer—haga—hagan**.

The **tú** Imperative is always formed by dropping the **-s** from the 2nd-person singular of the Present Indicative: **cuentas** *you tell*—**¡cuenta!** *tell!*, **pides** *you ask for*—**¡pide!** *ask for!* There are a few important exceptions, shown on p.36.

TABLES OF IRREGULAR VERBS, TYPICAL RADICAL CHANGING VERBS AND EXAMPLES OF VERBS AFFECTED BY SPELLING CHANGES

The Indicative Present and Preterit and the Present Subjunctive are always shown in full, whether they are regular or not. The endings of the Future and Conditional tenses are the same for all verbs. The endings of the

Imperfect Indicative are all regular, with very few exceptions (**ir** and **ser**). The Imperfect Subjunctive endings are always the same as for regular verbs.

1. **Abolir** *to abolish*

This, and a few verbs like it, is a defective verb. Forms in which the ending does not begin with **i** are not used.

Infinitive **abolir**   *Gerund* **aboliendo**

Past Participle **abolido**   *Imperative* **abolid.** ***Abole** *is not found*

INDICATIVE

Present	*Imperfect*	*Preterit*
not found	**abolía**	**abolí**
not found	etc.	**aboliste**
not found		**abolió**
abolimos		**abolimos**
abolís		**abolisteis**
not found		**abolieron**

Future	*Conditional*
aboliré	**aboliría**
etc.	etc.

SUBJUNCTIVE

Present	*Imperfect*
no forms	**aboliera/aboliese**
in use	etc.

2. **Adquirir** *to acquire*

Radical changing verb. Only **inquirir** *to enquire* is conjugated the same way.

Infinitive **adquirir**   *Gerund* **adquiriendo**

Past Participle **adquirido**   *Imperative* **adquiere adquirid**

INDICATIVE

Present	Imperfect	Preterit
adquiero	adquiría	adquirí
adquieres	etc.	adquiriste
adquiere		adquirió
adquirimos		adquirimos
adquirís		adquiristeis
adquieren		adquirieron

Future	Conditional
adquiriré	adquiriría
etc.	etc.

SUBJUNCTIVE

Present	Imperfect
adquiera	adquiriera/adquiriese
adquieras	etc.
adquiera	
adquiramos	
adquiráis	
adquieran	

3. **Aislar** *to isolate*

The **i** is written with an accent when it is stressed. The accent was introduced in 1959 and does not appear in books printed before then.

Infinitive **aislar** *Gerund* **aislando**

Past Participle **aislado** *Imperative* **aísla aislad**

INDICATIVE

Present	Imperfect	Preterit
aíslo	aislaba	aislé
aíslas	etc.	aislaste
aísla		aisló
aislamos		aislamos
aisláis		aislasteis
aíslan		aislaron

Future	Conditional
aislaré	**aislaría**
etc.	*etc.*

SUBJUNCTIVE

Present	Imperfect
aísle	**aislara/aislase**
aísles	*etc.*
aísle	
aislemos	
aisléis	
aíslen	

4. **Andar** *to walk/go about*

Infinitive **andar**	*Gerund* **andando**
Past Participle **andado**	*Imperative* **anda andad**

Present	Imperfect	Preterit
ando	**andaba**	**anduve**
andas	*etc.*	**anduviste**
anda		**anduvo**
andamos		**anduvimos**
andáis		**anduvisteis**
andan		**anduvieron**

Future	Conditional
andaré	**andaría**
etc.	*etc.*

SUBJUNCTIVE

Present	Imperfect
ande	**anduviera/anduviese**
andes	*etc.*
ande	
andemos	
andéis	
anden	

5. **Argüir** *to argue (a point)*

The dieresis on the **u** shows that it is pronounced as **w**.

Infinitive **argüir**   *Gerund* **arguyendo**
Past Participle **argüido**   *Imperative* **arguye argüid**

INDICATIVE

Present	*Imperfect*	*Preterit*
arguyo	argüía	argüí
arguyes	etc.	argüiste
arguye		arguyó
argüimos		argüimos
argüís		argüisteis
arguyen		arguyeron

Future	*Conditional*
argüiré	argüiría
etc.	etc.

SUBJUNCTIVE

Present	*Imperfect*
arguya	arguyera/arguyese
arguyas	etc.
arguya	
arguyamos	
arguyáis	
arguyan	

6. **Asir** *to grasp/seize*

Infinitive **asir**   *Gerund* **asiendo**
Past Participle **asido**   *Imperative* **ase, asid**

Forms containing **g** are usually avoided.

INDICATIVE

Present	*Imperfect*	*Preterit*
(asgo)	asía	así
ases	etc.	asiste

Present, continued		Preterit, continued
ase		asió
asimos		asimos
asís		asisteis
asen		asieron

Future	Conditional
asiré	asiría
etc.	etc.

SUBJUNCTIVE

Present	Imperfect
(asga)	asiera/asiese
(asgas)	etc.
(asga)	
(asgamos)	
(asgáis)	
(asgan)	

7. Averiguar *to ascertain*

The dieresis shows that the **u** is not silent.

Infinitive **averiguar**   Gerund **averiguando**
Past Participle **averiguado**   Imperative **averigua averiguad**

INDICATIVE

Present	Imperfect	Preterit
averiguo	averiguaba	averigüé
averiguas	etc.	averiguaste
averigua		averiguó
averiguamos		averiguamos
averiguáis		averiguasteis
averiguan		averiguaron

Future		Conditional
averiguaré		averiguaría
etc.		etc.

SUBJUNCTIVE

Present	Imperfect
averigüe	averiguara/averiguase
averigües	etc.
averigüe	
averigüemos	
averigüéis	
averigüen	

8. **Caber** *to fit into*

Infinitive **caber**	*Gerund* **cabiendo**
Past Participle **cabido**	*Imperative* **cabe cabed**

INDICATIVE

Present	Imperfect	Preterit
quepo	cabía	cupe
cabes	etc.	cupiste
cabe		cupo
cabemos		cupimos
cabéis		cupisteis
caben		cupieron

Future	Conditional
cabré	cabría
etc.	etc.

SUBJUNCTIVE

Present	Imperfect
quepa	cupiera/cupiese
quepas	etc.
quepa	
quepamos	
quepáis	
quepan	

9. **Caer** *to fall*

Infinitive **caer**   *Gerund* **cayendo**
Past Participle **caído**   *Imperative* **cae caed**

INDICATIVE

Present	*Imperfect*	*Preterit*
caigo	**caía**	**caí**
caes	*etc.*	**caíste**
cae		**cayó**
caemos		**caímos**
caéis		**caísteis**
caen		**cayeron**

Future	*Conditional*
caeré	**caeriá**
etc.	*etc.*

SUBJUNCTIVE

Present	*Imperfect*
caiga	**cayera/cayese**
caigas	*etc.*
caiga	
caigamos	
caigáis	
caigan	

10. **Cambiar** *to change*

Regular: the **i** is always pronounced like **y**. However, many verbs ending in **-iar** are conjugated like **liar** (no. 28).

Infinitive **cambiar**   *Gerund* **cambiando**
Past Participle **cambiado**   *Imperative* **cambia cambiad**

INDICATIVE

Present	*Imperfect*	*Preterit*
cambio	**cambiaba**	**cambié**
cambias	*etc.*	**cambiaste**

Present, continued	*Preterit, continued*
cambia	cambió
cambiamos	cambiamos
cambiáis	cambiasteis
cambian	cambiaron

Future	*Conditional*
cambiaré	cambiaría
etc.	etc.

SUBJUNCTIVE

Present	*Imperfect*
cambie	cambiara/cambiase
cambies	etc.
cambie	
cambiemos	
cambiéis	
cambien	

11. **Cerrar** *to shut/close*

Radical changing verb.

Infinitive **cerrar**	*Gerund* **cerrando**
Past Participle **cerrado**	*Imperative* **cierra cerrad**

INDICATIVE

Present	*Imperfect*	*Preterit*
cierro	cerraba	cerré
cierras	etc.	cerraste
cierra		cerró
cerramos		cerramos
cerráis		cerrasteis
cierran		cerraron

Future	*Conditional*
cerraré	cerraría
etc.	etc.

SUBJUNCTIVE

Present	Imperfect
cierre	cerrara/cerrase
cierres	*etc.*
cierre	
cerremos	
cerréis	
cierren	

12. **Cocer** *to boil*

Radical changing verb conjugated like **mover** but with spelling change **c** > **z** before **o** or **a**.

Infinitive **cocer**	*Gerund* **cociendo**
Past Participle **cocido**	*Imperative* **cuece coced**

INDICATIVE

Present	Imperfect	Preterit
cuezo	cocía	cocí
cueces	*etc.*	cociste
cuece		coció
cocemos		cocimos
cocéis		cocisteis
cuecen		cocieron

Future	Conditional
coceré	cocería
etc.	*etc.*

SUBJUNCTIVE

Present	Imperfect
cueza	cociera/cociese
cuezas	*etc.*
cueza	
cozamos	
cozáis	
cuezan	

13. **Construir** *to build*

The **y** between vowels should be noted.

Infinitive **construir** *Gerund* **construyendo**
Past Participle **construido** *Imperative* **construye construid**

INDICATIVE

Present	*Imperfect*	*Preterit*
construyo	construía	construí
construyes	etc.	construiste
construye		construyó
construimos		construimos
construís		construisteis
construyen		construyeron

Future	*Conditional*
construiré	construiría
etc.	etc.

SUBJUNCTIVE

Present	*Imperfect*
construya	construyera/construyese
construyas	etc.
construya	
construyamos	
construyáis	
construyan	

14. **Contar** *to count/tell a story*

Radical changing verb.

Infinitive **contar** *Gerund* **contando**
Past Participle **contado** *Imperative* **cuenta contad**

INDICATIVE

Present	*Imperfect*	*Preterit*
cuento	contaba	conté
cuentas	etc.	contaste

Present, continued		*Preterit, continued*
cuenta		contó
contamos		contamos
contáis		contasteis
cuentan		contaron

Future	*Conditional*
contaré	contaría
etc.	etc.

SUBJUNCTIVE

Present	*Imperfect*
cuente	contara/contase
cuentes	etc.
cuente	
contemos	
contéis	
cuenten	

15. Continuar *to continue*

The **u** is stressed when possible.

Infinitive **continuar** *Gerund* **continuando**
Past Participle **continuado** *Imperative* **continúa continuad**

INDICATIVE

Present	*Imperfect*	*Preterit*
continúo	continuaba	continué
continúas	etc.	continuaste
continúa		continuó
continuamos		continuamos
continuáis		continuasteis
continúan		continuaron

Future		*Conditional*
continuaré		continuaría
etc.		etc.

SUBJUNCTIVE

Present	Imperfect
continúe	continuara/continuase
continúes	etc.
continúe	
continuemos	
continuéis	
continúen	

16. **Dar** *to give*

Infinitive **dar** *Gerund* **dando**
Past Participle **dado** *Imperative* **da dad**

INDICATIVE

Present	Imperfect	Preterit
doy	daba	di
das	dabas	diste
da	daba	dio *(no accent)*
damos	dábamos	dimos
dais	dabais	disteis
dan	daban	dieron

Future	Conditional
daré	daría
etc.	etc.

SUBJUNCTIVE

Present	Imperfect
dé	diera/diese
des	etc.
dé	
demos	
deis	
den	

17. **Decir** *to say*

Infinitive **decir** *Gerund* **diciendo**
Past Participle **dicho** *Imperative* **di decid**

INDICATIVE

Present	Imperfect	Preterit
digo	decía	dije
dices	*etc.*	dijiste
dice		dijo
decimos		dijimos
decís		dijisteis
dicen		dijeron

Future	Conditional
diré	diría
etc.	*etc.*

SUBJUNCTIVE

Present	Imperfect
diga	dijera/dijese
digas	*etc.*
diga	
digamos	
digáis	
digan	

18. Discernir *to discern*

Radical changing verb. This pattern (**e > ie**) is rare in the **-ir** conjugation but common in the **-er** conjugation.

Infinitive **discernir** *Gerund* **discerniendo**
Past Participle **discernido** *Imperative* **discierne discernid**

INDICATIVE

Present	Imperfect	Preterit
discierno	discernía	discerní
disciernes	*etc.*	discerniste
discierne		discernió
discernimos		discernimos
discernís		discernisteis
disciernen		discernieron

Future	*Conditional*
discerniré	**discerniría**
etc.	etc.

SUBJUNCTIVE

Present	*Imperfect*
discierna	**discerniera/discerniese**
disciernas	etc.
discierna	
discernamos	
discernáis	
disciernan	

19. **Dormir** *to sleep*

Only **morir** *to die* (past. participle **muerto**) is conjugated similarly.

Infinitive **dormir**
Past Participle **dormido**

Gerund **durmiendo**
Imperative **duerme dormid**

INDICATIVE

Present	*Imperfect*	*Preterit*
duermo	**dormía**	**dormí**
duermes	etc.	**dormiste**
duerme		**durmió**
dormimos		**dormimos**
dormís		**dormisteis**
duermen		**durmieron**

Future	*Conditional*
dormiré	**dormiría**
etc.	etc.

SUBJUNCTIVE

Present	*Imperfect*
duerma	**durmiera/durmiese**
duermas	etc.
duerma	

Present, continued
durmamos
durmáis
duerman

20. Erguir(se) *to rear up/sit up straight*

Conjugated like **sentir** but with the normal spelling
change **ie > ye** at the beginning of words.
The alternative forms are conjugated like **pedir**.

Infinitive **erguir**   *Gerund* **irguiendo**
Past Participle **erguido**   *Imperative* **yergue/irgue erguid**

INDICATIVE

Present	*Imperfect*	*Preterit*
yergo/irgo	**erguía**	**erguí**
yergues/irgues	*etc.*	**erguiste**
yergue/irgue		**irguió**
erguimos		**erguimos**
erguís		**erguisteis**
yerguen/irguen		**irguieron**

Future	*Conditional*
erguiré	**erguiría**
etc.	*etc.*

SUBJUNCTIVE

Present	*Imperfect*
yerga/irga	**irguiera/irguiese**
yergas/irgas	*etc.*
yerga/irga	
yergamos/irgamos	
yergáis/irgáis	
yergan/irgan	

21. Errar *to wander/err*

Conjugated like **cerrar** but with regular spelling change
ie > ye at the beginning of words.

Infinitive **errar**   *Gerund* **errando**
Past Participle **errado**   *Imperative* **yerra errad**

INDICATIVE

Present	*Imperfect*	*Preterit*
yerro	erraba	erré
yerras	etc.	erraste
yerra		erró
erramos		erramos
erráis		errasteis
yerran		erraron

Future	*Conditional*
erraré	erraría

SUBJUNCTIVE

Present	*Imperfect*
yerre	errara/errase
yerres	etc.
yerre	
erremos	
erréis	
yerren	

22. **Estar** *to be*

Infinitive **estar**   *Gerund* **estando**
Past Participle **estado**   *Imperative* **estate estaos**

INDICATIVE

Present	*Imperfect*	*Preterit*
estoy	estaba	estuve
estás	etc.	estuviste
está		estuvo
estamos		estuvimos
estáis		estuvisteis
están		estuvieron

Future	Conditional
estaré	**estaría**
etc.	*etc.*

SUBJUNCTIVE

Present	Imperfect
esté	**estuviera/estuviese**
estés	*etc.*
esté	
estemos	
estéis	
estén	

23. **Gruñir** *to growl*

The diphthongs **ió** and **ie** become **ó** and **e** after **ñ**.
Infinitive **gruñir**   *Gerund* **gruñendo**
Past Participle **gruñido**   *Imperative* **gruñe gruñid**

INDICATIVE

Present	Imperfect	Preterit
gruño	**gruñía**	**gruñí**
gruñes	*etc.*	**gruñiste**
gruñe		**gruñó**
gruñimos		**gruñimos**
gruñís		**gruñisteis**
gruñen		**gruñeron**

Future	Conditional
gruñiré	**gruñiría**
etc.	*etc.*

SUBJUNCTIVE

Present	Imperfect
gruña	**gruñera/gruñese**
gruñas	*etc.*
gruña	
gruñamos	

Present, continued
gruñáis
gruñan

24. Haber (auxiliary verb or *there is/are*)

The 3rd-person present is **hay** when it means *there is/are*.

Infinitive **haber**	*Gerund* **habiendo**
Past Participle **habido**	*Imperative not found*

INDICATIVE

Present	*Imperfect*	*Preterit*
he	había	hube
has	etc.	hubiste
ha (hay)		hubo
hemos		hubimos
habéis		hubisteis
han		hubieron

Future	*Conditional*
habré	habría
etc.	etc.

SUBJUNCTIVE

Present	*Imperfect*
haya	hubiera/hubiese
hayas	etc.
haya	
hayamos	
hayáis	
hayan	

25. Hacer *to do/to make*

Infinitive **hacer**	*Gerund* **haciendo**
Past Participle **hecho**	*Imperative* **haz haced**

INDICATIVE

Present	Imperfect	Preterit
hago	hacía	hice
haces	etc.	hiciste
hace		hizo
hacemos		hicimos
hacéis		hicisteis
hacen		hicieron

Future	Conditional
haré	haría
etc.	etc.

SUBJUNCTIVE

Present	Imperfect
haga	hiciera/hiciese
hagas	etc.
haga	
hagamos	
hagáis	
hagan	

26. **Ir** *to go*

Infinitive **ir**	Gerund **yendo**
Past Participle **ido**	Imperative **ve id**

The **vosotros** imperative of **irse** is **idos**, not the expected *'íos'*.

INDICATIVE

Present	Imperfect	Preterit
voy	iba	fui *(no accent)*
vas	ibas	fuiste
va	iba	fue *(no accent)*
vamos	íbamos	fuimos
vais	ibais	fuisteis
van	iban	fueron

Future	Conditional
iré	**iría**
etc.	etc.

SUBJUNCTIVE

Present	Imperfect
vaya	**fuera/fuese**
vayas	etc.
vaya	
vayamos	
vayáis	
vayan	

27. Jugar *to play (a game)*

The only verb in which stressed **u** becomes **ue**.

Infinitive **jugar** *Gerund* **jugando**
Past Participle **jugado** *Imperative* **juega jugad**

INDICATIVE

Present	Imperfect	Preterit
juego	**jugaba**	**jugué**
juegas	etc.	**jugaste**
juega		**jugó**
jugamos		**jugamos**
jugáis		**jugasteis**
juegan		**jugaron**

Future	Conditional
jugaré	**jugaría**
etc.	etc.

SUBJUNCTIVE

Present	Imperfect
juegue	**jugara/jugase**
juegues	etc.
juegue	

Present, continued
juguemos
juguéis
jueguen

28. **Liar** *to tie up in a bundle*

The **i** may be stressed. Compare **cambiar.**

Infinitive **liar**   *Gerund* **liando**
Past Participle **liado**   *Imperative* **lía liad**

INDICATIVE

Present	*Imperfect*	*Preterit*
lío	**liaba**	**lié**
lías	*etc.*	**liaste**
lía		**lió**
liamos		**liamos**
liáis		**liasteis**
lían		**liaron**

Future	*Conditional*
liaré	**liaría**
etc.	*etc.*

SUBJUNCTIVE

Present	*Imperfect*
líe	**liara/liase**
líes	*etc.*
líe	
liemos	
liéis	
líen	

29. **Lucir** *to show off* (transitive)

c > **zc** before **o** or **a.**

Infinitive **lucir**   *Gerund* **luciendo**
Past Participle **lucido**   *Imperative* **luce lucid**

INDICATIVE

Present	Imperfect	Preterit
luzco	lucía	lucí
luces	etc.	luciste
luce		lució
lucimos		lucimos
lucís		lucisteis
lucen		lucieron

Future	Conditional
luciré	luciría

SUBJUNCTIVE

Present	Imperfect
luzca	luciera/luciese
luzcas	etc.
luzca	
luzcamos	
luzcáis	
luzcan	

30. Maldecir *to curse*

Conjugated like **decir** except for the Past Participle,
Imperative, Future and Conditional.

Infinitive **maldecir**   *Gerund* **maldiciendo**
Past Participle **maldecido**   *Imperative* **maldice maldecid**

INDICATIVE

Present	Imperfect	Preterit
maldigo	maldecía	maldije
maldices	etc.	maldijiste
maldice		maldijo
maldecimos		maldijimos
maldecís		maldijisteis
maldicen		maldijeron

Future	Conditional
maldeciré	**maldeciría**
etc.	etc.

SUBJUNCTIVE

Present	Imperfect
maldiga	**maldijera/maldijese**
maldigas	etc.
maldiga	
maldigamos	
maldigáis	
maldigan	

31. **Mover** *to move*

Radical changing verb.

Infinitive **mover**	*Gerund* **moviendo**
Past Participle **movido**	*Imperative* **mueve, moved**

INDICATIVE

Present	Imperfect	Preterit
muevo	**movía**	**moví**
mueves	etc.	**moviste**
mueve		**movió**
movemos		**movimos**
movéis		**movisteis**
mueven		**movieron**

Future	Conditional
moveré	**movería**
etc.	etc.

SUBJUNCTIVE

Present	Imperfect
mueva	**moviera/moviese**
muevas	etc.
mueva	
movamos	

Present, continued
mováis
muevan

32. Oír *to hear*

Infinitive **oír**   *Gerund* **oyendo**
Past Participle **oído**   *Imperative* **oye oíd**

INDICATIVE

Present	*Imperfect*	*Preterit*
oigo	**oía**	**oí**
oyes	*etc.*	**oíste**
oye		**oyó**
oímos		**oímos**
oís		**oísteis**
oyen		**oyeron**

Future	*Conditional*
oiré	**oiría**
etc.	*etc.*

SUBJUNCTIVE

Present	*Imperfect*
oiga	**oyera/oyese**
oigas	*etc.*
oiga	
oigamos	
oigáis	
oigan	

33. Oler *to smell*

Conjugated like **mover,** but the diphthong **ue** is always written **hue** at the beginning of a word.

Infinitive **oler**   *Gerund* **oliendo**
Past Participle **olido**   *Imperative* **huele oled**

INDICATIVE

Present	Imperfect	Preterit
huelo	olía	olí
hueles	etc.	oliste
huele		olió
olemos		olimos
oléis		olisteis
huelen		olieron

Future	Conditional
oleré	olería
etc.	etc.

SUBJUNCTIVE

Present	Imperfect
huela	oliera/oliese
huelas	etc.
huela	
olamos	
oláis	
huelan	

34. **Pagar** *to pay*

Regular **-ar** verb, but with spelling changes. The silent *u* keeps the **g** hard (like the g in **hago**).

Infinitive **pagar**   *Gerund* **pagando**
Past Participle **pagado**   *Imperative* **paga pagad**

INDICATIVE

Present	Imperfect	Preterit
pago	pagaba	pagué
pagas	etc.	pagaste
paga		pagó
pagamos		pagamos
pagáis		pagasteis
pagan		pagaron

Future	Conditional
pagaré	**pagaría**
etc.	*etc.*

SUBJUNCTIVE

Present	Imperfect
pague	**pagara/pagase**
pagues	*etc.*
pague	
paguemos	
paguéis	
paguen	

35. **Parecer** *to seem*

The change **c > zc** before **a** or **o** affects most verbs ending in **–cer** (common exceptions are **vencer, ejercer, torcer, cocer**).

Infinitive **parecer**	*Gerund* **pareciendo**
Past Participle **parecido**	*Imperative* **parece pareced**

INDICATIVE

Present	Imperfect	Preterit
parezco	**parecía**	**parecí**
pareces	*etc.*	**pareciste**
parece		**pareció**
parecemos		**parecimos**
parecéis		**parecisteis**
parecen		**parecieron**

Future	Conditional
pareceré	**parecería**
etc.	*etc.*

SUBJUNCTIVE

Present	Imperfect
parezca	**pareciera/pareciese**
parezcas	*etc.*

Present, continued
parezca
parezcamos
parezcáis
parezcan

36. Pedir *to ask for*
Radical changing verb.

Infinitive **pedir**	*Gerund* **pidiendo**
Past Participle **pedido**	*Imperative* **pide pedid**

INDICATIVE

Present	*Imperfect*	*Preterit*
pido	pedía	pedí
pides	etc.	pediste
pide		pidió
pedimos		pedimos
pedís		pedisteis
piden		pidieron

Future	*Conditional*
pediré	pediría
etc.	etc.

SUBJUNCTIVE

Present	*Imperfect*
pida	pidiera/pidiese
pidas	etc.
pida	
pidamos	
pidáis	
pidan	

37. Perder *to lose*
Radical changing verb.

Infinitive **perder**	*Gerund* **perdiendo**
Past Participle **perdido**	*Imperative* **pierde perded**

INDICATIVE

Present	Imperfect	Preterit
pierdo	perdía	perdí
pierdes	etc.	perdiste
pierde		perdió
perdemos		perdimos
perdéis		perdisteis
pierden		perdieron

Future	Conditional
perderé	perdería
etc.	etc.

SUBJUNCTIVE

Present	Imperfect
pierda	perdiera/perdiese
pierdas	etc.
pierda	
perdamos	
perdáis	
pierdan	

38. Poder *to be able*

Infinitive **poder**	Gerund **pudiendo**
Past Participle **podido**	Imperative not found

INDICATIVE

Present	Imperfect	Preterit
puedo	podía	pude
puedes	etc.	pudiste
puede		pudo
podemos		pudimos
podéis		pudisteis
pueden		pudieron

Future		Conditional
podré		podría
etc.		etc.

SUBJUNCTIVE

Present	*Imperfect*
pueda	pudiera/pudiese
puedas	etc.
pueda	
podamos	
podáis	
puedan	

39. **Poner** *to put*

Infinitive **poner**	*Gerund* **poniendo**
Past Participle **puesto**	*Imperative* **pon poned**

The **tú** *imperative of compounds takes an accent:* **compón, pospón.**

INDICATIVE

Present	*Imperfect*	*Preterit*
pongo	ponía	puse
pones	etc.	pusiste
pone		puso
ponemos		pusimos
ponéis		pusisteis
ponen		pusieron

Future	*Conditional*
pondré	pondría
etc.	etc.

SUBJUNCTIVE

Present	*Imperfect*
ponga	pusiera/pusiese
pongas	etc.
ponga	
pongamos	
pongáis	
pongan	

40. **Poseer** *to possess*

Note unstressed **i** > **y** between vowels.

Infinitive **poseer**   *Gerund* **poseyendo**
Past Participle **poseído**   *Imperative* **posee, poseed**

INDICATIVE

Present	*Imperfect*	*Preterit*
poseo	poseía	poseí
posees	etc.	poseíste
posee		poseyó
poseemos		poseímos
poseéis		poseísteis
poseen		poseyeron

Future	*Conditional*
poseeré	poseería
etc.	etc.

SUBJUNCTIVE

Present	*Imperfect*
posea	poseyera/poseyese
poseas	etc.
posea	
poseamos	
poseáis	
posean	

41. **Producir** *to produce*

c > **zc** before **a** and **o**, and irregular Preterit. All verbs whose Infinitive ends in **-ducir** conjugate like this verb.

Infinitive **producir**   *Gerund* **produciendo**
Past Participle **producido**   *Imperative* **produce producid**

INDICATIVE

Present	*Imperfect*	*Preterit*
produzco	producía	produje
produces	etc.	produjiste

Present, continued
produce
producimos
producís
producen

Preterit, continued
produjo
produjimos
produjisteis
produjeron

Future	*Conditional*
produciré	**produciría**
etc.	*etc.*

SUBJUNCTIVE

Present	*Imperfect*
produzca	**produjera/produjese**
produzcas	*etc.*
produzca	
produzcamos	
produzcáis	
produzcan	

42. **Prohibir** *to prohibit*

The **i** of the stem is written with an accent when it is stressed (this spelling rule was introduced in 1959 so the accent does not appear in texts printed before then).

Infinitive **prohibir** *Gerund* **prohibiendo**
Past Participle **prohibido** *Imperative* **prohíbe prohibid**

INDICATIVE

Present	*Imperfect*	*Preterit*
prohíbo	**prohibía**	**prohibí**
prohíbes	*etc.*	**prohibiste**
prohíbe		**prohibió**
prohibimos		**prohibimos**
prohibís		**prohibisteis**
prohíben		**prohibieron**

Future	*Conditional*
prohibiré	**prohibiría**
etc.	*etc.*

SUBJUNCTIVE

Present	*Imperfect*
prohíba	**prohibiera/prohibiese**
prohíbas	*etc.*
prohíba	
prohibamos	
prohibáis	
prohíban	

43. **Proteger** *to protect*

Regular verb with spelling changes.

Infinitive **proteger**	*Gerund* **protegiendo**
Past Participle **protegido**	*Imperative* **protege proteged**

INDICATIVE

Present	*Imperfect*	*Preterit*
protejo	**protegía**	**protegí**
proteges	*etc.*	**protegiste**
protege		**protegió**
protegemos		**protegimos**
protegéis		**protegisteis**
protegen		**protegieron**

Future	*Conditional*
protegeré	**protegería**
etc.	*etc.*

SUBJUNCTIVE

Present	*Imperfect*
proteja	**protegiera/protegiese**
protejas	*etc.*
proteja	

Present, continued
protejamos
protejáis
protejan

44. Querer *to want/love*

Infinitive **querer**	*Gerund* **queriendo**
Past Participle **querido**	*Imperative* **quiere quered**

INDICATIVE

Present	*Imperfect*	*Preterit*
quiero	quería	quise
quieres	etc.	quisiste
quiere		quiso
queremos		quisimos
queréis		quisisteis
quieren		quisieron

Future	*Conditional*
querré	querría
etc.	etc.

SUBJUNCTIVE

Present	*Imperfect*
quiera	quisiera/quisiese
quieras	etc.
quiera	
queramos	
queráis	
quieran	

45. Regir *to govern/direct*

Conjugated like **pedir** but with predictable spelling changes.

Infinitive **regir**	*Gerund* **rigiendo**
Past Participle **regido**	*Imperative* **rige regid**

INDICATIVE

Present	Imperfect	Preterit
rijo	regía	regí
riges	etc.	registe
rige		rigió
regimos		regimos
regís		registeis
rigen		rigieron

Future	Conditional
regiré	regiría
etc.	etc.

SUBJUNCTIVE

Present	Imperfect
rija	rigiera/rigiese
rijas	etc.
rija	
rijamos	
rijáis	
rijan	

46. **Reír** *to laugh*

Conjugated like **pedir**.

Infinitive **reír**
Past Participle **reído**

Gerund **riendo**
Imperative **ríe reíd**

INDICATIVE

Present	Imperfect	Preterit
río	reía	reí
ríes	etc.	reíste
ríe		rió
reímos		reímos
reís		reísteis
ríen		rieron

Future	Conditional
reiré	**reiría**
etc.	*etc.*

SUBJUNCTIVE

Present	Imperfect
ría	**riera/riese**
rías	*etc.*
ría	
riamos	
riáis	
rían	

47. **Reñir** *to scold*

Conjugated like **pedir,** but **ió** becomes **ó** and **ie** becomes **e** after **ñ**.

Infinitive **reñir** *Gerund* **riñendo**
Past Participle **reñido** *Imperative* **riñe reñid**

INDICATIVE

Present	Imperfect	Preterit
riño	**reñía**	**reñí**
riñes	*etc.*	**reñiste**
riñe		**riñó**
reñimos		**reñimos**
reñís		**reñisteis**
riñen		**riñeron**

Future	Conditional
reñiré	**reñiría**
etc.	*etc.*

SUBJUNCTIVE

Present	Imperfect
riña	**riñera/riñese**
riñas	*etc.*
riña	

Present, continued
riñamos
riñáis
riñan

48. **Reunir** *to bring together/call a meeting*

The **u** is written with an accent when stressed. The verb
rehusar *to refuse* is similar: **rehúso, rehúsa, rehusamos,**
etc. The accent was introduced in 1959 and is not seen in
books printed before then.

Infinitive **reunir**   *Gerund* **reuniendo**
Past Participle **reunido**   *Imperative* **reúne reunid**

INDICATIVE

Present	*Imperfect*	*Preterit*
reúno	**reunía**	**reuní**
reúnes	etc.	**reuniste**
reúne		**reunió**
reunimos		**reunimos**
reunís		**reunisteis**
reúnen		**reunieron**

Future	*Conditional*
reuniré	**reuniría**
etc.	etc.

SUBJUNCTIVE

Present	*Imperfect*
reúna	**reuniera/reuniese**
reúnas	etc.
reúna	
reunamos	
reunáis	
reúnan	

49. **Rezar** *to pray*

Regular -**ar** verb with spelling changes.

Infinitive **rezar** *Gerund* **rezando**
Past Participle **rezado** *Imperative* **reza rezad**

INDICATIVE

Present	*Imperfect*	*Preterit*
rezo	**rezaba**	**recé**
rezas	etc.	**rezaste**
reza		**rezó**
rezamos		**rezamos**
rezáis		**rezasteis**
rezan		**rezaron**

Future	*Conditional*
rezaré	**rezaría**
etc.	etc.

SUBJUNCTIVE

Present	*Imperfect*
rece	**rezara/rezase**
reces	etc.
rece	
recemos	
recéis	
recen	

50. **Roer** *to gnaw*

Infinitive **roer** *Gerund* **royendo**
Past Participle **roído** *Imperative* **roe roed**

INDICATIVE

Present	*Imperfect*	*Preterit*
roo	**roía**	**roí**
roes	etc.	**roíste**
roe		**royó**

Present, continued	*Preterit, continued*
roemos	**roímos**
roéis	**roísteis**
roen	**royeron**

The alternative first-person singular present forms **royo** *and* **roigo** *are rarely seen.*

Future	*Conditional*
roeré	**roería**
etc.	*etc.*

SUBJUNCTIVE

Present	*Imperfect*
roa (roiga, roya)	**royera/royese**
roas (roigas, royas)	*etc.*
roa (roiga, roya)	
roamos (roigamos, royamos)	
roáis (roigáis, royáis)	
roan (roigan, royan)	

Bracketed forms are rarely found.

51. **Saber** *to know*

Infinitive **saber**   Gerund **sabiendo**
Past Participle **sabido**   Imperative **sabe sabed**

INDICATIVE

Present	*Imperfect*	*Preterit*
sé	**sabía**	**supe**
sabes	*etc.*	**supiste**
sabe		**supo**
sabemos		**supimos**
sabéis		**supisteis**
saben		**supieron**

Future	*Conditional*
sabré	**sabría**
etc.	*etc.*

SUBJUNCTIVE

Present	*Imperfect*
sepa	supiera/supiese
sepas	etc.
sepa	
sepamos	
sepáis	
sepan	

52. Sacar *to take out/extract*

Regular -**ar** verb with spelling changes.

Infinitive **sacar**	*Gerund* **sacando**
Past Participle **sacado**	*Imperative* **saca sacad**

INDICATIVE

Present	*Imperfect*	*Preterit*
saco	sacaba	saqué
sacas	etc.	sacaste
saca		sacó
sacamos		sacamos
sacáis		sacasteis
sacan		sacaron

Future	*Conditional*
sacaré	sacaría
etc.	etc.

SUBJUNCTIVE

Present	*Imperfect*
saque	sacara/sacase
saques	etc.
saque	
saquemos	
saquéis	
saquen	

53. **Salir** *to go out/leave*

Infinitive **salir**   *Gerund* **saliendo**
Past Participle **salido**   *Imperative* **sal salid**

INDICATIVE

Present	*Imperfect*	*Preterit*
salgo	**salía**	**salí**
sales	*etc.*	**saliste**
sale		**salió**
salimos		**salimos**
salís		**salisteis**
salen		**salieron**

Future	*Conditional*
saldré	**saldría**
etc.	*etc.*

SUBJUNCTIVE

Present	*Imperfect*
salga	**saliera/salieses**
salgas	*etc.*
salga	
salgamos	
salgáis	
salgan	

54. **Seguir** *to follow*

Infinitive **seguir**   *Gerund* **siguiendo**
Past Participle **seguido**   *Imperative* **sigue seguid**

INDICATIVE

Present	*Imperfect*	*Preterit*
sigo	**seguía**	**seguí**
sigues	*etc.*	**seguiste**
sigue		**siguió**

Present, continued		*Preterit, continued*
seguimos		seguimos
seguís		seguisteis
siguen		siguieron

Future	*Conditional*
seguiré	seguiría
etc.	*etc.*

SUBJUNCTIVE

Present	*Imperfect*
siga	siguiera/siguiese
sigas	*etc.*
siga	
sigamos	
sigáis	
sigan	

55. **Sentir** *to feel*

Radical changing verb.

Infinitive **sentir**	*Gerund* **sintiendo**
Past Participle **sentido**	*Imperative* **siente sentid**

INDICATIVE

Present	*Imperfect*	*Preterit*
siento	sentía	sentí
sientes	*etc.*	sentiste
siente		sintió
sentimos		sentimos
sentís		sentisteis
sienten		sintieron

Future	*Conditional*
sentiré	sentiría
etc.	*etc.*

SUBJUNCTIVE

Present	*Imperfect*
sienta	sintiera/sintiese
sientas	*etc.*
sienta	
sintamos	
sintáis	
sientan	

56. **Ser** *to be*

Infinitive **ser**	*Gerund* **siendo**
Past Participle **sido**	*Imperative* **sé sed**

INDICATIVE

Present	*Imperfect*	*Preterit*
soy	era	fui
eres	eras	fuiste
es	era	fue
somos	éramos	fuimos
sois	erais	fuisteis
son	eran	fueron

The accent on the third-person Preterit forms **fuí** *and* **fué** *was abolished in the spelling reforms of 1959.*

Future	*Conditional*
seré	sería
etc.	*etc.*

SUBJUNCTIVE

Present	*Imperfect*
sea	fuera/fuese
seas	fueras/fueses
sea	fuera/fuese
seamos	fuéramos/fuésemos
seáis	fuerais/fueseis
sean	fueran/fuesen

57. Tañer *to chime*

ió is simplified to **ó** and **ie** to **e** as usual after **ñ**. This change also affects verbs ending in **-llir** like **bullir** *to seethe*.

Infinitive **tañer**	Gerund **tañendo**
Past Participle **tañido**	Imperative **tañe tañed**

INDICATIVE

Present	Imperfect	Preterit
taño	tañía	tañí
tañes	*etc.*	tañiste
tañe		tañó
tañemos		tañimos
tañéis		tañisteis
tañen		tañeron

Future	Conditional
tañeré	tañería
etc.	*etc.*

SUBJUNCTIVE

Present	Imperfect
taña	tañera/tañese
tañas	*etc.*
taña	
tañamos	
tañáis	
tañan	

58. Tener *to have*

Infinitive **tener**	Gerund **teniendo**
Past Participle **tenido**	Imperative **ten tened**

INDICATIVE

Present	Imperfect	Preterit
tengo	tenía	tuve
tienes	*etc.*	tuviste

Present continued	*Preterit continued*
tiene	tuvo
tenemos	tuvimos
tenéis	tuvisteis
tienen	tuvieron

Singular imperative of compounds ends in -én: detener *detain/stop* **detén**, retener *retain* **retén**.

Future	*Conditional*
tendré	tendría
etc.	etc.

SUBJUNCTIVE

Present	*Imperfect*
tenga	tuviera/tuviese
tengas	etc.
tenga	
tengamos	
tengáis	
tengan	

59. **Traer** *to bring*

Infinitive **traer**	*Gerund* **trayendo**
Past Participle **traído**	*Imperative* **trae traed**

INDICATIVE

Present	*Imperfect*	*Preterit*
traigo	traía	traje
traes	etc.	trajiste
trae		trajo
traemos		trajimos
traéis		trajisteis
traen		trajeron

Future	*Conditional*
traeré	traería
etc.	etc.

SUBJUNCTIVE

Present	*Imperfect*
traiga	**trajera/trajese**
traigas	*etc.*
traiga	
traigamos	
traigáis	
traigan	

60. **Valer** *to be worth*

Infinitive **valer**	*Gerund* **valiendo**
Past Participle **valido**	*Imperative* **vale valed**

INDICATIVE

Present	*Imperfect*	*Preterit*
valgo	**valía**	**valí**
vales	*etc.*	**valiste**
vale		**valió**
valemos		**valimos**
valéis		**valisteis**
valen		**valieron**

Future	*Conditional*
valdré	**valdría**
etc.	*etc.*

SUBJUNCTIVE

Present	*Imperfect*
valga	**valiera/valiese**
valgas	*etc.*
valga	
valgamos	
valgáis	
valgan	

61. **Vencer** *to defeat*

Regular verb with spelling changes.

Infinitive **vencer**   *Gerund* **venciendo**
Past Participle **vencido**   *Imperative* **vence venced**

INDICATIVE

Present	*Imperfect*	*Preterit*
venzo	vencía	vencí
vences	etc.	venciste
vence		venció
vencemos		vencimos
vencéis		vencisteis
vencen		vencieron

Future	*Conditional*
venceré	vencería
etc.	etc.

SUBJUNCTIVE

Present	*Imperfect*
venza	venciera/venciese
venzas	etc.
venza	
venzamos	
venzáis	
venzan	

62. **Venir** *to come*

Infinitive **venir**   *Gerund* **viniendo**
Past Participle **venido**   *Imperative* **ven venid**

INDICATIVE

Present	*Imperfect*	*Preterit*
vengo	venía	vine
vienes	etc.	viniste
viene		vino
venimos		vinimos
venís		vinisteis
vienen		vinieron

Future	Conditional
vendré	vendría
etc.	etc.

SUBJUNCTIVE

Present	Imperfect
venga	viniera/viniese
vengas	etc.
venga	
vengamos	
vengáis	
vengan	

63. **Ver** *to see*

Infinitive **ver**	*Gerund* **viendo**
Past Participle **visto**	*Imperative* **ve ved**

INDICATIVE

Present	Imperfect	Preterit
veo	veía	vi
ves	etc.	viste
ve		vio *(no accent)*
vemos		vimos
veis		visteis
ven		vieron

Future	Conditional
veré	vería
etc.	etc.

SUBJUNCTIVE

Present	Imperfect
vea	viera/viese
veas	etc.
vea	

Present, continued
veamos
veáis
vean

64. **Yacer** *to lie (as in 'he lay there'. This verb is archaic.)*

Infinitive **yacer**   *Gerund* **yaciendo**
Past Participle **yacido**   *Imperative* **yace/yaz yaced**

INDICATIVE

Present	*Imperfect*	*Preterit*
yazco	**yacía**	**yací**
yaces	*etc.*	**yaciste**
yace		**yació**
yacemos		**yacimos**
yacéis		**yacisteis**
yacen		**yacieron**

The alternative first-person singular present forms **yago/yazgo**
are rarely seen.

Future	*Conditional*	
yaceré		**yacería**

Present	*Imperfect*
yazca (yazga, yaga)	**yaciera/yaciese**
yazcas (yazgas, yagas)	*etc.*
etc.	

65. **Zurcir** *to darn*

Regular verb with spelling changes.

Infinitive **zurcir**   *Gerund* **zurciendo**
Past Participle **zurcido**   *Imperative* **zurce zurcid**

INDICATIVE

Present	*Imperfect*	*Preterit*
zurzo	zurcía	zurcí
zurces	etc.	zurciste
zurce		zurció
zurcimos		zurcimos
zurcís		zurcisteis
zurcen		zurcieron

Future	*Conditional*
zurciré	zurciría
etc.	etc.

SUBJUNCTIVE

Present	*Imperfect*
zurza	zurciera/zurciese
zurzas	etc.
zurza	
zurzamos	
zurzáis	
zurzan	

LIST OF IRREGULAR AND RADICAL CHANGING VERBS

A few regular verbs that are affected by regular spelling changes are included. Numerous rare or archaic verbs are omitted. The number identifies the model verbs printed on pp.254–302.

Pronominal (i.e. 'reflexive') infinitives are not shown unless the pronominal form is the more usual form.

abastecer to supply   **parecer (35)**
abolir to abolish   **(1)**
aborrecer to detest   **parecer (35)**

abrir *to open*	past participle **abierto**
absolver *to absolve*	**mover (31)** past participle **absuelto**
abstenerse *to abstain*	**tener (58)**
abstraer *to abstract*	**traer (59)**
acentuar *to accentuate*	**continuar (15)**
acertar *to hit the mark*	**cerrar (11)**
acontecer *to occur*	**parecer (35)**
acordar *to agree upon*	**contar (14)**
acostarse *to go to bed*	**contar (14)**
actuar *to act*	**continuar (15)**
adherir *to adhere*	**sentir (55)**
adolecer *to be ill*	**parecer (35)**
adormecer *to put to sleep*	**parecer (35)**
adquirir *to acquire*	**(2)**
advertir *to warn*	**sentir (55)**
aferrarse *to grasp*	**cerrar (11);** may be conjugated regularly
agradecer *to thank*	**parecer (35)**
agredir *to assault*	**abolir (1)**
agriar *to sour*	**cambiar (10)**
aguar *to spoil*	**averiguar (7)**
aislar *to isolate*	**aislar (3)**
alentar *to encourage*	**cerrar (11)**
aliar *to ally*	**liar (28)**
almorzar *to lunch*	**contar (14);** z>c before e
amanecer *to dawn*	**parecer (35)**
amnistiar *to amnesty*	**liar (28)**
ampliar *to enlarge*	**liar (28)**
andar *to walk*	**(4)**
anochecer *to grow dark*	**parecer (35)**
ansiar *to yearn for*	**liar (28)**
anteponer *to put in front*	**poner (39)**
aparecer *to appear*	**parecer (35)**
apetecer *to crave*	**parecer (35)**
apostar *to bet*	**contar (14)**

apretar *to squeeze*	cerrar (11)
aprobar *to approve,* *pass* (exam.)	contar (14)
argüir *to argue*	(5)
arraigar *to establish*	pagar (34)
arrendar *to lease*	cerrar (11)
arrepentirse *to repent*	sentir (55)
ascender *to ascend*	perder (37)
asentar *to settle*	cerrar (11)
asentir *to assent*	sentir (55)
asir *to grasp*	(6)
atender *to attend*	perder (37)
atenerse *to abide by*	tener (58)
atenuar *to attenuate*	continuar (15)
atraer *to attract*	traer (59)
atravesar *to cross*	cerrar (11)
atribuir *to attribute*	construir (13)
avenir *to reconcile*	venir (62)
aventar *to fan*	cerrar (11)
avergonzar *to shame*	contar (14), z>c before e, and diphthong spelt üe, e.g. subjunctive avergüence
averiar *to spoil*	liar (28)
bendecir *to bless*	maldecir (30)
biografiar *to write* *biography*	liar (28)
caber *to fit in*	(8)
caer *to fall*	(9)
calentar *to heat*	(11)
carecer *to lack*	parecer (35)
cegar *to blind*	cerrar (11); g>gu before e
ceñir *to girdle*	reñir (47)
cerrar *to close*	cerrar (11)
circunscribir *to* *circumscribe*	past participle circunscrito
cocer *to cook*	(12)

coger *to catch*	**proteger (43)**
colar *to filter*	**contar (14)**
colegir *to infer*	**regir (45)**
colgar *to hang*	**contar (14) g>gu** before **e**
comenzar *to begin*	**cerrar (11) z>c** before **e**
compadecer *to pity*	**parecer (35)**
comparecer *to appear*	**parecer (35)**
competir *to compete*	**pedir (36)**
complacer *to please*	**parecer (35)**
componer *to compose*	**poner (39)**
comprobar *to check*	**contar (14)**
comunicar *to communicate*	**sacar (52)**
concebir *to conceive*	**pedir (36)**
conceptuar *to deem*	**continuar (15)**
concernir *to concern*	**discernir (18)**; third person only
concertar *to harmonize*	**cerrar (11)**
conciliar *to reconcile*	**cambiar (10)**
concluir *to terminate*	**construir (13)**
concordar *to reconcile*	**contar (14)**
condescender *to condescend*	**perder (37)**
conducir *to drive*	**producir (41)**
conferir *to confer*	**sentir (55)**
confesar *to confess*	**cerrar (11)**
confiar *to entrust*	**liar (28)**
confluir *to come together*	**construir (13)**
conmover *to move (emotionally)*	**mover (31)**
conocer *to know*	**parecer (35)**
conseguir *to achieve*	**seguir (54)**
consentir *to consent*	**sentir (55)**
consolar *to console*	**contar (14)**
consonar *to harmonize*	**contar (14)**
constituir *to constitute*	**construir (13)**
constreñir *to restrict*	**reñir (47)**

construir *to build*	(13)
contar *to count, tell*	(14)
contener *to contain*	tener (58)
continuar *to continue*	(15)
contradecir *to contradict*	decir (17)
contraer *to contract*	traer (59)
contrahacer *to forge*	hacer (25)
contravenir *to contravene*	venir (62)
contribuir *to contribute*	construir (13)
convalecer *to convalesce*	parecer (35)
convencer *to convince*	vencer (61)
convenir *to agree*	venir (62)
convertir *to convert*	sentir (55)
corregir *to correct*	regir (45)
corroer *to corrode*	roer (50)
costar *to cost*	contar (14)
crecer *to grow*	parecer (35)
creer *to believe*	poseer (40)
criar *to rear*	liar (28)
cubrir *to cover*	past participle **cubierto**
dar *to give*	(16)
decaer *to decay*	caer (9)
decir *to say*	(17)
decrecer *to diminish*	parecer (35)
deducir *to deduce*	producir (41)
defender *to defend*	perder (37)
deferir *to relegate*	sentir (55)
demoler *to demolish*	mover (31)
demostrar *to demonstrate*	contar (14)
denegar *to reject*	cerrar (11) **g>gu** before **e**
denostar *to revile*	contar (14)
derretir *to melt*	pedir (36)
desacertar *to be wrong*	cerrar (11)
desacordar *to put out of tune*	contar (14)
desafiar *to challenge*	liar (28)

desalentar *to dishearten*   **cerrar (11)**

desandar *to retrace steps*   **andar (4)**

desaparecer *to disappear*   **parecer (35)**

desaprobar *to disapprove of*   **contar (14)**

desasosegar *to unsettle*   **cerrar (11) g>gu** before **e**

desatender *to disregard*   **perder (37)**

descender *to descend*   **perder (37)**

descolgar *to take down*   **contar (14) g>gu** before **e**

descollar *to stand out*   **contar (14)**

descomedirse *to be rude*   **pedir (36)**

descomponer *to break down into parts*   **poner (39)**

desconcertar *to disconcert*   **cerrar (11)**

desconocer *not to know*   **parecer (35)**

desconsolar *to distress*   **contar (14)**

descontar *to discount*   **contar (14)**

desconvenir *to disagree*   **venir (62)**

describir *to describe*   past participle **descrito**

descubrir *to discover*   past participle **descubierto**

desempedrar *to take up stones*   **cerrar (11)**

desenraizar *to uproot*   **aislar (3)**

desentenderse *to pretend not to know about*   **perder (37)**

desenterrar *to unearth*   **cerrar (11)**

desenvolver *to unwrap*   **mover (31)**; past participle **desenvuelto**

desfallecer *to weaken*   **parecer (35)**

deshacer *to unmake*   **hacer (25)**

desleír *to dissolve*   **reír (46)**

deslucir *to tarnish*   **lucir (29)**

desmembrar *to dismember*   **cerrar (11)**

desmentir *to deny*   **sentir (55)**

desmerecer *not to deserve* **parecer (35)**

desobedecer *to disobey* **parecer (35)**

desoír *to disregard* **oír (32)**

despedir *to fire* **pedir (36)**

despertar *to awake* **cerrar (11)**

desplegar *to unfold* **cerrar (11); g>gu** before **e**; now often regular

despoblar *to depopulate* **contar (14)**

desproveer *to deprive of* **poseer (40)**; past participle **desprovisto** or **desproveído**

desterrar *to exile* **cerrar (11)**

destituir *to dismiss* **construir (13)**

destruir *to destroy* **construir (13)**

desvariar *to rave* **liar 28**

desvergonzarse *to lose all shame* **contar (14); z>c** before **e**; diphthong spelt **üe**

desviar *to divert, throw off course* **liar (28)**

desvirtuar *to spoil* **continuar (15)**

detener *to stop, detain* **tener (58)**

detraer *to separate* **traer (59)**

devolver *to give back* **mover (31)**; past participle **devuelto**

diferir *to differ* **sentir (55)**

digerir *to digest* **sentir (55)**

diluir *to dilute* **construir (13)**

discernir *to discern* **(18)**

disentir *to dissent* **sentir (55)**

disminuir *to diminish* **construir (13)**

disolver *to dissolve* **mover (31)**; past participle **disuelto**

disponer *to dispose* **poner (39)**

distender *to distend* **perder (37)**

distraer *to distract* **traer (59)**

distribuir *to distribute* **construir (13)**

divertir *to amuse* **sentir (55)**

doler *to hurt*	mover (31)
dormir *to sleep*	(19)
efectuar *to effect*	continuar (15)
ejercer *to exercise*	vencer (61)
elegir *to elect, to choose*	regir (45)
embebecer *to fascinate*	parecer (35)
embellecer *to embellish*	parecer (35)
embestir *to charge* (e.g. bull)	pedir (36)
embravecer *to infuriate*	parecer (35)
embrutecer *to brutalize*	parecer (35)
empedrar *to pave*	cerrar (11)
empequeñecer *to dwarf*	parecer (35)
empezar *to start*	cerrar (11); z>c before e
empobrecer *to impoverish*	parecer (35)
enaltecer *to extol*	parecer (35)
enardecer *to impassion*	parecer (35)
encanecer *to get gray/grey hair*	parecer (35)
encarecer *to extol*	parecer (35)
encender *to ignite*	perder (37)
encerrar *to shut in*	cerrar (11)
encomendar *to commend*	cerrar (11)
encontrar *to find, meet*	contar (14)
encubrir *to cloak, hush up*	past participle **encubierto**
endurecer *to harden*	parecer (35)
enflaquecer *to make thin*	parecer (35)
enfriar *to chill*	liar (28)
enfurecer *to infuriate*	parecer (35)
engrandecer *to enlarge*	parecer (35)
engreírse *to grow smug*	reír (46)
engrosar *to swell (a quantity)*	contar (14); now usually regular
enloquecer *to madden*	parecer (35)
enmendar *to emend*	cerrar (11)
enmudecer *to silence*	parecer (35)

ennegrecer *to blacken* — parecer (35)
ennoblecer *to ennoble* — parecer (35)
enorgullecer *to make proud* — parecer (35)
enriquecer *to enrich* — parecer (35)
ensombrecer *to darken* — parecer (35)
ensordecer *to deafen* — parecer (35)
entender *to understand* — perder (37)
enternecer *to soften* — parecer (35)
enterrar *to bury* — cerrar (11)
entreabrir *to half open* — past participle **entreabierto**
entreoír *to hear faintly* — oír (32)
entretener *to distract* — tener (58)
entrever *to glimpse* — ver (63) third-person present singular **entrevé**
entristecer *to sadden* — parecer (35)
envanecer *to make vain* — parecer (35)
envejecer *to age* — parecer (35)
enviar *to send* — liar (28)
envilecer *to debase* — parecer (35)
envolver *to wrap up* — mover (31) past participle **envuelto**
equivaler *to be equal* — valer (60)
erguir *to straighten up* — (20)
errar *to wander* — (21)
escabullirse *to slip away* — gruñir (23)
escalofriarse *to shiver* — liar (28)
escarmentar *to teach a lesson* — cerrar (11)
escarnecer *to scoff* — parecer (35)
escocer *to annoy, hurt* — cocer (12)
escribir *to write* — past participle **escrito**
esforzarse *to strive* — contar (14) z>c before **e**
esparcir *to strew, scatter* — zurcir (65)
espiar *to spy on* — liar (28)
establecer *to establish* — parecer (35)

estar *to be*	(22)
estremecer *to shake*	parecer (35)
europeizar *to Europeanize*	aislar (3)
evacuar *to evacuate*	averiguar (7) (no dieresis)
evaluar *to evaluate*	continuar (15)
exceptuar *to except*	continuar (15)
excluir *to exclude*	construir (13)
expedir *to ship*	pedir (36)
exponer *to expose*	poner (39)
extasiar *to enrapture*	liar (28)
extender *to extend*	perder (37)
extraer *to extract*	traer (59)
extraviar *to mislead*	liar (28)
fallecer *to pass away*	parecer (35)
favorecer *to favor/favour*	parecer (35)
fiar *to entrust, give credit*	liar (28)
florecer *to flourish*	parecer (35)
fluctuar *to fluctuate*	continuar (15)
fluir *to flow*	construir (13)
fortalecer *to strengthen*	parecer (35)
forzar *to force*	contar (14) z>c before **e**
fotografiar *to photograph*	liar (28)
fregar *to scrub*	cerrar (11) g>gu before **e**
freír *to fry*	reír (46); past participle **frito**
fruncir *to pucker*	zurcir (65)
gemir *to groan*	pedir (36)
gloriar(se) *to glory*	liar (28)
gobernar *to govern*	cerrar (11)
graduar *to grade*	continuar (15)
gruñir *to growl*	(23)
guarecer *to protect*	parecer (35)
guarnecer *to equip*	parecer (35)
guiar *to guide*	liar (28)
haber auxiliary for forming compound tenses, or there *is/are*	(24)

habituar *to make accustomed to*	**continuar (15)**
hacer *to do, make*	**(25)**
hastiar *to weary*	**liar (28)**
heder *to reek*	**perder (37)**
helar *to freeze*	**cerrar (11)**
henchir *to cram, stuff*	**pedir (36)**
hender *to cleave*	**perder (37)**
hendir = **hender**	**discernir (18)**
herir *to wound*	**sentir (55)**
herrar *to shoe, brand*	**cerrar (11)**
hervir *to boil*	**sentir (55)**
holgar *to take one's ease*	**contar (14) g>gu** before **e**
hollar *to trample*	**contar (14)**
huir *to flee*	**construir (13)**
humedecer *to dampen*	**parecer (35)**
impedir *to impede*	**pedir (36)**
imponer *to impose*	**poner (39);** imperative singular **impón**
incensar *to incense*	**cerrar (11)**
incluir *to include*	**construir (13)**
indisponer *to indispose*	**poner (39)**
individuar *to individualize*	**continuar (15)**
inducir *to induce*	**producir (41)**
infatuar *to make big-headed*	**continuar (15)**
inferir *to infer*	**sentir (55)**
influir *to influence*	**construir (13)**
ingerir *to ingest*	**sentir (55)**
inquirir *to investigate*	**adquirir (2)**
insinuar *to hint*	**continuar (15)**
instituir *to institute*	**construir (13)**
instruir *to instruct*	**construir (13)**
interferir *to interfere*	**sentir (55)**
interponer *to interpose*	**poner (39)**
intervenir *to intervene*	**venir (62)**

introducir *to insert*   **producir (41)**
intuir *to intuit*   **construir (13)**
invertir *to invest*   **sentir (55)**
ir *to go*   **(26)**
izar *to raise (flag)*   **rezar (49)**. All verbs ending in **-izar** conjugate like **rezar**.

jugar *to play*   **(27)**
languidecer *to languish*   **parecer (35)**
leer *to read*   **poseer (40)**
liar *to tie up in a bundle*   **(28)**
llegar *to arrive*   **pagar (34)**
llover *to rain*   **mover (31)**; usually only 3rd person

lucir *to sport, show off*   **(29)**
maldecir *to curse*   **(30)**
manifestar *to manifest*   **cerrar (11)**
mantener *to maintain*   **tener (58)**
mecer *to rock (a child)*   **vencer (61)**
medir *to measure*   **pedir (36)**
mentar *to mention by name*   **cerrar (11)**
mentir *to lie*   **sentir (55)**
merecer *to merit*   **parecer (35)**
merendar *to eat an afternoon snack*   **cerrar (11)**
moler *to grind*   **mover (31)**
morder *to bite*   **mover (31)**
morir *to die*   **dormir (19)**; past participle **muerto**
mostrar *to die*   **contar (14)**
mover *to move*   **(31)**
mullir *to fluff up*   **gruñir (23)**
nacer *to be born*   **parecer (35)**
negar *to deny*   **cerrar (11) g>gu** before **e**
nevar *to snow*   **cerrar (11)**; usually 3rd person only

obedecer *to obey*	**parecer (35)**
obtener *to obtain*	**tener (58)**
ofrecer *to offer*	**parecer (35)**
oír *to hear*	**(32)**
oler *to smell*	**(33)**
oponer *to oppose*	**poner (39)**
oscurecer *to darken*	**parecer (35)**
pacer *to graze*	**parecer (35)**
padecer *to suffer*	**parecer (35)**
palidecer *to pale*	**parecer (35)**
parecer *to seem*	**(35)**
pedir *to ask for*	**(36)**
pensar *to think*	**cerrar (11)**
perecer *to perish*	**parecer (35)**
permanecer *to remain*	**parecer (35)**
perpetuar *to perpetuate*	**continuar (15)**
perseguir *to pursue*	**seguir (54)**
pertenecer *to belong*	**parecer (35)**
pervertir *to pervert*	**sentir (55)**
plegar *to fold*	**cerrar (11); g>gu** before **e**
poblar *to people/populate*	**contar (14)**
poder *to be able*	**(38)**
podrir *to rot*	variant of **pudrir**; **-u-** used for all forms save past participle **podrido**
poner *to put*	**(39)**
poseer *to possess*	**(40)**
posponer *to postpone*	**poner (39)**
predecir *to foretell*	**decir (17)**
predisponer *to predispose*	**poner (39)**
preferir *to prefer*	**sentir (55)**
prescribir *to prescribe*	past participle **prescrito**
presuponer *to presuppose*	**poner (39)**
prevalecer *to prevail*	**parecer (35)**
prevaler *to take advantage of*	**valer (60)**

prevenir *to prepare*	**venir (62)**
prever *to foresee*	**ver (63)**; third-pers. present singular **prevé**
probar *to prove*	**contar (14)**
producir *to produce*	**(41)**
proferir *to utter* (usually cries, insults)	**sentir (55)**
prohibir *to prohibit*	**(42)**
promover *to promote*	**mover (31)**
proponer *to propose*	**poner (39)**
proseguir *to continue*	**seguir (54)**
prostituir *to prostitute*	**construir (13)**
proteger *to protect*	**(43)**
proveer *to supply*	**poseer (40)**; past participle **provisto/proveído**
provenir *to arise from*	**venir (62)**
pudrir *to rot*	regular; see **podrir**
puntuar *to punctuate/mark*	**continuar (15)**
quebrar *to snap*	**cerrar (11)**
querer *to want/love*	**(44)**
reaparecer *to reappear*	**parecer (35)**
reblandecer *to soften*	**parecer (35)**
recaer *to relapse*	**caer (9)**
recocer *to warm up (food)*	**cocer (12)**
recomendar *to recommend*	**cerrar (11)**
reconocer *to recognize*	**parecer (35)**
reconvenir *to reprimand*	**venir (62)**
recordar *to remember/remind*	**contar (14)**
recostar(se) *to lean back*	**contar (14)**
redituar *to yield*	**continuar (15)**
reducir *to reduce*	**producir (41)**
reelegir *to re-elect*	**regir (45)**
referir *to refer*	**sentir (55)**
reforzar *to reinforce*	**contar (14)**; z>c before e

refregar *to rub/scrub*	**cerrar (11); g>gu** before **e**
regar *to water*	**cerrar (11); g>gu** before **e**
regir *to govern*	**(45)**
rehacer *to redo*	**hacer (25)**
rehusar *to refuse*	**reunir (48)**
reír *to laugh*	**(46)**
rejuvenecer *to rejuvenate*	**parecer (35)**
remendar *to mend*	**cerrar (11)**
remorder *to grieve* (transitive)	**mover (31)**
remover *to stir up/Lat. Am. to remove*	**mover (31)**
rendir *to yield*	**pedir (36)**
renegar *to deny strongly*	**cerrar (11); g>gu** before **e**
renovar *to renew*	**contar (14)**
reñir *to scold*	**(47)**
repetir *to repeat*	**pedir (36)**
replegar *to fold over*	**cerrar (11); g>gu** before **e**
reponer *to replace*	**poner (39)**
reprobar *to reprove*	**contar (14)**
reproducir *to reproduce*	**producir (41)**
requebrar *to flatter*	**cerrar (11)**
requerir *to require*	**sentir (55)**
resarcir *to compensate for*	**zurcir (65)**
resentirse *to resent*	**sentir (55)**
resfriar *to chill*	**liar (28)**
resollar *to wheeze*	**contar (14)**
resolver *to resolve*	**mover (31);** past participle **resuelto**
resonar *to echo*	**contar (14)**
resplandecer *to gleam*	**parecer (35)**
restablecer *to re-establish*	**parecer (35)**
restituir *to return*	**construir (13)**
retemblar *to shudder*	**cerrar (11)**
retener *to retain*	**tener (58)**

retorcer *to twist*	**cocer (12)**; c>z before **a, o**
retraer *to draw in*	**traer (59)**
retribuir *to pay*	**construir (13)**
reunir *to bring together*	**(48)**
reventar *to burst*	**cerrar (11)**
reverdecer *to grow green again*	**parecer (35)**
revertir *to revert*	**sentir (55)**
revestir *to put on (clothes)*	**pedir (36)**
revolar *to flutter about*	**contar (14)**
revolcarse *to knock over*	**contar (14)** c>qu before **e**
revolver *to turn over*	**mover (31);** past participle **revuelto**
rezar *to pray*	**(49)**
robustecer *to strengthen*	**parecer (35)**
rociar *to sprinkle*	**liar (28)**
rodar *to roll*	**contar (14)**
roer *to gnaw*	**(50)**
rogar *to request*	**contar (14);** g>gu before **e**
romper *to break*	past participle **roto**
saber *to know*	**(51)**
sacar *to take out*	**(52)**
salir *to come out/leave*	**(53)**
satisfacer *to satisfy*	**hacer (25)**
seducir *to seduce*	**producir (41)**
segar *to reap*	**cerrar (11)** g>gu before **e**
seguir *to follow*	**(54)**
sembrar *to show*	**cerrar (11)**
sentar *to seat*	**cerrar (11)**
sentir *to feel*	**(55)**
ser *to be*	**(56)**
serrar *to saw*	**cerrar (11)**
servir *to serve*	**pedir (36)**
situar *to situate*	**continuar (15)**
sobre(e)ntender *to infer*	**perder (37)**
sobreponer *to put on top*	**poner (39)**

sobresalir *to jut out*	**salir (53)**
sobrevenir *to happen suddenly*	**venir (62)**
sofreír *to fry lightly*	**reír (46)**; past participle **sofrito**
soldar *to solder*	**contar (14)**
soler *to be used to*	**mover (31)** future, conditional and past and future subjunctives not used
soltar *to release*	**contar (14)**; past participle **suelto**
sonar *to sound*	**contar (14)**
sonreír *to smile*	**reír (46)**
soñar *to dream*	**contar (14)**
sosegar *to calm*	**cerrar (11)** g>gu before e
sostener *to support*	**tener (58)**
subarrendar *to sublease*	**cerrar (11)**
subscribir	see **suscribir**
substituir	see **sustituir**
substraer	see **sustraer**
subvenir *to defray costs*	**venir (62)**
subvertir *to subvert*	**sentir (55)**
sugerir *to suggest*	**sentir (55)**
suponer *to suppose*	**poner (39)**
suscribir *to subscribe*	past participle **suscrito**
sustituir *to substitute*	**construir (13)**
sustraer *to remove*	**traer (59)**
tañer *to chime*	**(57)**
temblar *to tremble*	**cerrar (11)**
tender *to tend*	**perder (37)**
tener *to have*	**(58)**
tentar *to tempt*	**cerrar (11)**
teñir *to dye*	**reñir (47)**
torcer *to twist*	**cocer (12)**; c>z before a, o
tostar *to toast*	**contar (14)**
traducir *to translate*	**producir (41)**
traer *to bring*	**(59)**

tra(n)scender *to transcend* perder (37)

transcribir *to transcribe* past participle **transcrito**

transferir *to transfer* sentir (55)

transgredir *to transgress* abolir (1); sometimes regular

transponer *to transpose* poner (39)

trasegar *to switch round* cerrar (11); g>gu before e

traslucir *to hint at* lucir (29)

trastrocar *to switch round* contar (14); c>qu before e

trocar *to barter* contar (14); c>qu before e

tronar *to thunder* contar (14)

tropezar *to stumble* cerrar (11); z>c before e

tullir *to maim* gruñir (23)

vaciar *to empty* liar (28)

valer *to be worth* (60)

valuar *to value* continuar (15)

variar *to vary* liar (28)

vencer *to win/conquer* (61)

venir *to come* (62)

ver *to see* (63)

verter *to pour out* perder (37)

vestir *to clothe* pedir (36)

volar *to fly* contar (14)

volcar *to upset* contar (14); c>qu before e

volver *to return* mover (31); past participle **vuelto**

yacer *to lie* (i.e. *lie down*) (64)

zaherir *to mortify* sentir (55)

zambullir *to plunge* gruñir (23)

zurcir *to darn* (65)

Glossary of Grammatical Terms

A few terms not used in this book but often found in Spanish grammars are also included. Terms printed in bold characters are defined elsewhere in the glossary.

Abstract noun A **noun** that refers to something that is not a person or concrete object. The following are abstract nouns: *liberty, impatience, innocence*.

Accent Strictly speaking, the various signs written over certain vowels in Spanish and many other languages, e.g. in the words **café, averigüe**. It is often confusingly used to mean stress; see **Stressed Syllable**.

Active see **Passive**

Adjectival Participles Adjectives formed from some (but by no means all) Spanish verbs by adding -ante, -ente or -iente, e.g. **preocupante** *worrying*, **hiriente** *wounding*.

Adjective A word that describes a noun, e.g. *a good* book, **un *buen* libro**.

Adverb A word that describes a verb, an adjective or another adverb: *he did it well*, **lo hizo *bien***; *terribly tired*, **terriblemente cansado**; *very quickly*, **muy deprisa**.

Agreement Agreement in Spanish is of three kinds:

(1) **Number agreement**: the fact that a singular noun or pronoun requires a singular adjective, verb or article, and a plural noun or pronoun a plural adjective, verb or article:

El buen alumno *trabaja* mucho *The good student works hard*

Los buenos alumnos *trabajan* mucho *The good students work hard*

(2) **Person agreement**: the fact that a first-person subject requires a first-person verb and so on:

Person	Singular	Plural
First	**Yo quiero** *I want*	**Nosotros queremos** *We want*
Second	**Tú quieres** *You want*	**Vosotros queréis** *You want*
Third	**Ella quiere** *She wants*	**Ellos quieren** *They want*

(3) **Gender agreement**: the fact that masculine nouns require masculine adjectives, articles or pronouns, and feminine nouns require feminine adjectives, articles or pronouns:

Masculine	*un* **muchacho** *rubio a blond boy* *este* **libro** *rojo this red book*
Feminine	*una* **muchacha** *rubia a blond girl* *esta* **casa** *blanca this white house*

Anterior Preterit Tense See **Pretérito anterior**

Apposition Two nouns or noun phrases placed side by side so that the second expands the meaning of the first: *Don Quixote,* **the greatest Spanish novel**. The words in bold are said to be 'in apposition' to the first part of the phrase.

Articles Words meaning *the* or *a/an*. See **Definite Article** and **Indefinite Article**.

Attributive Adjective In Spanish, an adjective that specifies the type or purpose of a noun: **la industria hotelera** *the hotel industry*, **problemas sindicales** *trade-union problems*. English regularly expresses the same construction by joining nouns together, e.g. *police dog, baseball game*.

Auxiliary verb A verb used to form a **Compound Tense** The most common auxiliary verbs in English are *to have* as in *I* **have** *said*, and *to be* as in *I* **am** *saying*. The Spanish equivalents are **haber** as in **yo** *he* **dicho** and **estar** as in **yo** *estoy* **diciendo**.

Cardinal numbers The ordinary numbers used for counting, e.g. *one*, *two*, *three*, etc. See also **Ordinal Numbers**.

Ceceo See **Seseo**.

Clause A group of words that forms part of a sentence and includes a **Finite Verb:** *I'll finish it before she arrives* contains two clauses, *I'll finish it* and *before she arrives*. Often a sentence consists of only one clause, cf. *Jack ate an apple*. Among the types of clause mentioned in this grammar are **Main Clause, Subordinate Clause** and **Relative Clause**, each separately defined below.

Collective Noun A noun that, although it may be singular in form, refers to a group of people or things: *flock*, *crowd*, *committee*, *crew*, *majority*, *dozen*, etc.

Comparative Forms of adjectives and adverbs that indicate a *more* or *less* intense quality: *better*, *worse*, *more intelligent*, *less beautiful*, **mejor**, **peor**, **más inteligente**, **menos bello**, etc.

Compound noun A noun formed from two or more nouns joined together: *fire alarm*, *cat-hair*, *fish soup*, *database design textbook*. As the examples show, English can make complex compound nouns, but Spanish has only a few, e.g. **año luz** *light year*, **perro policía** *police-dog*. Generally Spanish creates such nouns either by using **de** *of*—**manual de diseño de bases de datos**—or by using an **Attributive Adjective** (q.v.): **problemas** *estudiantiles* *student problems*.

Compound tenses Tense forms of verbs created in English by using the verb *have* plus a past participle, and in Spanish by using **haber** plus a past participle: *I have done, had finished, I will have left,* **he hecho, había terminado, habré salido**.

Conditional Sentence One that includes a condition and a result, e.g. *if it rains we'll stay at home, if it had rained we would have stayed at home*. Occasionally the *if*-clause is omitted: *it would be have been nice* (i.e. if some condition or other had been met).

Conditional tense The tense of a verb used to express what might or could happen or have happened: *I would be angry, He would have realized,* **me enojaría, se habría dado cuenta**.

Conjugation The general pattern that a verb's forms follow. There are three conjugations in Spanish corresponding to **Infinitives** ending in **-ar**, **-er** and **-ir**. All regular verbs belong to one of these conjugations. Radical changing and irregular verbs follow one of these conjugations in most forms, but some forms are unpredictable.

Conjunction Words or phrases (**Relative Pronouns** excepted) that connect words, phrases and clauses within a sentence. In the following sentence the words in bold are conjunctions: *I bought a shirt **and** a tie, **but when** she saw them, Mary said **that** she didn't like them, **so** I took them back, **although** I liked them myself*.

Consonant Simply defined as all the sounds in a language that are not vowels, i.e. in English and Spanish the sounds corresponding to all the letters of the alphabet except *a, e, i, o, u* and *y* when the latter is pronounced like *i*. See also **Vowel and Semi-vowel**.

Continuous The name given to Spanish verb forms consisting of **estar** plus a gerund, e.g. **estoy fumando** *I'm smoking*. See also **Progressive**.

Definite Article in English *the*, in Spanish **el, la, los, las** when used with the same meaning as the English word.

Demonstrative Adjective A special type of adjective used to point to something: in English *this*, *that* and *those*, in Spanish **este/esta/estos/estas, ese/esa/esos/esas, aquel/aquella/aquellos/aquellas**.

Demonstrative Pronoun A special type of pronoun used to point to something, e.g. *I don't want **this one**, I want **that one***. In Spanish they usually have the same form as **Demonstrative Adjectives**, but are usually distinguished in writing by an accent. See p.138.

Diphthong In Spanish, a combination of a **Vowel** (q.v.) and a **Semi-vowel** (q.v.), e.g. the **oy** in **soy** or the **ue** in **bueno**.

Direct Object A noun or pronoun that directly experiences the action of a verb: *He hit **me**, Jack saw **Mary**, I wrote **it***. See also **Indirect Object**.

Direct Question see **Indirect Question**.

Feminine see **Gender**

Finite Verb Form A verb form that shows **Tense**, **Person** and **Number**, e.g. *he walked* (Third-person, Past and Singular), **iremos** *we'll go* (First-person, Future and Plural). See also **Non-Finite Verb Form**.

First Person see **Person**

Future Perfect Tense Tense forms that refer to an event that *will have* happened by a certain time: ***I will have died** of hunger by the time you finish cooking dinner*.

Future Tense Strictly speaking, the tense form that refers to the future, usually taken in Spanish to mean forms like **hablaré, iremos**. The term is not very helpful because both Spanish and English have several different ways of expressing the future, cf. *we're going tomorrow*, *we'll go tomorrow, we're going to go tomorrow, we go tomorrow, we're to go tomorrow.*

Gender In Spanish, the fact that nouns and pronouns are either 'masculine' or 'feminine'. Gender is usually obvious if the word refers to a male or a female human being, but all Spanish nouns are either feminine or masculine, even when they refer to sexless objects: **el libro** *book*, **el fusil** *rifle*, **el árbol** *tree* are masculine nouns, **la cama** *bed*, **la cartucha** *cartridge* and **la flor** *flower* are feminine. In the case of such nouns, grammatical gender has obviously got nothing to do with sex. See also **Agreement**.

Generic 'Referring to a whole class or every member of a set of things.' In the sentence *I hate beer/oysters/politics*, the three nouns are said to be generic nouns since they refer to substances, things or abstractions in general. Compare **Partitive**.

Gerund The Spanish verb form created by replacing the ending of the **Infinitive** by -**ando** or -**iendo**, depending on **Conjugation**, e.g. **hablando, durmiendo**. The gerund is one of the **Non-Finite Verb Forms** of Spanish and corresponds to some of the uses of the English verb form ending in *-ing*.

Historic Present The **Present Tense** used to make a past event sound dramatic, cf. *There I **am** resting after all my hard work when she **walks** in and **tells** me I'm lazy!*

Imperative See **Mood**.

Imperfect Subjunctive The name traditionally given to the simple (i.e. non-compound) verb forms of the past of the Spanish subjunctive. Examples: **hablara/ hablase, dijeran/dijesen**. See also **Mood**.

Imperfect Tense A Spanish past tense formed by adding a set of endings (**-aba, -abas, -aba** or **-ía, -ías, -ía,**

etc.) to the **Stem** of the verb. It usually expresses either habitual actions in the past—**yo fumaba mucho** *I used to* smoke *a lot*—or events that were in progress at the time but had not yet ended, cf. *I was smoking a lot*.

Impersonal Pronouns Pronouns that refer to unidentifiable persons or things, e.g. *someone, something, anyone,* **alguien, algo, cualquiera**, etc.

Impersonal se One of the many uses of the pronoun **se** as a rough equivalent of the English *one, people*: **se vive mejor en España** *people live better in* Spain, **se come bien en Francia** *people eat well in France.* Compare **Passive se**.

Indefinite Article In English *a/an*, in Spanish **un/una/unos/unas** when used with the same meaning as their English counterparts.

Indicative Mood See **Mood**.

Indirect Object The noun or pronoun that acquires, hears or in some way receives the **Direct Object** (q.v.) of a verb. The word *him* or **le** is the Indirect Object in these sentences and the words in bold italics are the Direct Object: *I sent him **the letter**/***le** enviaron ***la carta**, *she told him **the truth**/***ella **le** dijo **la verdad***. In Spanish an Indirect Object can also lose as well as receive: **le** robaron ***mil pesetas*** *they stole 1,000 ptas from him*, **se le** cae el pelo *his hair's falling out* (literally *his hair is falling out* (**caerse**) *from him*).

Indirect Question A question included in a **Subordinate Clause** (q.v.) in a sentence. It is normally introduced by some such expression as *I wonder . . . , Do you know where . . . , I'll ask him when . . . .* Direct question: *When is he coming?*, Indirect Question *I don't know **when he is coming***.

Infinitive The 'dictionary form' of a verb, which always ends in **-r** in Spanish, e.g. **hablar, comer, vivir**. It often corresponds to the English form preceded by *to—to speak, to eat , to live*—and sometimes to the form ending in *-ing*, as in **fumar es malo para la salud** *smoking is bad for the health*. It is a **Non-Finite-Verb Form** (q.v.).

Interrogative A feature of words that ask questions, like *why?* (adverb), *when?* (adverb), *who?* (pronoun), *which?* (adjective), Spanish **¿por qué?, ¿cuándo?, ¿quién?, ¿qué?, ¿cuál?**

Intransitive Verb a verb that has no **Direct Object** present or implied: *I go, she came* are intransitive, as are their Spanish equivalents, **voy, vino**: one cannot go *someone* or come *something*. 'Transitive' and 'Intransitive' are often descriptions of the use of a verb rather than of its inherent nature, since many so-called intransitive verbs can take a direct object and then become transitive, cf. *he slept ten hours*, Spanish **durmió diez horas**, or Spanish **lo durmieron** *they put him to sleep*. See also **Transitive verbs**.

Irregular Verb A verb whose forms cannot always be predicted from the usual pattern. English *go-went-gone, sleep-slept*, Spanish **soy, eres, es** are typical examples.

Main Clause A Clause (q.v.) that could stand alone as a sentence. In *I stood up when she came in*, the words *I stood up* could form a sentence on their own and therefore form the Main Clause; *when she came in* cannot form a sentence without the addition of more words, and is therefore a **Subordinate Clause** (q.v.).

Masculine see **Gender**.

Modal Verbs A verb that indicates the 'mood' of another, e.g. *I **may** go* (possibility), *you **ought to** do it* (obligation), *she **can't** come* (possibility). The main

Spanish Modal Verbs are **poder, deber, tener que, soler**.

Mood The traditional name given to the three different forms that Spanish and English verbs can take according to the use being made of the verb:

   Indicative Mood, used for making statements: *it's raining, you said it,* **yo hablo español**

   Subjunctive Mood, almost obsolete in English, but much used in Spanish to show that the verb expresses something hoped, wanted, feared, approved, disapproved, possible or, after **Subordinators** (q.v.) something that has or had not yet happened, e.g. **quiero que** *vayas I want you to go*, **espero que** *venga I hope that he comes*, **antes de que** *saliera* **el avión** *before the plane left.* The subjunctive occasionally occurs in English, e.g. *if I were you, it is necessary that this be done quickly, if this be true.*

   Imperative Mood: The form of a verb used to express a command or order: *tell me the truth,* **dime la verdad**.

Non-Finite Verb Forms Verb forms that cannot express Person, Tense or Number, e.g. *living, to live, lived*—three forms that do not tell us who lived when and how many people were involved. In Spanish the non-finite verb forms are the **Gerund**, the **Infinitive** and the **Past Participle**.

Noun A word that names a person, object or abstraction, e.g. *Peter, woman, table, hope, freedom.* See also **Abstract Noun, Collective Noun**.

Number In grammar, the state of being either singular (i.e. referring to only one person or thing) or plural (referring to more than one).

Object Pronouns in Spanish, pronouns like **me, te, nos, os** that refer either to the **Direct Object** or the **Indirect Object** (q.v.). **Le** and **les** are also object pronouns, although in standard Spanish they usually (but by no means always) refer only to the Indirect Object.

Ordinal Numbers Numerals that indicates the order in which something appears, e.g. *first/primero, second/segundo, hundredth/***centésimo.** Compare **Cardinal Number**.

Partitive 'Referring only to a part of something, not to the whole'. In *Don't forget to buy bread/oysters* the words *bread* and *oysters* are Partitive Nouns: they imply *some* bread, *some* oysters, not all the bread or oysters that exist. Compare **Generic**.

Passive The opposite of **Active**. An active sentence that can be made passive must contain a **Subject**, a **Transitive Verb** and optionally a **Direct Object**: *A car ran him down/***Lo atropelló un coche.** The equivalent Passive Sentence makes the direct object into the subject: *He was run down by a car/***Fue atropellado por un coche.** See also **Passive se**.

Passive se One of the uses of the Spanish pronoun **se** to make the equivalent of a **Passive** (q.v.) sentence: **estos libros se publicaron en España** *these books were published in Spain*.

Past Participle The part of the verb used to form **Compound Tenses** and **Passive** sentences. In English it usually ends in **-ed**, in Spanish **-ado** or **-ido**, although there are exceptions in both languages, cf. *broken/***roto,** *seen/***visto.** It is a **Non-Finite Verb Form** (q.v.).

Perfect Tense The **Compound Tense** formed in English with the present tense of *to have* plus the **Past Participle,** in Spanish from the present tense of **haber** plus the past participle, e.g. *he has seen,* **ha visto.** It is often called the **pretérito perfecto** in Spanish.

Perfect Tense Continuous (or Continuous Perfect Tense) The tense formed in English with the **Perfect Tense** of *to be* plus the *-ing* form, in Spanish with the perfect tense of **estar** plus the **Gerund**, e.g. *he has been thinking*, **ha estado pensando**.

Perfect of Recency The use of the **Perfect Tense** in Spanish (as opposed to the **Preterit Tense**) to show that an event occurred recently (e.g. since midnight). This is more typical of Spain than Latin America.

Person See **Agreement**

Personal a The term used in Spanish grammar to refer to the preposition **a** when used before **Direct Objects** that refer to human beings, e.g. **vi a Mario** *I saw Mario*. See p.157.

Personal Pronouns Subject pronouns and **Object Pronouns** referring to people or things, e.g. *I*/**yo**, *you*/**tú**/**usted**, *he*/**él**, or *me*/**me**, *him*/**lo**/**le**, *us*/**nos**, etc.

Phrase A meaningful group of words in a sentence that does not contain a **Finite Verb**, e.g. the bold words in *I arrived **at ten o'clock***.

Pluperfect Conditional The tense formed in Spanish by using the **Conditional** form of **haber** + the **Past Participle**: **habrían sido** *they would have been*. The **-ra** form of **haber** may also be used: **hubieran sido** *they would have been*.

Pluperfect Subjunctive The **Subjunctive** version of the Spanish **Pluperfect** (q.v.), formed from the **-ra** or **-se** form of **haber** + the **Past Participle**, e.g. **si me hubieras visto** *if you had seen me*.

Pluperfect Tense The tense formed in English with the past of **had** plus the **Past Participle**, e.g. *I had done*, and in Spanish with the **Imperfect** of **haber** and the **Past Participle**, e.g. **yo había hecho**.

Possessive Adjective An adjective that indicates possession, i.e. *my*/**mi**, *your*/**tu/vuestro/su**, *his*/**su**, *our*/**nuestro**, etc.

Possessive Pronoun A pronoun that indicates possession. English examples are *mine, yours, hers*; Spanish examples are **el mío, el tuyo, el suyo**, etc.

Prefix A letter or letters that usually have no meaning in isolation but are added at the beginning a word to change the meaning, e.g. *pre-* in *pre-school, re-* in *represent*.

Preposition A word used before a noun to relate it to the rest of the phrase or sentence, e.g. *on*/**en**, *with*/**con**, *without*/**sin**, *against*/**contra**, etc. In English a preposition can come at the end of a clause or sentence: *the girl he's going out with*. In Spanish a preposition must precede the word it refers to: **la chica con la que sale**.

Prepositional Phrase A phrase used like a **Preposition**, e.g. *on behalf of*/**de parte de**, *in return for*/**a cambio de**.

Present Continuous The name usually given in Spanish grammar to the tense form based on the present of **estar** plus the **Gerund**, e.g. **está cantando** *he is singing*. See also **Progressive**.

Present Participle In Spanish, the name sometimes given to **Adjectival Participles** (q.v.). In English, the name sometimes given to the *-ing* form of verbs, e.g. *walking, riding*.

Present Tense The name given to the verb form that indicates events that are happening in the present, e.g. **hablo** *I speak/I'm speaking*. The name is misleading since in both languages this tense form can also be used for future, timeless and even past actions. See also **Present Continuous, Historic Present**.

Preterit (British spelling 'Preterite') The name given in English to the simple Past Tense in Spanish that denotes a completed action, e.g. **hablé** *I spoke*, **tuve** *I got*, **dijimos** *we said*. In Spanish this tense is often called the **pretérito indefinido**.

Pretérito anterior The Spanish name for the tense form made with the **Preterit** of **haber** and the **Past Participle**, e.g. **hubo hablado** *he had said*. It is nowadays used only in literary styles.

Progressive The name usually given to English verb forms made with *to be* and the *-ing* form of a verb, e.g. *he was singing*, *they are shouting*. The rough Spanish equivalent is the **Continuous**.

Pronominal verb A Spanish verb that has an **Object Pronoun** that is of the same person and number as the subject, e.g. **me afeito** *I'm shaving (myself)*, **te vas** *you're leaving*, **se murieron** *they died*. Traditionally these were called 'reflexive verbs', but the term **Reflexive** correctly refers to just one possible meaning of a Pronominal Verb, not to the *form* of the verb.

Pronoun A word, e.g. *he*, *she*, it, *they*, I, **yo**, **tú**, that stands for a noun.

Radical-changing verb In Spanish, verbs that have regular endings but unpredictable vowel changes in certain forms, e.g. **contar** *to tell*, **cuento** *I tell* but **contamos** *we tell*, or **pedir** *to ask for*, **pido** *I ask for*, **pedí** *I asked for*, **pidió** *he asked for*, etc.

Reciprocal One of the meanings that a plural Spanish **Pronominal Verb** can have. The action is done to or for *one another*, e.g. **se quieren** *they love one another*.

Reflexive One of the meanings of a Spanish **Pronominal Verb** which shows that an the action is done by the subject to him or herself, e.g. **me lavo** *I wash myself*.

Regular Verb A verb whose various forms are all predictable from the pattern used by its **Conjugation** (q.v.). Typical Spanish examples are **hablar, comer** and **vivir,** which have no irregularities or exceptions.

Relative Clause A clause that modifies or restricts the meaning of a noun or pronoun that occurred earlier in the sentence, e.g. *I was talking to the woman **who lives over the road,** That's the girl **that/whom I saw yesterday.** In Spanish Relative clauses are always introduced by a **Relative Pronoun** (q.v.), but the pronoun can sometimes be omitted in English, cf. *that's the girl I saw yesterday*.

Relative Pronoun A class of words that introduce a **Relative Clause** (q.v.). English relative pronouns are *who, whom, which, that;* Spanish equivalents are **que, el que, quien, el cual.**

Second Person See **Person**

Semi-Vowel A special kind of vowel that acts like a consonant. There are two Spanish semi-vowels, one pronounced like the *y* of *yes* as in **bien,** the other like the *w* of *wood* as in **bueno.** When a semi-vowel is attached to a **Vowel,** a **Diphthong** is formed.

Seseo In Spanish pronunciation, the use of an s sound where Spaniards from Central and Northern Spain use a sound like the *th* of *think,* e.g. in words like **cinco** *five,* **atroz** *atrocious.* Most Andalusians and Canary Islanders and all Latin Americans use **seseo.** Use of the *th* sound is called **ceceo.**

Simple Tense A one-word tense form of a verb, e.g. *he does,* **sabe, toma.** It is the opposite of **Compound Tense** (q.v.).

Stem The part of a verb to which the various endings that indicate Tense, Person and Mood are added. The stem of *kissing* is *kiss: kissed, kisses.* The stem of **hablar** is

habl: habl*amos*, habl*aron*, habl*ando* etc. Some irregular verbs have no single identifiable stem, e.g. **ser—soy, eres, fui,** etc.

Stressed Syllable The **Syllable** of a word spoken most loudly. Stress is crucial to meaning in both Spanish: and English: compare **hablo** *I speak* with **habló** *he spoke* or the two pronunciations of *invalid* in *the invalid had an invalid ticket.*

Subject The noun or pronoun that performs the action of verb or about which the verb phrase makes a statement: **Mary** *got up late,* **I** *am getting tired,* **Miguel** *conoce a* **Antonia.**

Subjunctive See **Mood.**

Subordinate Clause A clause in a sentence that depends on a **Main Clause** to make sense. In *Jane got up before the sun rose*, the subordinate clause *before the sun rose* cannot stand alone as a sentence, whereas the main clause *Jane got up* can.

Subordinator A **Conjunction** used to introduce a **Subordinate Clause**, e.g. *I did it* **before** *you did,* *Peter phoned* **when** *she arrived,* *I paid* **although** *I wasn't pleased.*

Suffix A letter or letters that (usually) have no meaning in isolation but are added to the end of a word to change the meaning, e.g. *-ness* in *smallness,* **-ito** in **perrito.**

Superlative The form of an adjective or adverb that shows that the quality referred to is the most intense of all: *Molly is the* **brightest** *student, you're the* **best,** *Molly es* **la más inteligente,** *tú eres* **el mejor.** See also **Comparative.**

Syllable In Spanish, a portion or element of a word that contains one **Vowel** sound (**Diphthongs** and **Triphthongs** counting as one vowel). **Es** contains one syllable, **era** contains two and **habitación** contains four (**ió** being a diphthong and counting as one vowel).

Tense The form of a verb that indicates *when* the action takes place. *I went*/**yo iba**/**yo fui**/**yo he ido** are all past tenses of various kinds, *I'll go*/*I will go*/*I'm going to go* are different types of future tense.

Third Person See **Person**.

Transitive Verb A verb that can have a **Direct Object**. The following verbs are transitive: *I hit him*, **La vi** *I saw her*. *I yawned*/**bostecé** is **Intransitive** since we cannot yawn something or someone.

Triphthong The combination of a **Semi-Vowel**, a **Vowel** and another **Semi-Vowel**, e.g. **uéi** in **continuéis** (pronounced 'way').

Verb A word that explains what the **Subject** of a clause or sentence does: *I eat fish*, *You tell tall stories*.

Vowel The sounds of a language that are not classified as consonants and which, in the case of Spanish, can form a **Syllable** (q.v.) on their own or in combination with consonants. Spanish has five vowels: **a, e, i, o, u**. English has the same number of vowel signs, but they are pronounced in more than a dozen different ways.

| Index

Prepositional phrases like **en contra, con motivo de, debajo de** are listed in alphabetical order on pp.166–183. Only a few important English prepositions are included here. The rest are listed with their Spanish equivalents on pp. 183–6.

For individual Spanish verbs not listed here, see the list on pp. 303–319.

a, before direct object (**a personal**), 157; other uses, 160
a, an, 87
a lo mejor, 32
a medida que, 30
a pesar de que, 24, 32
a que, 31
abolir, 254
acá, 152
acaso, 33
Accent: spelling rules, 222ff
according to, see **según**
adentro, 152
Adjectival Participles, e.g. **amante, hiriente, convincente**), 59
Adjectives, 127; forms of 127–31; agreement, 131; comparison, 132; use of **-ísimo,** 134; position of, 135; change of meaning with **ser** or **estar,** 80
Adverbs, 148; comparison of 151
Affective Suffixes, 208
after, see **después de que**
afternoon, 230

afuera, 152
Age, 201
ago, 206
ahí, 152
aislar, 256
algo, 121
alguien, 120
alguno, 121
allá, 152
allí, 152
alone, 236
Alphabet, 222
already, see **ya**
although, see **aunque**
American, 230
and, 190
andar, forms, 256
another, see **otro**
Anterior Preterit tense, 18
antes de, 165, 23
antes de que, 30
any, 231; see also **cualquiera**
anyone, see **alguien, nadie**
anyone who . . ., 119
aquel & aquél, 138–9
aquello, 140
aquí, 152
ardiendo, 54
Articles, see Definite Article, Indefinite Article
as if, see **como si**
as . . . as, 134
at, see pp.183–6
Augmentative Suffixes, 209
aun and **aún**, 232
aunque, 32
averiguar, 259

be, see **ser**, **estar**
beber, 243
because, see **porque**
become, 232
billón, 193, 194
bueno, 131
but, 187
by, 184

caber, 259
caer, forms, 259; compared with **caerse**, 75
cambiar, 260
can, 60, 63; see also **poder**, **saber**
Cardinal Numbers, 191
Castilian, 237
-cer, verbs ending in, 249,
cerrar, 261
cien, **ciento**, 193
Collective Nouns, 102
como, 187; = *if*, 41
cómo, 202
como si, 32
Comparison, see Adjectives, Adverbs
Compound Tenses, forms, 250, 2; uses, 9–11; **tengo hecho**, etc., 16
con, 166
con tal de que, 24, 31
Conditional Sentences, 40
Conditional Tense, uses, 12, 40; forms, 251
conducir, see **producir**
Conjunctions, 187
conmigo, 106
consigo, 106
construir, 263
contar, 263
contigo, 106

continuar, 264
Continuous Forms of Verbs, 13
contra, 168
Countries, Definite Article with, 86
cuál, 203–4
cualquier(a), 122
cuán, 146
cuando, 24, 30
cuándo, 202
cuanto, 134
cuánto, 201
cuyo, 125

dar, 265
Dates, 200
Days of the Week, 199
de, 168; **es difícil** *de* **hacer**, 50
de ahí que, 31
de forma que, 31
de manera que, 31
de modo que, 31
de que, 233
deber, 61
Definite Article, 82
dejar, 26
delante de, 171
Demonstrative Adjectives and Pronouns, 138
dentro, 152
desde, 205–7; 171, 17, 30
desde hace, 205
despite, see **a pesar de (que)**
después de que, 17, 24, 30
Dieresis, 222
Diminutive suffixes, 208
Diphthongs, 215, 225
do, see **hacer**

dónde, 202
dormir, 267
durante, 172

e, see **y**
el/la/los/las = *the*, 82
el cual, 125
el de, etc., 120
el que, etc. = 'the one who', 119; = relative pronoun,
    124
él, 107, 104, 106
ella(s), 107, 104, 106
ellos, 107, 104, 106
en caso de que, 31
en caso de, 24
en, 172
entre, 175, 107
ese & **ése**, 138-9
eso, 140
Estados Unidos, 86, 230
estar forms, 269; compared with **ser**, 77; compared
    with **hay**, 81; used to form passive, 66; with gerund,
    13
este & **éste**, 138-9
esto, 140
even, 232
evening, 230
except, see **salvo que**, **excepto que**
excepto que, 31
excepto, 107

feliz, 79
for, see pp.183-6; in phrases like *for three weeks*, 205
Fractions, 196
from, see pp. 183-6
fuera, 152;

fuera de, 176
Future Indicative Tense; uses, 11; forms, 251
Future Subjunctive, 22

Gender of Nouns, 91ff
Gerund, 51; not used as noun, 50; in phrases like **estar cantando**, 13; compared with English *-ing* form, 234
Glossary, 321
go, see **ir**
gran(de), 131
gustar, 235

haber de, 62
haber que, 62
haber, forms, 271; = 'there is/are', 80; in compound tenses, 250; see also Perfect, Pluperfect
hablar, 240
hacer, forms, 271; = *ago*, 206
hacerse = *become*, 232
hacia, 176
hasta, 176;
hasta que, 31
have, see **tener, haber**
hay (special form of verb **haber**, q.v.), 80
her = pronoun, 109ff, esp. 111; = 'of her' (possessive), 141ff
here, 152
hers, 143
him, 109ff, esp. 111
hirviendo, 54
his, 141ff
Historic Present, 6
how old are you?, 201
how, 146, 202
however, 34
hube hecho, etc., 18

I, see **yo**
if, 40
igual, 34
-illo, 208
Imperative, 36
Imperfect IndicativeTense, forms, 250; uses, 7
Imperfect Subjunctive tense, forms, 252–3; uses, 22, 17;
    -ra and **-se** forms compared, 22; **-ra** form for condi-
    tional, 13, 42. See also Subjunctive Mood
Impersonal Pronouns, see Indefinite Pronouns
Impersonal **se**, see **se**
in case, see **en caso de que; por si**
in order to, see **para que, a que**
in, see pp.183–6
incluso, 232
Indefinite Pronouns (**algo, alguien, alguno**, etc.), 119
Indicative Mood, 18
Infinitive, 42 to replace subjunctive, 23, 48; as imperative,
    39; prepositions with, 44; after **ver, oír**, 49
-ing form of English verbs, 234, 51
inside, 152
ir, forms, 272; with gerund, 53; **ir a** + infinitive to form
    future tense, 11
Irregular Verbs, 254–319
irse, 75
-ísimo, 134
it's me, it's you, etc., 118
it, 109ff, esp. 111
-ito, 208

jamás, 154
jugar, 273

la/las = *the*, 82; = *her, it*, 109ff, esp. 111
Languages, use of definite article with, 86
Latin America(n), 230

le/les, 109ff, esp. 111

less, 132ff

like, as in *I like chocolate*, 235

llevar, as in **llevo meses aquí** *I've been here for months*, 205

lo pronoun, 109ff, esp. 111; = neuter pronoun, 145; with adjectives and adverbs, 146

lo de, 120

lo que, 120

los = *the*, 82; = *them*, 109ff., esp. 111

make, see **hacer**

malo, 131

más que, más de, 133

maybe, 32

mayor, 133

me, 109ff

Measurements, 201

mediante, 177

mejor, 132

menor, 133

menos que, menos de, 133

mi, 141

mí, 106

mientras (que), 31

mil, 193

mío, 143

Modal Verbs (**poder, deber, hay que, haber de, querer, tener que**, etc.), 60

Months, 199

Mood, 18; see also Indicative, Subjunctive, and Imperative Mood

more, 132ff

mover, 276

must, 61, 62

my, 141

nada, 154
nadie, 154
Negation, 154
neither, 155
Neuter Articles, 145
Neuter Pronouns, 145
never, 154
ni, 155
ninguno, 155
no one, 154
no, 154
nor, 155
nomás, 156
Non-Finite Verb Forms, 42
none, see **ninguno**; see also *any*
norteamericano, 230
nos, 109
nosotros/nosotras, 107, 104, 106
not, 154
nothing, 154
Nouns, gender of, 91; nouns that refer to females, 97;
       plural of, 100
nowhere, 154
nuestro, 141
Numerals, 191ff
nunca, 154

o, u, 187
Object Pronouns, forms, 105; uses 109ff; position of, 113;
       position with imperative, 38; order of, 113; redun-
       dant pronouns 117; emphasis of 118
of, see pp. 183–6
oír, forms, 277; Infinitive with, 49
ojalá, 35
on, see pp.183–6
one, = numeral, 191; = pronoun 71, 123

one another, 69
only, 236
or, 187
Ordinal Numerals, 194
os, 105, 109ff
other, see **otro**
otro, 89
our, ours, 141ff
outside, 152

para, 177
para que, 24
Passive *se*, 64ff.
Passive Voice, 64
Past Participle, 55
pedir, forms, 280; with Subjunctive, 25
pegar, 112
Pejorative Suffixes, 210
peor, 132
perder, 280
Perfect Indicative Tense, forms, 250; uses, 7, 205
perhaps, 32
permitir, subjunctive with, 25
pero, 187
Personal **a**, 157
Personal Pronouns, 104
Pluperfect Indicative Tense, forms 250; uses 11; **-ra** form
     of, 17
Pluperfect Subjunctive, 21, 42;
Plural of nouns, 100
poder, forms, 281; uses, 60
poner, 282; **ponerse** = *become*, 232
por, 178
por si, 31
porque, 188, 32
por qué, 188

poseer, 283

posiblemente, 33

Possessive Adjectives & Pronouns, 141; replacement by definite article, 85

Prepositions, list of 160; use after infinitives, 43. For a list of English prepositions with Spanish equivalents see pp.183–6

Present Indicative Tense, uses, 4 (the forms must be learned from the tables on pp. 240–302)

Present Subjunctive Tense, forms, 251; uses, see Subjunctive Mood

Preterit Tense, 6 (the forms should be learned from the tables on 240–302)

primero, 131, 191

producir, 283

prohibir, forms, 284; subjunctive with, 25

Pronominal (i.e. 'Reflexive') Verbs, 66ff; unclassifiable pron. verbs like **bajarse**, **irse**, 75

Pronouns, Personal, 104; see also Object Personal Pronouns, Subject Personal Pronouns

Pronunciation, 214

pues, 189

puesto que, 32, 189

Punctuation, 227

que = relative pronoun, 124; = conjunction, 189; compared with **de que**, 233; = *than*, 132

qué, 203–4

querer, forms, 286; as modal verb, 62; subjunctive with, 25

Questions, 202

quien = 'the person who', 'anyone who' 119

quién, 202

quizá(s), 33

-ra Pluperfect, 17; **-ra** Subjunctive, see Imperfect subjunctive

Radical Changing Verbs, 253ff
recién, 150
Reciprocal Verbs, 69
Redundant Pronouns, 117
Reflexive Verbs, see Pronominal Verbs
regresar(se), 76
Regular Verb forms, 239–50
reír, 287
Relative Pronouns and Clauses, 124
reunir, 289

saber, forms, 291; = 'to know how to', 63
sacar, 292
salir, forms, 293; compared with **salirse**, 76
salvo que, 31
san(to), 131
se, 66ff; Impersonal **se**, 71; Passive **se**, 73, 70; **se admira a . . .**, 70, 74
Seasons, 199
seguir, 293
según, 31, 106
sentir, 294; with subjunctive, 26
señor, señora, señorita, 85
ser, forms, 295; compared with **estar**, 77; to form the passive, 64
si, 40
sí (pronoun), 106
sin, 182
sin que, 31
since, (time) see **desde**; = *because*, see **puesto que, porque, como, pues**
sino, 187
siquiera, 155
so, see **de manera que, de modo que; tan**
sobre, 182
soler, 63

348 | Index

solo, sólo, 236
some, 236
someone, see **alguien, alguno**
something, see **algo**
Spanish, 237
still, = *yet*, 232
su, sus, 141ff
Subject Personal Pronouns, 107ff; emphasis 118
Subjunctive Mood, forms, 21, 251; uses, 20; replacement
　by infinitive, 23; use after words meaning: *want,
　order, ask, oblige, cause, insist, allow, forbid,* 25; *need,
　possible/ impossible; emotions* 26; *value judgments,* 27;
　denials, 27; *doubt, fear,* 28; *the fact that,* 28; *perhaps,*
　32; *use after subordinators,* 29; *use in relative clauses,*
　34; *use as imperative,* 35, 37
Subordinators; subjunctive with, 29
Superlative, see Adjectives, Adverbs (comparison of); sub-
　junctive with, 35
suyo, 143

tal vez, 33
tan, tan como, 133
tarde, 230
te, 109ff.
Telephone Numbers, 194
tener que, 62
tener, 296
tengo hecho, etc., 16
Tense Agreement, 23
that as in *that book*, 138; as in *the book that I read*, 125; as
　in *he said that . . .*, 189
the, 82
their, theirs, 141ff
them, 109ff, esp. 111
there, 152, see also *there is/are*
there is, there are, 80

these 138
they, 107
this 138
those, 138
ti 106
Time, 197
to be, 77
to, see pp.183–6
traer, 297
tras 183
Triphthongs, 216, 225
tu, 141
tú, 108, 107
tuyo, 143

u, see **o**
ü, 222
United States, see **Estados Unidos**
uno = *a/an*, 87; = a pronoun, 123; = number one; 193
unos/unas, 89
until, see **hasta**
us, 109ff
usted/ustedes, 109, 107, 104, 106

vencer, 249, 298
venir, 299
ver, forms, 300; infinitive with, 48; gerund with, 55
Verbs (See also individual tenses, Mood); types of 3;
    Regular, 240ff; Irregular, 253ff; Spelling rules, 249;
    Hints for learners, 250
vivir, 246
volverse, 76; = *become*, 232
vos, 108
vosotros/vosotras, 109, 107, 104, 106
vuestro, 141ff

want, see **querer**
we, see **nosotros**
what's the time?, 197
what, 203
what, 203
whatever, 34
when, see **cuando**
whenever, 34
where, 202
which = relative pronoun, 124; = *what?*, *which of?*, 203–4
whichever, 34
while, see **mientras (que)**
whoever, 34
whose = relative pronoun, 125
why, 188
with, see pp. 183–6
without, , see pp. 183–6
Word Order, 211
would, 237

y, 190
ya, 238
ya que, 32
yet, 232
yo, 107, 104
you, see **tú, vosotros, usted, te, lo/las, os**
our, yours, 141ff

This book is due for return on or before the last date shown
above: it may, subject to the book not being reserved by
another reader, be renewed by personal application, post, or
telephone, quoting this date and details of the book.

HAMPSHIRE COUNTY COUNCIL
County Library   100%
                        recycled paper